Sri Lanka

**Land, people
and economy**

Sri Lanka

Land, people and economy

B.L.C. Johnson and M. Le M. Scrivenor

 Heinemann · London · Exeter New Hampshire

To Delia

Published in Great Britain 1981 by
Heinemann Educational Books Ltd
22 Bedford Square, London WC1B 3HH

Published in the U.S.A. 1981 by
Heinemann Educational Books Inc.
4 Front Street, Exeter, New Hampshire 03833

British Library C.I.P. Data
Johnson, Basil Leonard Clyde
  Sri Lanka.
  1. Sri Lanka – Description and travel
  I. Title   II. Scrivenor, M Le M
  915.49′3   DS489

  ISBN 0-435-35489-2

Library of Congress Cataloging in Publication Data

Johnson, B. L. C. (Basil Leonard Clyde), 1919–
  Sri Lanka, land, people, and economy.

  Bibliography: p.
  Includes index.
  1. Sri Lanka – Economic conditions. 2. Sri
Lanka – Description and travel. 3. Agriculture –
Economic aspects – Sri Lanka. I. Scrivenor,
M. LeM. II. Title.
HC424.J65   330.9549′303   81–2504
ISBN 0-435-35489-2   AACR2

Photoset and printed in Malta by Interprint Limited

Contents

Acknowledgements

Through the kindness and interest of Mr K. B. Ekanayake, then of the Sri Lanka High Commission in Canberra, we were introduced to Dr Wickrema Weerasooria, Secretary of the Ministry of Plan Implementation in Colombo, who took us under his wing. He did us the very great favour of asking his Director of Regional Development, a former academic geographer, Mr K. P. G. M. Perera, to help us find out what we wanted to know and to see what we wanted to see. This he did with unfailing considerateness and patience. Throughout the Sri Lanka administration, whether in Colombo or in the district kachcheris, and in all our contacts with estates, private business, farmers and fishermen, factories and institutes we met with the same helpfulness and generosity of spirit. Mr E. F. Dias Abeyesinghe, High Commissioner for Sri Lanka in Australia, kindly read the manuscript and made valuable comments. The authors, however are entirely responsible for the views expressed.

We have cause also to be grateful to many academic colleagues in Sri Lanka among them particularly Dr Hiran D. Dias, Dr H. N. C. Fonseka, Professor B. L. Panditaratna, Vice Chancellor of the University at Peradeniya, Professor K. M. de Silva and Mr P. Silva. It is sad to record that another Sri Lanka geographer, Professor K. Kularatnam, who kindly received us in 1978, has since died. No one undertaking a study of Sri Lanka can fail to become deeply indebted to that doyen of the country's geographers, Mr B. H. Farmer of St John's College, Cambridge, and Director, Centre of South Asian Studies.

In Australia, our thanks are due to the Sri Lanka High Commissioner and to his staff, and to Mr D. S. Abeyagunawardene, an ex-patriate who diligently and effectively racked his brains to answer our innumerable questions. We have also to thank Mr Kevin Cowan for his patient drawing and redrawing of the figures. The following kindly assisted with photographic material: Professor Martyn Webb (University of Western Australia), nos 7, 130; Mr M. P. A. Jayatillake (Forest Department, Sri Lanka), nos 89, 90, 91, 92; and the Ministry of Information in Colombo, nos 119 and 121.

To the Australian National University we are grateful for the study leave which made the essential field work possible.

At a more personal level we are most appreciative of the hospitality of Mr and Mrs Hubert Congreve of Newburgh Estate who put us up and put up with us on several occasions in their beautiful bungalow near Ella; of Mr and Mrs Ernie Silva of Yuillefield Estate; and of Mr L. M. de W. Tillekeratne of the T.R.I.

Finally we dedicate this book to the wife of one of the authors and the close friend of the other, who shared some of the joys of exploration in Sri Lanka but who with great forebearance allowed the geographers to get on with the job.

B.L.C.J.

M. Le M.S.

Colombo
February 1980

Preface

The little tropical island of Sri Lanka, smaller than Scotland or Tasmania and half the size of the State of New York, is a country of remarkable variety of climate and landscape. A long history of contact with mainland South Asia and with three European trading empires in succession has endowed Sri Lanka with strands of several cultures, religions and languages. Following many centuries as a mercantile colony of Portugal, the Netherlands and Britain, Sri Lanka achieved independence after World War II. This book tries to review, against the island's range of environmental conditions, the way in which its people are now developing their economy, and the degree to which past indigenous and exotic elements persist in the present patterns of man's occupance.

List of Tables

Note: Rounding-off of figures may result in apparent small discrepancies between the sum of the items and the total shown.

List of Figures

Chapter 1

The Cultural and Environmental Heritage

Introduction

Compared with its near neighbours, Sri Lanka,* or Ceylon (Fig. 1.1) enjoys a modestly high standard of living.

Sri Lanka owes its present level of development

*Sri Lanka replaced Ceylon as the official name of the island nation in 1972, but seemingly without prejudice to the earlier title. For trade purposes, notably for tea, the name Ceylon is retained, and it appears in the title of the Central Bank and of many institutes. The new name 'Lanka' comes from the Indian epic *Ramayana*, 'Sri' being an honorific prefix. 'Sri Lanka' is used adjectivally without change, and the simple form 'Lankan' also seems to be accepted.

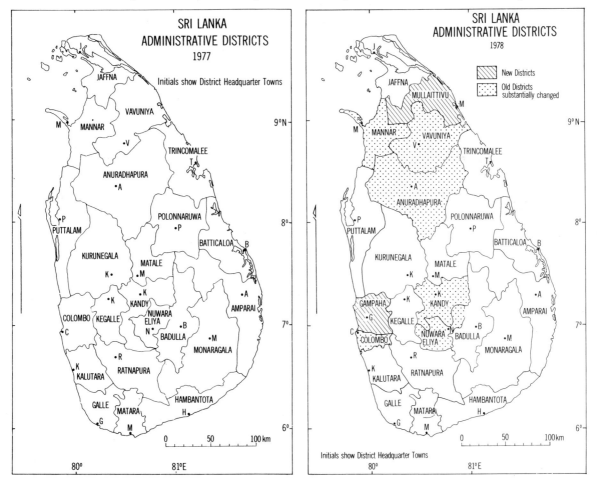

1.1 Sri Lanka, administrative Districts (a) 1977, (b) 1978. From 1978 two new Districts, Mullaittivu in the north, and Gampaha in the northern part of Colombo District, have been promulgated. Minor adjustments have been made in some other Districts, notably in Nuwara Eliya and Kandy. At the time of writing statistical data were only available for the Districts shown for 1977 in Fig. 1.1(a).

in large measure to a combination of climatic and locational factors that made it attractive commercially and strategically to several European imperial powers over the centuries. To traders, Asian and European, plying between the Middle East and the East African coast on the one hand, and Malaya and the Indonesian and Philippine Archipelagos on the other, Sri Lanka provided havens midway across the Indian Ocean (Fig. 1.2). Arabs, Malays, and probably Chinese used the island as a convenient entrepôt situated bet-

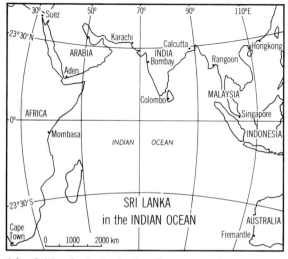

1.2   Sri Lanka in the Indian Ocean

ween the gateways to European trade on the one hand and the Straits of Malacca leading to the Indonesian Spice Islands and to China's sphere of influence on the other. The Portuguese, entering the Indian Ocean round the Cape of Good Hope, similarly made landfalls on Sri Lanka and on the Indian mainland, developing them not only as ports of call for vessels plying to the Spice Islands and China, but also, from the sixteenth century, as trading posts to obtain the cinnamon and other condiments produced in the island's near equatorial climate. The Dutch followed in the mid-seventeenth century with similar intent, and then the French, but briefly. Finally the British came at the turn of the eighteenth century to protect their strategic interests. With the opening of the Suez Canal in 1867 and the expansion of British Imperial interests and steam-driven seapower, Sri Lanka entered a new phase of strategic importance as a coaling station from which to control the Indian Ocean, and to provision vessels plying

the sea routes to China, Japan, Australia and New Zealand. British interests invested heavily in Sri Lanka's development as a vast plantation, first of coffee, then of tea and rubber.

During World War II the island played its last vital role in super-power strategy as a forward naval and air base against the Japanese who had invaded Malaya, Indonesia and Burma, and were threatening India. When Sri Lanka gained political independence in 1948 it soon lost most of its former maritime significance, a process hastened by the development of air travel. Air services between Europe and East Asia and Australasia tend to bypass the island.

Sri Lanka's position *vis-à-vis* India is viewed more closely in Figure 1.3. Although less than 30 km of shoal-studded sea divides the most proximate inhabited parts of Sri Lanka and India, the island has generally enjoyed a political existence independent of the mainland. As both Sri Lanka and India claim jurisdiction over the sea areas extending 12 miles (19.2 km) from their coasts the demarcation of their mutual boundary in Palk Strait has presented some problems. The possibility that oil might be found under the Gulf of Mannar has accentuated the issue. An agreed boundary has now been determined, following a line equidistant from the two coasts, passing one mile (1.6 km) west of the tiny island of Kachchativu (which is uninhabited except in March when Christian pilgrims from Sri Lanka and India visit a shrine dedicated to St Anthony).

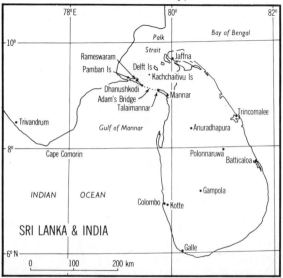

1.3   Sri Lanka and India

The People

The origins of the people of Sri Lanka are somewhat obscure. The earliest inhabitants were probably the ancestors of the Veddas, a once relatively primitive group now no longer recognised separately in the census, and who have effectively lost their identity by physical and cultural absorption into the Sinhalese populations. Anthropologists find affinities between the Veddas and some hill tribes of peninsular India and it is probable that, like the latter, they were in part absorbed and in part driven into the less attractive highlands by invading peoples. As a separate ethnic entity, the Veddas can be said to have disappeared already.

There are two distinct cultural groups forming the bulk of the population, the Sinhalese and the Tamils. The role of migration in the genesis of the Sinhalese people, much the larger of the two groups, is uncertain but tradition holds that they entered Sri Lanka from India at an early date.

1 The magnificent gilt-topped Buddhist dagoba at Mahiyangana on the right bank of the Mahaweli Ganga in Badulla District. (Fig. 4.12)

Possibly through continued contact with their homeland, they received Buddhist missionaries sent by Asoka, ruler of northern India in the third century BC. Thus the Sinhalese acquired their Buddhist religion and its associated Aryan language of Pali with its Brahmi script. The Sinhalese language, as it has since developed, has been much modified by fusion with Dravidian, linguistic elements derived from the Tamils, who came from South India and now constitute the largest minority group in the country.

Early History

The Sinhalese established an advanced civilisation in northern Sri Lanka during the first millennium of the Christian era. Close proximity to the Tamil country of southern India ensured some degree of cultural contact and physical mixture, probably from the very earliest days. It was customary for Sinhalese kings to seek brides from southern India, perhaps in an effort to preserve peaceable relations between the communities. Tamil incursions into the island were taking place probably as early as the second century BC when they are reported by the *Mahavamsa* chronicler as being routed from the Buddhists' sacred city, Anuradhapura, and not for the last time.

Ludowyk suggests that for several centuries after the introduction of Buddhism into Ceylon 'over large tracts of the northern plain Tamil and Sinhalese must have been indistinguishable from each other. In these years there were Tamil rulers who had been patrons of Buddhism, then flourishing in South India. Brahmins (high caste Hindus) were officials in the court of Sinhala kings, and the gods of the Hindu pantheon were respected by Hindu and Buddhist alike.'* These idyllic conditions of multiracial harmony must have been strained and ultimately shattered by the recurrence of Tamil aggression from the fifth century AD, when increasingly strong Hindu states in South India periodically sought to extend their power base to Sri Lanka.† In the fifth century AD the Sinhalese King Dhatusena, who built the great 5.6 km dam to form the Kala Wewa reservoir to

*Ludowyk, E. F. C. *The Story of Ceylon,* Faber and Faber, London, 1962, p. 58.
†de Silva, K. M. in de Silva K. M. (ed.), *Sri Lanka: a Survey,* Hurst, London, 1977, p. 37.

supply water to Anuradhapura, was again expelling the Tamils from that city. K. M. de Silva dates Sri Lanka's plural society from this phase of Tamil intervention in the island's political struggles.

The early Sinhalese were attracted to the drier northern and eastern threequarters of the island. The principal focus of settlement was the north-central lowlands, where the Buddhist kingdom of Rajarata was established by the third century BC and from which Buddhism probably spread to other 'kingdoms' such as Ruhuna in the southeast and to parts of the lowland west. Ruhuna was at some times independent, at others under the suzerainty of Rajarata. It seems that the wetter southwest quadrant of the island in general, and the highlands over 1,000 m in particular, were rather avoided by these settlers who perhaps found the dry areas easier to clear for irrigated paddy cultivation.

By the eleventh century AD, pressures from the Tamil Chola kingdom on the mainland reached the level of military invasion, and there began a period of progressive 'Tamilisation' of northern Ceylon, as a result of which the Sinhalese were eventually pushed southwards. For 75 years, in fact, Sri Lanka became a province of the Chola's South Indian kingdom.* In 1017 the South Indian Cholas captured the ancient and glorious Sinhalese capital of Anuradhapura, compelling the Sinhalese to move their capital which they then established at Polonnaruwa, 80 km to the southeast. Here developed a civilisation more strongly influenced by the Dravidian culture of the Tamils which achieved its 'golden age' under King Parakramabahu I (1153–86). Invasion and migration from India persisted in the twelfth century, resulting in the establishment of a strong Tamil kingdom in the far north, and the decay of the Rajarata kingdom of the Sinhalese by the thirteenth century. The Sinhalese capital was moved southward from the dry north progressively deeper into the wet southwest – to the rock fortress of Dambadeniya in the thirteenth century, to Kurunegala, to Gampola in the fourteenth century, and then to Kotte near Colombo by 1415.

With the dissolution of the old Rajarata kingdom many of its splendid feats of irrigation engineering fell into decay. From this time up to the arrival of the Portuguese early in the sixteenth century, there were three principal political foci in Sri Lanka. The Tamil kingdom in the far north was based on the Jaffna Peninsula and was separated by what is now a somewhat desolate region in the northern third of the island from the other two kingdoms. The Kandyan kingdom of Udarata occupied the eastern third of the island and the kingdom of Kotte the western part (see Fig. 1.4).

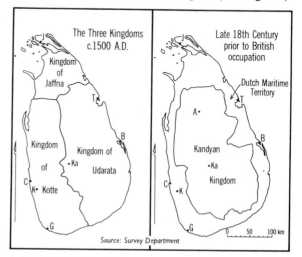

1.4   (a) The Three Kingdoms (b) Late eighteenth century

One can only speculate on the reasons for the decline of the golden age of Sinhalese civilisation in the dry parts of the island. Possibly the breakdown in administration consequent on repeated Tamil attacks allowed the irrigation system to fall into disrepair and so led to depopulation of the region. Farmer suggests that natural hazards in the form of flood and possibly the appearance of malaria could have been contributing factors.*

The Physical Environment of Early Settlement

It is appropriate to pause here to consider what kind of country it was that the Sinhalese and Tamils were striving to colonise, and by what agricultural techniques they were able to support themselves. The present-day map of population distribution probably bears very little similarity to the situation

*de Silva, K. M. *op. cit.*, p. 39.

*Farmer, B: H. *Ceylon, a Divided Nation*, Oxford University Press, London, 1963, p. 14.

2 A splendid example of Hindu temple architecture, the gopuram at Valvedditturai, Jaffna Peninsula, is elaborately adorned with painted plaster figures. Attendant priest in the foreground

more likely explanation is that the agricultural techniques, that may well have originated in India, and which were then available to the settler, were found to be adequately effective in supporting, within the dry areas, the population attained within the first millenium AD. The heavy forest cover of the wetter parts may have deterred settlement at this stage.

The map of mean annual rainfall (Fig. 1.5) shows the three-quarters of the island with less than 2,000 mm divided into a major northern half and a small southeastern section. Within the high rainfall area of the southwest the main hill masses stand out with over 2,500 mm, and one group of peaks receives over 5,000 mm.

Rainfall, through its influence on the growth of the natural vegetation and as a limiting factor in agricultural activity, has been the dominant but not the sole factor affecting man's occupance of

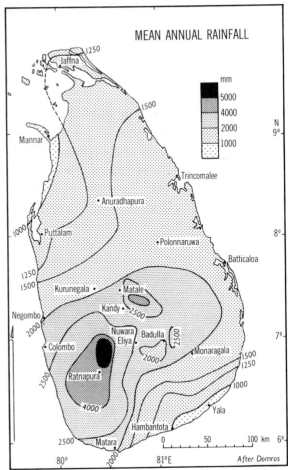

1.5 Mean annual rainfall

that obtained in AD 1500 immediately prior to the establishment of European contact with the island, and still less to that of AD 1000 when the Sinhalese kingdom based on Anuradhapura was at its height. The early Sinhalese settlers and after them the Tamils, who established their civilisations in the northern half of the island, did not occupy the areas which we today might regard as the most favourable to settlement. Why did the better watered southwest quadrant of the country remain for so long neglected? In so small an island, measuring very roughly 400 km by 240 km, it is unlikely that people in one part remained for long in ignorance of conditions in another. A

the land. Sri Lanka rises to 2,524 m in Pidurutalagala and there are 13 peaks exceeding 2,000 m. In the south-centre of the island the highlands rise to above 1,000 m over a roughly elliptical area measuring 80 km from east to west by 55 km north to south (Fig. 1.6). In addition to this continuous upland there are substantial areas northeast of Kandy, east of Badulla, and in the south in Ratnapura District which exceed this altitude. (For the location of districts and their headquarter towns see Fig. 1.1.)

Temperatures in the highlands are lower, of course (6°C and more below those in the surrounding low country) but whether it was the cooler climate, the high rainfall, or the heavy forest cover that discouraged them, the Sinhalese did not settle here except in the lower valleys, and the region awaited development by British plantation owners in the mid-nineteenth century.

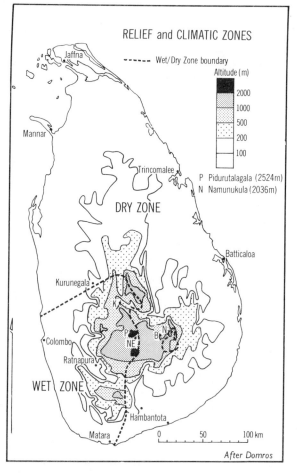

1.6   Relief, and climatic zones

Wet and Dry Zones

Conventionally and conveniently two distinct regions are recognised in Sri Lanka: a Wet and a Dry Zone. There has been much academic debate about which criteria most accurately determine the boundary between Wet and Dry Zones. In Figure 1.6 Wikkramatileke's definition has been adopted. This is based on the occurrence in the Dry Zone of an 'effective dry period' of three consecutive dry months each with less than 102 mm of actual rainfall, more often than not.* This boundary can be seen to approximate to the 2,000 mm isohyet between Negombo and Kurunegala, and also near Matara. Within the highlands however it approaches the 2,500 mm isohyet close to Nuwara Eliya, and approximates the boundary between areas dominated by the southwest and northeast monsoons. An outlier of the Wet Zone envelopes the Namunukula massif near Badulla in the Uva basin where the rainfall is also about 2,500 mm.

To many travellers from the drier parts of South India, 'dry' might seem an inappropriate epithet to apply to regions that receive mainly over 1,250 mm of rain, and only rarely below 1,000 mm. The driest parts of Sri Lanka are the northwest coast near Mannar, which receives an average of 964 mm, and the south coast, east of Hambantota, with an average of 923 mm at Yala. However, the general tendency is for areas of lower rainfall to experience greater variability. Even Trincomalee with a mean annual rainfall of 1,727 mm had actual totals ranging between 886 mm and 2,578 mm over 107 years of records.

In the north-central parts of the Dry Zone the observer is impressed by the apparent luxuriance of the woodland vegetation. Trees and shrubs with their deep-root systems are able to withstand periods of drought better than shallower-rooted field crops, and so cannot be taken as an entirely reliable index of the agricultural potentialities of the climate. For rain-fed agriculture the big problem has always been the unreliability of a rainfall which in some years is adequate but more often is less than a farmer needs to grow crops without the added insurance of irrigation. The rate

* Wikkramatileke, R. *Southeast Ceylon: Trends and Problems in Agricultural Settlement*, University of Chicago, Department of Geography, Research Paper 83, 1963, p. 30.

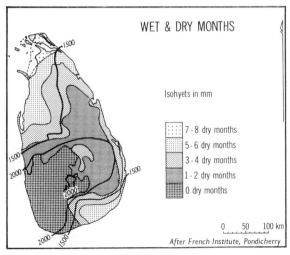

1.7 Wet and dry months

WET & DRY MONTHS

Isohyets in mm

7 - 8 dry months
5 - 6 dry months
3 - 4 dry months
1 - 2 dry months
0 dry months

0   50   100 km

After French Institute, Pondicherry

Using the concept of wet and dry months (a dry month having an average temperature [°C] exceeding twice the average rainfall [in mm]), biogeographers at the French Institute, Pondicherry, have compiled a map (Fig. 1.7) in which the region with no dry month coincides remarkably closely with the Wet Zone as defined by Wikkramatileke.

Climatic boundaries based on average values are at best imprecise having the character of zones of transition. The Wet Zone-Dry Zone boundary is no exception and there is a belt, broad in Kurunegala District in the north but narrower to the east of Matara in the south, where either Wet or Dry Zone conditions can occur.

of evaporation is always high, especially in the dry season when conditions may be aggravated, as far as crop growth is concerned, by the desiccating effect of the winds, particularly where the airflow is subsiding after its passage over the high country.

Seasonality

In most areas of Sri Lanka rainfall is markedly seasonal. The alternation in the direction of air flow between southwest and northeast is the basic key to this seasonality. As the maps of bi-monthly wind direction show (Fig. 1.8), the year may be

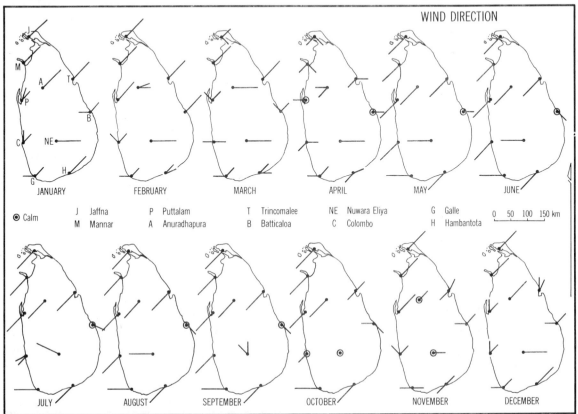

WIND DIRECTION

JANUARY   FEBRUARY   MARCH   APRIL   MAY   JUNE

⊙ Calm

J Jaffna   P Puttalam   T Trincomalee   NE Nuwara Eliya   G Galle
M Mannar   A Anuradhapura   B Batticaloa   C Colombo   H Hambantota

0   50   100   150 km

JULY   AUGUST   SEPTEMBER   OCTOBER   NOVEMBER   DECEMBER

1.8 Wind direction. Lines show dominant direction of winds towards locations marked.

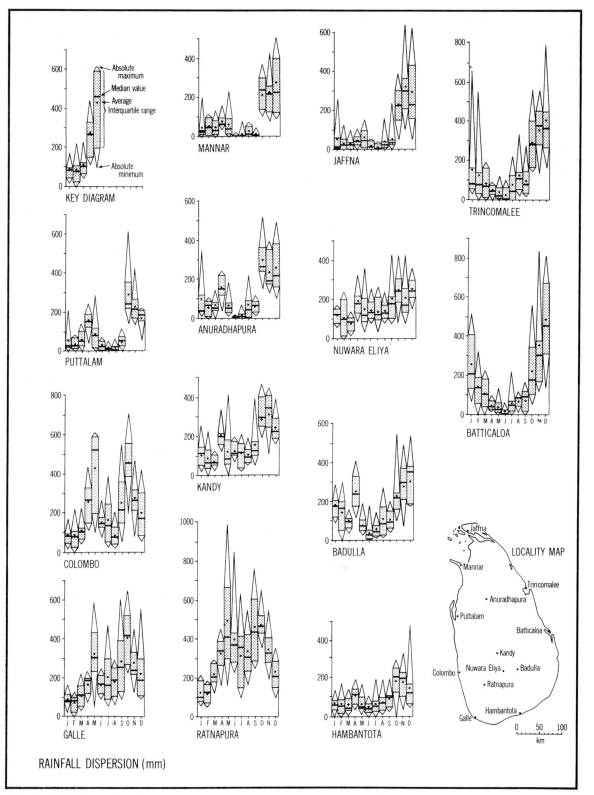

RAINFALL DISPERSION (mm)

1.9   Rainfall dispersion diagrams

divided into two major periods each of about five months, one dominated by the southwest monsoon (May–September) the other by the northeast monsoon (November–March). Between them, April and October show greater variation in wind direction, and it is the doldrum weather of these 'inter-monsoonal' months that accounts for the characteristic double rainfall maxima of the Wet Zone and the single maximum of much of the Dry Zone (Fig. 1.9). In the early months of the southwest monsoon from mid-April to June, the west-facing hill country is most thoroughly soaked, after which the rains slacken off somewhat. For agriculture, the southwest monsoon is the *yala* crop season. As Figure 1.10 shows, it is a period of very low rainfall throughout the Dry Zone, and what little precipitation occurs there is extremely unreliable.

From October to December most of the island enjoys an important period of rains, marking the start of the *maha* crop season which runs through to the end of March. At first, winds are variable and light, strengthening in December–January as the northeast monsoon or trade winds set in. For the Dry Zone *maha* is effectively the only wet season. Since a good deal of rain also falls at this time in the Wet Zone, the latter has no clear dry season; Colombo averages 88 mm in January and 96 mm in February, its months of lowest rainfall.

Early Settlement

The early settlers of Sri Lanka were concerned principally with the lowlands, and with the Dry Zone lowlands at that. The staple food, rice, was grown in irrigated fields in valley bottoms. Over many centuries hundreds of tanks and some elaborate and finely executed irrigation systems essential to guarantee a paddy crop in the Dry Zone were built. Today these old tanks are found throughout the Dry Zone (Fig. 1.11). While some have been abandoned through siltation or dilapidation, many others have been restored.

The greatest concentration of ancient tanks, and some of the largest – the inheritance from the kingdom of Rajarata – were in the north-central districts, including Anuradhapura and Polonnaruwa. They were also concentrated in the south of

Monaragala and the adjacent parts of Hambantota in what must have been a most populous district of the southern kingdom of Ruhuna.

The majority of these tanks were small reservoirs in the tributary valleys of the major rivers. Figure 1.12 shows the present day pattern of tanks and the paddy lands they support along the upper Kudahatu Oya and some of its tributaries, 25 km east of Anuradhapura. The proportion of land taken up by the tanks to the actual paddy area is almost 1:1. Particularly where tanks are 'beaded' along a minor river in this way, they are at risk when exceptionally heavy rainfall occurs since the failure of one structure may threaten others downstream.

Some of the most elegant irrigation engineering of pre-industrial times anywhere in the world is seen in the channels cut to lead water from a tank in one river basin to another in an adjacent one. The Yoda Ela, a part of which is seen in Figures 3.3 and 4.15, is the best example. It was built in the fifth century AD and restored in 1897 to supply the tanks at Anuradhapura from the Kala Wewa, a reservoir 87 km distant in the head waters of the Kala Oya catchment (see also Fig. 4.17). The overall gradient of the Yoda Ela averages less than 1:5000.

The simplest irrigation systems involved leading water from a submersible (and so generally flood-proof) weir or *anicut* built across a river. An *anicut* across the Mahaweli Ganga, first built in the sixth century and restored in 1940, now supplies water to the Minipe Scheme (see Fig. 4.12).

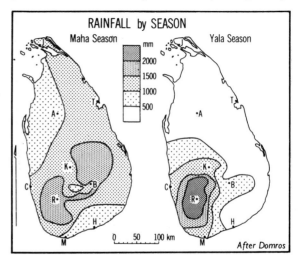

1.10 Rainfall in *maha* and *yala*

3　This elaborate Muslim mosque is in the heart of the Pettah area of old Colombo. Note beside the clock the loudspeaker through which the faithful are called to prayer. To the immediate left is a dealer in all kinds of dyes and chemicals

Another ancient *anicut* on the Amban Ganga, a major tributary of the Mahaweli, was first constructed in the twelfth century AD to feed the Parakrama Samudra, the tank system upon which the former capital city Polonnaruwa depended. It now feeds a system of tanks extending to Kantalai (Fig. 4.13). Giant's Tank in Mannar District has for centuries drawn water from an *anicut* on the Malwatu Oya (Aruvi Aru).

The absence of tanks in the Jaffna Peninsula may be explained by the occurrence there of permeable limestone at the surface. However, the presence of groundwater has enabled wells to be sunk to obtain water for domestic purposes and to irrigate intensively-cultivated crops. Rice here is rain-fed.

Supplementary to paddy farming the early cultivators, like their modern counterparts, utilised wooded interfluve areas to cultivate *chenas* (the Sinhala term for clearings for shifting cultivation). Crops such as the millet *kurakkan*, and the oil seed *gingelly* were grown. In their homestead gardens they no doubt cultivated fruit trees, spices and vegetables as is the practice today throughout Sri Lanka. Their economy was one of local self-sufficiency. What trade there was had little direct effect on the peasant. The export of gemstones, pearls and elephants by Arab and Chinese traders helped to enrich the king and his officials in the capital but, to quote Ludowyk, 'the kingdom's prosperity was based on the productivity of its rice fields'.*

Irrigation schemes on the scale developed in the north-central lowlands by the twelfth century AD depended for their continued success on an efficient and centralised administration. The proper maintenance of tank bunds, weirs and *elas* (canals) would have been beyond the means of villagers. The centuries of political disintegration which followed the relative stability of the Anuradhapura (250 BC – AD 1029) and Polonnaruwa (AD 1111–1215) periods saw the decay of many of the irrigation schemes and the impoverishment and probably the partial depopulation of what are now the districts of Anuradhapura and Polonnaruwa. From what must have been a quite highly centralised and unified island state, Sri Lanka lapsed into three weaker kingdoms. It is perhaps significant that the three kingdoms were located in areas where subsistence agriculture could be pursued without state initiative or control. Jaffna had its wells and rain-fed paddies, while the foci of the kingdoms of Kotte and Udarata (Kandy) lay mainly in the Wet Zone where paddy fields could be watered by diverting streams and impounding rainfall in bunded fields.

Arrival of the Portuguese

For perhaps three centuries there was little change in the situation, but in 1505 a new factor appeared on the scene. Up to this time the island's overseas

*Ludowyk, F. F. C. *op. cit.*, p. 77.

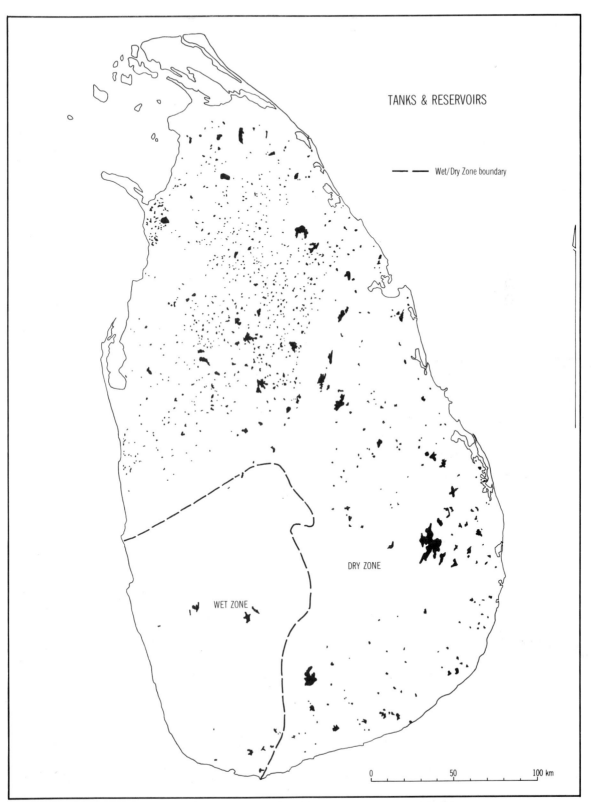

TANKS & RESERVOIRS

— — — Wet/Dry Zone boundary

DRY ZONE

WET ZONE

0   50   100 km

1.11 Tanks and reservoirs

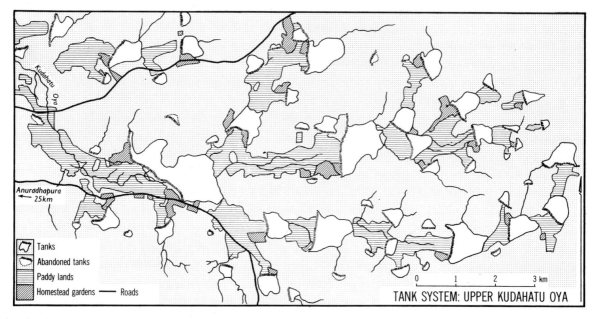

Tanks
Abandoned tanks
Paddy lands
Homestead gardens — Roads

0   1   2   3 km

TANK SYSTEM: UPPER KUDAHATU OYA

1.12   Tank system, Upper Kudahatu Oya

contacts had been primarily Asian. In the sixteenth century Christian Europe ceased to be content to leave this profitable commerce in Asian, especially Muslim Arab, hands. Following exploratory voyages in the late fifteenth century the Portuguese were quick to establish a chain of trading centres around the shores of the Indian Ocean. Their acquisition of Colombo in 1505 must be viewed in the wider context of other bases in Ormuz, Diu, Goa, Cochin, Madras, Hooghly, Chittagong, Bassein, Malacca and elsewhere, which formed the foundation of a century of trading monopoly. The arrival of the Portuguese to trade in the high-grade wild cinnamon that flourished in the south-west coastal lowlands, and for which Sri Lanka was the only source, saw the beginnings of an exotic commercial agricultural economy that was to reach its culmination under the British in the twentieth century. Cinnamon grew wild on the royal estates, and a labour force had to be found to peel the cinnamon sticks to obtain the commercially valuable bark. The Sinhalese Buddhist of whatever social level, while willing enough to labour on the land for himself and his family, had always tended to regard toil for another as distasteful. Whether or not this was the major reason, from the fourteenth and fifteenth centuries South Indian labourers were imported to peel cinnamon.

Portuguese interest focussed on the Wet Zone lowlands where cinnamon grew, but in addition to their main outlet, Colombo, they also held Mannar, Jaffna, Batticaloa and Trincomalee with fortified trading stations. The Sinhalese of the coastal lowlands were much affected by contact with the Portuguese. Many adopted Portuguese names and Christianity, perhaps under pressure but also to gain advantage by concealing their lower caste origins. Thus began the persisting distinction between Low Country Sinhalese, contaminated by a measure of Europeanisation, and the Kandyan Sinhalese of the kingdom of Kandy who held themselves aloof from Portuguese contact and maintained their traditional values and Buddhism. They remained independent until 1815. The death in 1597 of the king of Kotte, who in his will left to the Portuguese his assumed suzerainty over all the island (incomplete as his effective rule was), and the subjugation by the Portuguese of the kingdom of Jaffna in 1619, accentuated the polarisation between the invaders and the inland Kandyan kingdom.

The Dutch in Sri Lanka

Early in the seventeenth century European trade rivalry appeared on the scene when Portugal's main rivals, the Dutch, treated with the Kandyan king on how to rid the island of the Portuguese. By 1658 the Portuguese troops had left and their place was filled by the Dutch who followed a very similar trading policy. Besides cinnamon they sought *areca* nuts (betel nuts) and elephants. The cultural disparity between Low Country and Kandyan Sinhalese increased as westernisation proceeded in the coastal areas tributary to the trading stations. Intermarriage between Dutch officials and local women produced a new high 'caste', the Burghers, who still maintain their identity. Perhaps the most lasting contribution the Dutch made to Sri Lanka was to the codification of customary laws. By 1640 the Dutch were in Galle, by 1656 in Colombo and in Jaffna by 1658. On the south coast they built a fort at Matara and took control of Hambantota. Another fort was built in Mannar. Furthermore, they built forts on the east coast at Trincomalee and Batticaloa in their efforts to monopolise the trade of the Indian Ocean.

With the Dutch came the embryonic plantation system, as in the East Indies. Gardens of cinnamon were planted and this, with *areca* nuts, dominated

trade. Pepper vines and coffee trees were introduced, coconut planting increased, and commercially valuable field crops such as sugar cane and tobacco were encouraged. Under the Dutch, the idea of commercial plantation agriculture blossomed and their Sinhalese official class, the *Mudaliyars*, became wealthy land-holders in the process. The *Salagamas*, the cinnamon peelers, originating as low caste Indian weavers, also achieved wealth and status. The problem of feeding a partly nonsubsistence agricultural population made itself apparent. Rice had to be imported from India, and slave-labour was introduced from Tanjore (now in Tamilnadu) in an effort to reclaim some of the land which had been lost to paddy cultivation during the Portuguese period. Soldiers were brought in from Java and Amboina in the East Indies, the origin of the Malay element in the modern population. Like the Portuguese, the Dutch regarded the local Muslims as commercial rivals, banning them from Colombo, Galle and Matara but using them as middlemen and entrepreneurs in the pearl trade.

The Kandyan kingdom lay in the economic doldrums during the Dutch occupation of the maritime territory (Fig. 1.4). In the mid eighteenth century Buddhism experienced a revival under the influence of immigrant priests from Burma and

4 An old Christian church in the Dutch fort at Galle. Note the covered bullock cart, characteristic of the southwest, and the tourist car that helps attract foreign exchange to the island

Siam (Thailand) during the reign of a Tamil king, Kirti Sri.

By the end of the eighteenth century the effect of many decades of commercial activity and peace could be seen in the prosperity of the west coastal lowlands as compared with the Kandyan kingdom which retained its traditional economy. This dichotomy reinforced the separate identification of Kandyan and Low Country Sinhalese. Today the distinction has little or no political significance.

The events which led to the Dutch abandoning their possessions in Malaya were paralleled in Sri Lanka. The British, strongly established in Madras, were at war with France at the end of the eighteenth century and intense rivalry existed between them in the Indian Ocean for control of the naval bases essential to trading nations. Trincomalee first attracted the attention of the British who, having occupied it in 1782, lost it to the French, then regained it and handed it back to the Dutch in 1784 under the Treaty of Paris. In 1795 they reoccupied it in alliance with the king of Kandy in order to deny its use to the French.

5   The gate at the entrance to the fort at Matara is typical of several at other fortified ports established by the Dutch around the island

The British in Sri Lanka

With the overrunning of the Netherlands by the French, the British (in the form of the Madras Presidency of the East India Company) stepped in as a 'caretaker' of Dutch interests in Sri Lanka – as they did also in Malaya and the East Indies – and remained in possession thereafter. The Dutch territories, effectively the former Jaffna kingdom and the coastal belt, became a British Crown Colony in 1802, and thus began the third and last phase of domination by European powers. The Kandyan kingdom was not acquired by the British until 1815; and effective domination only came after a rebellion terminating in 1818 when, for the first time in at least a millenium, a unified administration of the island was achieved – albeit by an alien power.

The British accomplishment in Sri Lanka has been described as a modernisation of the structure laid down by the Dutch. A significant development in 1810 was to allow Europeans to own land in Sri Lanka, but until the possibilities for development in the interior were realised, following the construction of roads as a means to political control, little economic change occurred. A road was pushed through Kurunegala to Kandy in 1821 and a more direct route from Colombo to Kandy in 1825, into country where coffee could be grown.

With penetration of the Kandyan kingdom, direct rule by British government agents ultimately replaced indirect rule through traditional chiefs, bringing the former separate administration into line with that of the Low Country provinces and diminishing the cultural separateness of the Kandyan districts.

The Dutch had introduced cinnamon plantations alongside the mixed economy of wild cinnamon collecting and the cultivation by smallholders of export crops such as coffee, pepper, coconuts, sugar, cotton and tobacco. British colonial rule heralded a new era of plantation development, and a more specialised and commercialised economy evolved in much of the Wet Zone. Coffee was the crop of the new economy and was grown on Sinhalese smallholdings as well as European-owned estates. Booming in the 1840s, coffee reached an export peak in 1875 (43,514 tonnes from 101,200 ha) but it was hit by a fungus disease which ruined most of the trees in the late 1870s. Production fell to less than 9,144 tonnes by 1886. Botanists had long been active in search of alternative plantation crops however, and were ready first with cinchona and then tea to replace coffee, so enabling the whole complex infrastructure of the economy, including roads, railways and ports, to continue in profitable use. Tea planting, begun commercially in 1867, went ahead apace on both lowland plateaus and in the high country where much land was alienated to British private ownership after 1840 following the enactment of the Crown Lands Encroachment Ordinance. In some cases the villagers were certainly deprived of their traditional common woodland, in which they could pasture animals, cultivate *chenas* and, when population pressure compelled, build and cultivate paddy terraces. Rubber joined tea towards the end of the century to compete for the lower hill country and to add to the demand for plantation labour. The coffee harvest was seasonal and temporary Tamil labour was generally recruited in South India to work under extremely poor and unhealthy conditions. Thousands succumbed to malaria particularly when moving through the Dry Zone. For tea and rubber a more permanent work force was needed and, since the Sinhalese prejudice against wage labouring was still strong, the planters created settlements of Indian Tamils on their estates. These immigrants, separated by a thousand years of his-

tory from the 'Sri Lanka Tamils' of Jaffna, are culturally even more distinct than the latter from their Sinhalese neighbours. For five generations now they have lived on their estates, remote from their ancestral homeland yet largely out of contact with the citizens of Sri Lanka.

The Sinhalese attitude to wage labour on plantations is rooted in their traditional land holding system. In the villages much prestige goes with land ownership, and the laws and customs of succession decree that all children share in the property of their parents. To maintain one's rights of ownership it is unwise to move away permanently from the village. Furthermore, for the high castes at least, wage labour is regarded as unworthy. Thus the development of plantations imposed a marked cultural dualism on the pattern of local settlement in many mid-country and lowland areas. Great tracts of land were alienated to British plantation companies who set up estate settlements of Tamil labourers thereon under the management of resident British planters. Side by side with the estate settlements Sinhalese villages persisted, the Sinhalese living a completely separate existence though now somewhat constrained in their capacity to expand or to use 'waste land' by the pre-emption of such terrain by the planters. In the Up-country this problem hardly occurred since the British introduced Tamil labour to an unpopulated area.

European commercial impact – Portuguese, Dutch or British – was minimal upon the Dry Zone, since plantations could prosper only in the areas transitional to the Wet Zone. Administratively however, the British began to recognise some obligation to the indigenous economy of the Dry Zone from 1856, following an ordinance aimed to facilitate revival and enforcement of the ancient customs regarding the irrigation and cultivation of paddy lands. Twenty years later an attempt was made to establish an agricultural colony based on the restoration of Kala Wewa. This was the first of the many but not always successful efforts to make better use of the Dry Zone's irrigation potential and to make resettlement possible.

In Sri Lanka's overseas trade tea and rubber have held dominant positions since World War I (which gave a fillip to both) and in a worthy third place has stood another tree crop, coconuts. Of greater seniority than tea or rubber in Sri Lanka's economic history coconut growing remains mainly the preserve of Sinhalese estate owners and small-holders. It is extensive in the sandier coastal low-lands, especially in the 'coconut triangle' north-wards from near Colombo to Chilaw, and east to the Kurunegala-Matale border. Profits in coconut plantations have never compared with those to be gained from tea or rubber, which explains why European interest therein has been slight.

Independent Ceylon

In 1948 the British voluntarily relinquished their colonial rule and Sri Lanka achieved a state of unified independence. While superficially it may appear that independence has brought little change in the economy which is still dominated by the fluctuating fortunes of plantation commodities on the world market, there has been considerable movement away from the rigid dual economy of colonial times. Formerly, British capital and Indian Tamil labour generated profits and earnings which were in part repatriated and in part invested in the infrastructure of the plantation sector, but since the nationalisation of all but the small estates and the virtual disappearance of the British interest at the production level, the economy is becoming more integrated. It is also expanding in sectors pre-viously neglected – specifically the cultivation of the staple foodgrain rice, and the manufacture of goods for local consumption. As in many develop-ing countries, it is the outcome of the race between production and population increase that will determine the nation's welfare.

Population Growth

At the 1971 Census the population was 12.7 mil-lion, estimated to rise to 13.94 million in 1979, and projected to reach between 15.3 and 15.9 million by 1981. Table 1.1 summarises the demo-graphic history of Sri Lanka over the past hundred years since censuses were first taken.

Until World War II immigration from India played a major role in population growth, account-ing for between one and two-thirds of the increase in the decades up to 1921. Up to 1953 some 1.2 million immigrants from South India (in excess of those returning) had come to work on planta-tions and so to contribute substantially to the country's productivity. It is only since Indepen-dence that the direction of migrant flow has been reversed, as Indian Tamils seek repatriation and English-speaking Burghers and others find new homes in Australia and elsewhere.

Table 1.2 shows the trend of migration since 1871, with a reduced inward flow setting in follow-ing the world depression and during World War II, recovering thereafter for a while. The outflow became a flood from the 1950s for reasons discus-sed towards the end of this chapter.

Table 1.1   Population of Sri Lanka

Census year	Population (millions)	Average annual growth rate (per cent)	Inter-censal increase/ decrease due to migration (per cent)	Annual birth rate (per thousand)	Annual death rate (per thousand)	Natural increase (per cent per annum)
1871	2.4	–	–	–	–	–
1881	2.8	1.4	67	27	23	0.5
1891	3.0	0.9	42	29	24	0.5
1901	3.6	1.7	60	34	28	0.7
1911	4.1	1.4	34	38	29	0.9
1921	4.5	0.9	18	38	30	0.7
1931	5.3	1.7	19	40	27	1.3
1946	6.7	1.5	5	37	23	1.4
1953	8.1	2.8	5	38	17	2.1
1963	10.6	2.7	−1	37	10	2.7
1971	12.7	2.2	−5	33	8	2.5

Source: Department of Census and Statistics, *The Population of Sri Lanka*, Colombo, 1974.

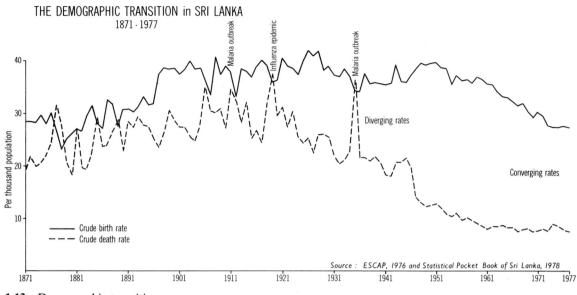

1.13 Demographic transition

Table 1.2 Inter-censal trend of migration, 1871–1971

Inter-censal period	Migration increase/decrease
1871–81	239,566
1881–91	103,791
1891–01	332,759
1901–11	184,249
1911–21	72,845
1921–31	151,276
1931–46	69,552
1946–53	112,201*
1953–63	−29,079
1963–71	−78,982*

Source: Sri Lanka Yearbook, Colombo, 1977.
*UNESCAP *Population of Sri Lanka,* Bangkok, 1976, gives 77,381 for 1946–53 and 100,228 for 1963–71.

Setting aside for a moment the effects of migration, it may be noted from Table 1.1 that the trends in birth and death rates and in the consequent rates of natural increase are characteristic of what is referred to as the 'demographic transition' (Fig. 1.13). In brief, this is a sequence of demographic phases through which a country passes as it changes from having an undeveloped pre-industrial society and economy to adopting advanced economic and medical technologies. In the nineteenth century birth and death rates were high, there being little attempt to control births, and medical services for the bulk of the population were minimal. Cholera, typhoid and malaria were endemic. Occasional epidemics, like the influenza that swept South Asia in 1919, and outbreaks of malaria as in 1911 and 1935, caused the death rate to fluctuate. Increasingly during the present century, and with accelerated effect following the advances in immunological science during World War I, the death rate has been reduced, although part of the fall may be attributed to better general nutrition. In the decades since World War II very significant falls in the death rate have been recorded, with corresponding extensions of life expectancy

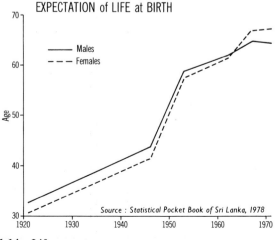

1.14 Life expectancy

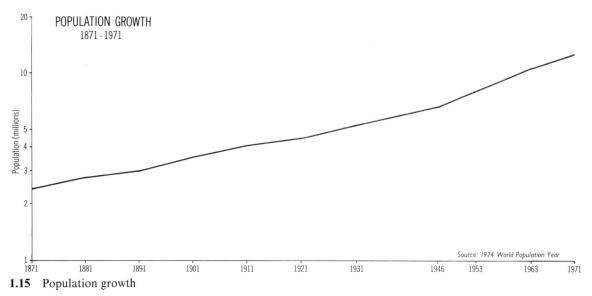

POPULATION GROWTH
1871 - 1971

Population (millions)

Source: *1974 World Population Year*

1.15   Population growth

to levels (67 for women, 64 for men) little short of those in highly developed countries (Fig. 1.14). Information in Table 1.1 indicates the upward trend in the rate of population increase to a peak in the period 1946–53, from which it has since subsided, but to a level still well above that of any inter-censal period prior to Independence. It was probably in Sri Lanka that the demographic impact of the insecticide DDT as a killer of the malaria-bearing *Anopheles* mosquito became first apparent. Prior to 1947 the island's population had been increasing at the relatively moderate rate of 1.6 per cent per annum. Immediately after World War II an extensive scheme of spraying

with DDT was undertaken which, along with other measures to improve health such as the use of antibiotics, led to a rapid reduction of the death rate and to an increased birth rate, and so to an upsurge in the rate of population increase. The general debilitation caused by malaria, and its effect on the birth rate through spontaneous abortion, was much reduced. The downward trend in death rates from 1921 has not been paralleled by birth rates which, until the most recent census, stood at between 37 and 40 per 1,000 of the total population.

Contributing substantially to the fall in death rates have been the reductions in infant and maternal mortality, mainly as a result of improvements in health care and the spread of hospital facilities. From levels ranging between 171 and 223 per thousand live births in the decade up to 1920, in-

6   A herd of cattle on the edge of dry woodland grazes paddy stubble during the fallow season near Pottuvil on the southeast coast in Amparai District

fant mortality has fallen to between 57 and 82 in the period 1951–60 and to between 45 and 51 in the years 1971–74. Maternal mortality has fallen from between 18.5 and 21.6 per thousand live births in 1921–25 to between 0.9 and 1.0 per cent in 1976–77. During the malaria epidemic of 1935 the infant mortality rate soared to 263 and maternal mortality to 26.5 per thousand live births. Typical of the course of the demographic transition elsewhere, change in the birth rate has lagged behind the reduction in the death rate so that for the half century 1911–61 the two rates have diverged, with consequent increase in the rates of natural increase. This reached a maximum of 2.8 per cent in 1953 and again in the period 1962–64 (Fig. 1.13), after which rates fell to 2.4 (up to 1968) and then to 2.2 per cent in 1969 and 1970, and to 1.9 per cent in 1974 and 1975. The rates then rose slightly to 2 per cent in 1976 and 2.1 per cent in 1977. The estimated rate for 1978 was 2.2 per cent.

These rates reflect not only the factors lowering death rates mentioned above but also some more positive factors encouraging family formation and reducing economic constraints on family size. New economic opportunities were created for young couples in the Dry Zone colonisation schemes and more generally, free schooling, school meals, subsidised rice prices and accessible health services signalled a new era for many.

Several factors appear to be affecting the current rates of natural increase, although the relative weight to be given to these factors is not yet certain. The age of marriage is rising; it is becoming rather less nearly universal and, through the increasing adoption of contraceptive practices, is becoming less fertile. Notwithstanding, Sri Lanka is still a very long way from zero population growth. Its population is still expanding quite rapidly and maintains an age-sex structure that puts a heavy burden of dependent children and aged people on the economically productive section of society. The age-sex 'pyramid' has the characteristic broad base and tapering apex of a less developed country (Fig. 1.16).

Half the population was less than 20 years old in 1971 and the dependency ratio in 1977 was 76 per cent, i.e. the population less than 15 or more than 65 years of age (43 per cent of the total) was supported by the 57 per cent in the economically active age range. The true level of dependency is probably much higher. Although many children may

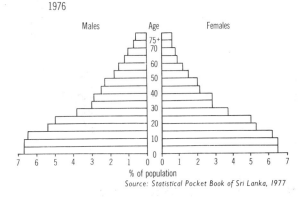

AGE-SEX PYRAMID
1976

Males   Age   Females

% of population
Source: *Statistical Pocket Book of Sri Lanka, 1977*

1.16 Age-sex pyramid

make some contribution to a family's income as helpers, adult women do not figure largely in the workforce, and even among the males there is much unemployment and underemployment. An ESCAP report calculated the *real* dependents per 100 employed persons as 248 (see Chapter 2.)*

Ethnic Structure

Not least among Sri Lanka's problems is that of welding into a national unity the several more or less distinct ethnic groups. Their population strength at the 1971 Census is shown in Table 1.3 and their distribution in Figure 1.17.

Table 1.3 Population by ethnic groups, 1971

Ethnic group	Number (thousands)		Per cent	
Low Country Sinhalese	5426	9,131	42.8	72.0
Kandyan Sinhalese	3705		29.2	
Sri Lanka Tamils		1,424		11.2
Indian Tamils		1,175		9.3
Sri Lanka Moors		828		6.5
Indian Moors		27		0.2
Burghers and Eurasians		45		0.4
Malays		43		0.3
Others		16		0.1
Total		12,689		100.0

Source: Statistical Pocket Book of Sri Lanka, Colombo 1978.

* The two most useful demographic surveys are UNESCAP, *Population of Sri Lanka*, Country Monograph Series No. 4., Bangkok, 1976, and Department of Census and Statistics, *The Population of Sri Lanka* (special publication for the 1974 World Population Year), Colombo 1974. Also valuable is Nimal Sanderatne, 'Socio-economic variables in Sri Lanka's demographic transition: an analysis of recent trends', *Staff Studies*, Central Bank of Ceylon Vol. 5, 1976, pp. 157–89.

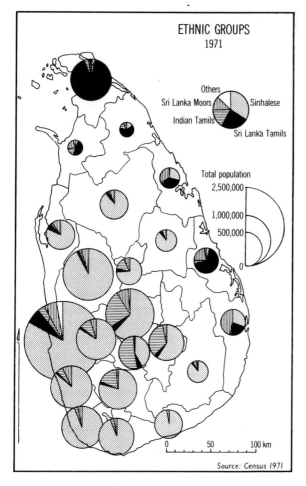

ETHNIC GROUPS
1971

Others
Sri Lanka Moors
Indian Tamils
Sinhalese
Sri Lanka Tamils

Total population
2,500,000

1,000,000

500,000

0

0   50   100 km

Source: Census 1971

1.17   Ethnic groups by District

Table 1.4   Distribution of ethnic groups by place of residence, 1971 (by per cent)
Urban, rural and estate

Ethnic group	Urban	Rural	Estate
Low Country Sinhalese	28.0	70.0	1.3
Kandyan Sinhalese	6.6	92.0	1.4
Sri Lanka Tamils	35.0	60.0	5.0
Indian Tamils	9.3	11.0	80.0
Sri Lanka Moors	44.0	55.0	0.7
Indian Moors	40.0	38.0	22.0
Burghers and Eurasians	80.0	17.0	2.7
Malays	75.0	22.0	2.7
Others	71.0	24.0	5.4
All groups	22.0	69.0	9.1

Source: UNESCAP, *Population of Sri Lanka, op. cit.*

Grouped together, the Kandyan and Low Country Sinhalese constitute 72 per cent of the total population, a level exceeded over the lowland Wet Zone and in the Dry Zone in all but the three northern and three eastern Districts. Nuwara Eliya, the upcountry tea-growing District, has only 41 per cent Sinhalese, and the neighbouring Districts of Kandy and Badulla, 62 and 59 per cent respectively. Figure 1.18 shows the distribution of the four largest ethnic groups by electorates. Sinhalese are here seen to be quite strongly represented in the developing colonies of the Dry Zone (See Fig. 4.11). The two Sinhalese groups are distinguished in their relative levels of urbanisation (Table 1.4), the Low Country Sinhalese understandably being much more given to urban living than the Kandyans who are 92 per cent rural.

Sri Lanka or 'Jaffna' Tamils (11.2 per cent of the total population) are in an overall majority in the three northernmost Districts of Mannar, Vavuniya and Jaffna (reaching 92 per cent in the latter) and in the east coast District of Batticaloa. Trincomalee and Amparai, adjoining Batticaloa to its north and south respectively, have 35 and 22 per cent Sri Lanka Tamils. In no other District do they exceed 6.5 per cent of the total. Their distribution is to be seen in Figures 1.18 and 1.19. Their commercial vigour as a group and their proclivities for education are reflected in their relatively high concentration in the urban sector compared with the Low Country Sinhalese, their major rivals (Table 1.4).

Indian Tamils (9.3 per cent of the total) are located mainly where they can find work on plantations, on which 80 per cent are resident (Fig. 1.18 and 1.20). They have little in common with the Sri Lanka Tamils. They reach 52 per cent of the District total in Nuwara Eliya (71 per cent of the Nuwara Eliya electorate) and 25 and 34 per cent in Kandy and Badulla Districts respectively. The Dry Zone District of Mannar has very small absolute numbers, and the 18 per cent of Indian Tamils there, and others scattered in the northern Districts, are generally migrants from the tea regions seeking economic opportunities.

In the past the total number of the Indian Tamil population has always been related to the prosperity of the plantation industry and until World War II a proportion of this group had been transitory. In recent decades, however, repatriation to their ancestral homeland has emerged as a

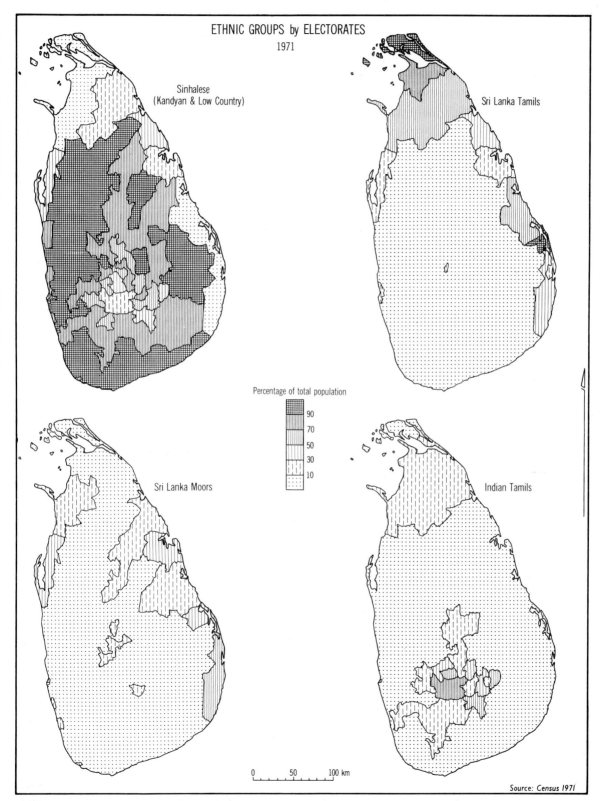

1.18 Ethnic groups, as percentage of total population: Sinhalese, Sri Lanka Tamils, Sri Lanka Moors, Indian Tamils

7 Aerial view of the lowlands in Colombo District showing the distinct separation of paddy cultivation on the flood plains from coconut and mixed homestead gardens on the low interfluves. Drainage of the paddy land is more necessary here than is irrigation; drainage channels follow the centre line of the flood plains. For the most part the paddy has only recently been planted and the fields are under water. (See Fig. 3.7)

new factor and their fate has been the subject of Indo-Sri Lanka discussions culminating in the Srimavo-Shastri Pact of 1964 under which Sri Lanka was to grant citizenship to 300,000 Indians, and India was to accept 525,000 (plus their natural increase in both cases) as repatriated workers, to whom they subsequently granted Indian citizenship. In 1974 the numbers were adjusted to 375,000 and 600,000 respectively and 1982 was set as the date by which the whole transaction would be completed.

The other community with substantial numbers is that of the Sri Lanka Moors (6.5 per cent of the total). (Fig. 1.18 and 1.21). As a group descended from sea-going Arabs arriving in the ninth to tenth centuries, and with strong fishing and trading interests, they exceed 23 per cent in the east coast districts of Trincomalee and Batticaloa, in Amparai (which latter has 45 per cent), and in Mannar on

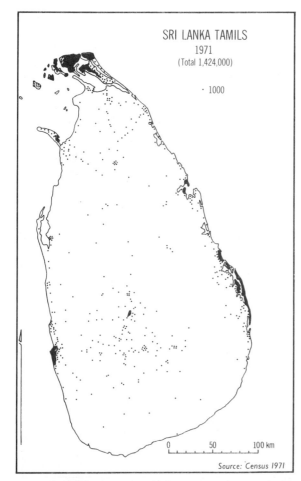

1.19   Distribution of Sri Lanka Tamils

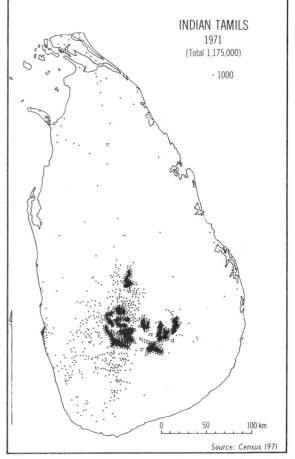

1.20   Distribution of Indian Tamils

the west coast. In Kalmunai electorate of Amparai District, they reach 69 per cent.

The small number of Indian Moors (27,000 or 0.2 per cent of the total population) came to Sri Lanka in the nineteenth century in search of work, and the Malays (0.3 per cent) were brought in earlier to serve as soldiers under the Dutch. The high birth rates of these Muslim groups is characteristic of their co-religionists elsewhere.

By contrast, the Burghers and Eurasians, totalling 0.4 per cent – the descendents of mixed marriages of Portuguese, Dutch or British colonists mainly with Low Country Sinhalese – have a very low birth rate. This is partly a consequence of the considerable emigration of members in the reproductive age groups, leaving behind an ageing population.

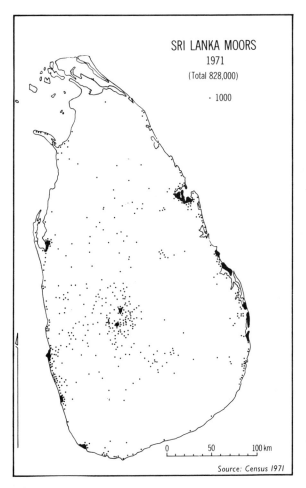

SRI LANKA MOORS
1971
(Total 828,000)

· 1000

0   50   100 km

Source: Census 1971

1.21   Distribution of Sri Lanka Moors

Religion

While the majority of the major groups adhere to their traditional religions – the Sinhalese to Buddhism, the Tamils to Hinduism – the effect of European colonial contact can be seen in almost 8 per cent of the population professing Christianity (over 80 per cent of these being Roman Catholics). They are mainly in the west coast Districts of Puttalam and Mannar where they account for 39 per cent of the total population. Colombo follows with almost 18 per cent of its population being Christian. Buddhism is the religion of over two-thirds of the total population, a proportion that has been rising with the revival of this faith as an element of Sinhalese nationalism following Independence. Hinduism, (18 per cent of the population), has been declining with the repatriation of Indian Tamils, while Islam (7 per cent) shows a recent fractional advance, though the percentage has varied only between 6.6 and 7.2 since 1881.

Both Buddhist and Hindu communities are stratified by caste. Among the Sinhalese there are four major castes which, although deriving from pre-Buddhist Hinduism, now carry no religious sanctions. They are merely functional in origin but still have some connotation in terms of traditional social status, affecting marriage and social mobility in particular. At the top are the *goyigamas* (the cultivators), followed by the *karavas* (fishermen) the *salagamas* (the cinnamon peelers, coming from the *chaliyas* or weavers), and the *duravas* (toddy tappers). There are many other minor castes like tailors, barbers, domestic servants etc. The Tamils have castes similar to those of South India, ranging from the priestly *brahmin* through superior and inferior cultivating castes (*vellala* and *koviyar*, and numerous others) to the untouchables, or *harijans,* at the lowest rank of the system.

The Ethnic Problem

No study of Sri Lanka today can ignore the issue of ethnic disharmony which has become increasingly acute since Independence and is the nation's major political problem. Whatever its roots in the past, there persists today a deep-seated antipathy between the Sinhalese (72 per cent of the population) and the Sri Lanka Tamils (11 per cent). While the present government under President J. R. Jayewardene's statesmanlike leadership appears to be creating a climate for reconciliation to take place between the two groups, it will take a generation of mutual tolerance and respect to unify the nation.*

The acuteness of the ethnic problem lies in the severe competition that exists for the economic opportunities available to the nation's elites. The Sri Lanka Tamils had achieved under the British an enviable position in the professions and the administration, where their numbers proportionately far exceeded their share in the population. Following Independence, the Sinhalese majority began to demand at least its proportionate share in tertiary education and the careers to which a university degree provides the entree. The procedures from time to time adopted to guarantee to the Sinhalese a 'fair' share of university places appear unfair to the Sri Lanka Tamils who sometimes see candidates with lesser academic qualifications gaining places ahead of themselves, particularly in prestigious faculties like medicine, engineering and science.

The Tamils also feel discriminated against in lesser fields of employment, but for the mass of the electorate, however, the ethnic issue is of a political rather than economic nature. Most Sinhalese Buddhists have heard in their religious instruction translations of the *Mahavamsa*, the part-historical chronicle dating from about the sixth century AD, from which they gain a 'conception of themselves as the chosen guardians of Buddhism, and of Sri Lanka itself, "a place of special sanctity for the Buddhist religion"', and a view of the Tamils as 'the implacable enemy'.† Despite this, 'the fact is that the Sinhalese, though an overwhelming majority of the population in the island, nevertheless have a minority complex *vis-à-vis* the Tamils; they feel encircled by the more than 50 million Tamil-speaking people in Tamilnadu and Sri Lanka'.*

Some Sinhalese politicians have played upon these sensibilities for their own political advantage, sometimes quite unscrupulously fomenting feeling against the Tamils, both Sri Lanka and Indian, to justify discriminatory policies. The language issue has been the one in which the Tamils have suffered the most overt discrimination since Independence. Fuel has been added to the flame of Tamil resentment of Sinhalese linguistic policies by the failure of Sinhalese political leaders on several occasions to honour their promises that both Sinhala and Tamil would be recognised as national languages. From time to time this issue has been a major cause of riots and bloodshed. As recently as 1972 a new Constitution made Sinhala the single official language, thus denying to the Tamils the use of their own tongue for official purposes. Although the Constitution promulgated in 1978 moderated some of the earlier legislation, accepting both Sinhala and Tamil as national languages while upholding the former as the official language, it will take some time before the Tamils are convinced that a new era of harmony has begun.

In their reaction to Sinhalese nationalist policies the Sri Lanka Tamils have come to demand a measure of autonomy under the slogan of *Eelam*, a 'separate state for the indigenous Tamils'.† While there may be an historical argument for claiming the Jaffna region as Tamil territory where once the Kingdom of Jaffna existed, it cannot be extended to the east coast districts. Here, although they are the major ethnic group, only in Batticaloa are they in an absolute majority.

Another contentious territorial issue is that of the infiltration of Sinhalese colonists into regions of the Dry Zone regarded by the Tamils as theirs by occupation. They feel threatened by impending overpopulation of the lands they occupy, particularly in Jaffna, and 'have not been given equal opportunity for settlement in these projects as colonists'. Furthermore, 'non-Sinhalese squatters on Government land here are not shown the same tolerance that Sinhalese squatters have enjoyed in recent times'.‡

---

* Two papers by Professor K. M. de Silva present as balanced a view of this intractable problem as the authors have been able to find. The first reviews the situation at its worst, before the fall of Mrs Bandaranaike's regime in 1977; the second discusses some of the improvements under the current Jayewardene regime.
  (i) 'Discrimination in Sri Lanka' in V. Venhoven (ed.), *Case Studies on Human Rights and Fundamental Freedoms: a World Survey*, The Hague, Martinus Nijhoff, vol. 3, 1976, pp. 73–119.
  (ii) 'Political and Constitutional Change in Sri Lanka', in *The Round Table*, No. 273, January 1979, pp. 49–57.
† de Silva, K. M., *op. cit.* 1976, p. 74.

* *Ibid*, p. 87.
† de Silva, K. M., *op. cit.* 1979, p. 53.
‡ de Silva, K. M., *op. cit.* 1978, p. 101.

Education and Literacy

It is somewhat ironic that education, so often regarded as the panacea for the ills of underdevelopment, itself becomes a bone of contention in this the best-educated of the countries of South Asia. Over-education in academic curricula may well be doing the country a disservice by adding to the numbers of educated unemployed, a fertile soil for disaffection. The 1971 census showed that 72 per cent of the males and 67 per cent of the females aged 10–14 were at school, levels that compare very favourably with standards elsewhere in South Asia. The high proportion of girls in school is particularly noteworthy.

The percentage of the age group 10–14 at school in 1971 by Districts is shown for boys and girls separately in Figure 1.22. Jaffna and the urbanised Districts in the southwest have the best showing for both sexes. The lowest rates of participation are found in the hill country tea-growing Districts, the east coast Districts of Batticaloa and Amparai (strongly Muslim) and the least developed Monaragala District. The disparity between the sexes is most marked in the areas with large Muslim communities, in which girls tend to be kept away from school after puberty.

That 78.5 per cent of the population ten years old and over are literate (86 per cent of the males, 71 per cent of the females) bears witness to the long-held respect for education in the island. Colombo District, with 88 per cent literate, leads the field in

8   The beach at Galkanda, north of Ambalangoda in Galle District. Outrigger fishing boats are drawn up in the shade of the coconut palms, with the fishermen's huts behind. The concrete structure in the foreground is the seaward end of a drainage channel cut through the beach ridge to enable flood waters to escape to the sea. (Fig. 4.28)

which again Batticaloa trails on 57 per cent (Fig. 1.23). Apart from the latter District, where two-thirds of the males over ten years of age are literate, no District has less than three-quarters, and eight western Districts have over 85 per cent of males literate. Female literacy rates are less impressive, falling to less than 52 per cent in Nuwara Eliya and Badulla (with large Indian Tamil populations) and in the strongly Muslim east coastal Districts of Batticaloa and Amparai.

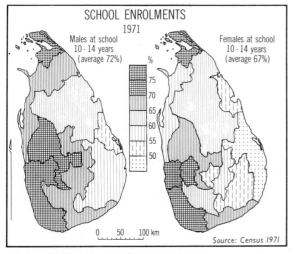

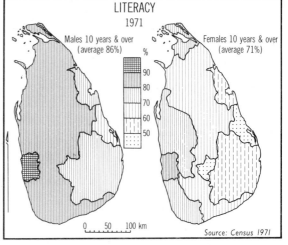

1.22   School enrolments

1.23   Literacy

Government and Politics

Sri Lanka, then Ceylon, gained independence on 4 February 1948 as a Dominion within the British Commonwealth under the statesmanship of D.S. Senanayake who 'sought the reconciliation of the majority and minority ethnic and religious groups within the context of an all-island policy'.* In 1972 it became a Republic.

Up to the present, elections have generally led to the party in power being unseated and replaced by the opposition, sometimes a coalition of parties. One major objective of the revised Constitution promulgated in 1978 is to bring about greater stability by introducing a measure of proportional representation which will make electoral landslides highly improbable in future. Parliament is made up of 196 members. The President, directly elected by the People, is Head of State, Head of the Executive and of the Government, and the Commander-in Chief of the Armed Forces. The President, who is responsible to Parliament and is Head of the Cabinet of Ministers, appoints as Prime Minister a Member of Parliament.

That the 1978 Constitution, brought in by a 'rightist' United National Party (UNP), should describe the State as a Democratic Socialist Republic is some indication of where the centre of gravity of Sri Lanka politics lies. The alternative party of government in the past, the Sri Lanka Freedom Party (SLFP), leans well to the left of that centre. In terms of policies, J. Jupp describes the UNP as following a line more akin to those of the countries of Southeast Asia in encouraging private enterprise and foreign investment while the SLFP tends to the Indian model, imitated at times by

Pakistan and Bangladesh, of placing more reliance on development through the public sector. Since Independence all governments have, however, been committed to a fair degree of welfare politics.

Under the SLFP in coalition with the Trotskyist Lanka Sama Samaja Party (LSSP), policies were pursued to nationalise major economic enterprises, thus removing foreign commercial controls. Subsidised and even free rice rationing and other social welfare measures held the support of the masses despite much unemployment. It has been the SLFP that has most ruthlessly promoted Sinhalese-Buddhist nationalism. On the whole, recent UNP policies have been more reconciliatory to the Sri Lanka and Indian Tamils as the latest constitution shows, and the country's best hope lies in the statesmanship of its President, Mr J. R. Jayewardene.

9   Near Ella in Badulla District, in the southeastern part of the central highlands. A narrow belt of paddy fields, carefully levelled and bunded to hold rainfall, occupies the valley floor. The near slopes are planted with tea where patches of mixed trees hide the homesteads of the paddy farmers; a small field of sugar cane (left centre) and tussocky grass on the steepest slope. In the distance the higher slopes are partly in tea, through which estate roads can be seen zig-zagging, or under *patana* grass. The tea factory on the sky line is well located to benefit from the winds which help the withering process

*de Silva, K. M. in an entry on Sri Lanka's history in *The Far East and Australasia 1977–78*, Europa Publications, London 1978, p. 951. This section draws also on the same writer's edited volume *Sri Lanka: A Survey*, Hurst, London, 1977.

Other valuable sources are: Wriggins, W. Howard *Ceylon: Dilemmas of a New Nation*, Princeton, N. J., 1960 (Dr Wriggins, US Ambassador to Sri Lanka in 1978 graciously discussed modern issues with one of the authors); Mendis, G. C. *Ceylon Today and Yesterday*, Associated Newspapers of Ceylon, Colombo, 1957; Coelho, V. *Across the Palk Strait*, Madras, 1976 (Mr Coelho was a former Indian High Commission Official in Sri Lanka); Jupp, J. *Sri Lanka, Third World Democracy*, Frank Cass, London, 1978.

For an understandably partisan but perhaps necessary corrective of majority bias see Schwarz, W. *The Tamils of Sri Lanka*, Minority Rights Group Report No. 25, London, 1975.

Chapter 2

The Wealth of the Nation

Introduction

The island republic of Sri Lanka may be regarded as the most fortunate of the countries of South Asia in its overall level of development. On Independence, Sri Lanka found itself with a well developed but largely British-owned plantation industry, the exports of which paid for the import of the half of its food that it did not grow itself and almost all the manufactured goods it used. Today the country's major problems are associated with adjusting its economy, based upon rather limited natural resources, to meet the needs of a rapidly increasing and increasingly articulate population, and to respond to the challenges and opportunities of its political independence.

In this chapter we examine the occupational structure of Sri Lanka's work force; the sectoral make-up of the gross national product (GNP), and of exports and imports; the changing pattern of trade; and finally, the general living standards of the people.

Occupations

The occupations of the employed population according to the 1971 Census are shown in Table 2.1 and Figure 2.1.

Half the total were engaged in primary production, 20 per cent of the total being cultivators of the three major export tree crops: tea, rubber and coconuts. In tea-growing there were slightly more women than men, and in only one other activity, textile manufacture, did they outnumber men. In the estate sector, 64 per cent of women aged ten and over were in the work force. For the rural sector as a whole, almost 28 per cent of women worked as against 21 per cent in the urban

areas, there being greater opportunities for women to find agricultural work, paid or unpaid, than urban jobs. There was a negligible difference between rural and urban rates of male participation in the work force which stood at 68.9 and 68.3 per

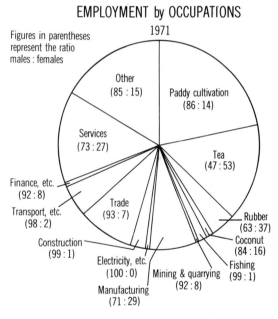

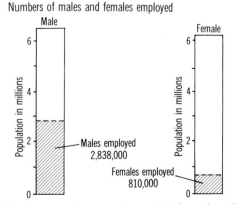

2.1 Employment by occupations, 1971 *Source: Census 1971*

Table 2.1   Major occupations, 1971
(thousands and per cent of total employed)

Occupation by Industrial Group	Total	%	Male	%	Female	%
Total employed	3,649	100	2,838	78	810	22
Agriculture, hunting, forestry, fishing	1,829	50	1,328	36	501	14
paddy cultivation	803	22	689	19	114	3.1
tea cultivation	559	15	266	7	294	8
rubber cultivation	138	3.8	87	2.4	51	1.4
coconut cultivation	43	1.2	36	1.0	7	0.2
fishing	54	1.5	54	1.5	0.7	
others	230	6.3	196	5.3	34	0.9
Mining and quarrying	13	0.4	12	0.3	1	
Manufacturing	339	9	240	7	99	2.7
food, drink and tobacco	72	2	59	1.6	13	0.4
textiles	99	2.7	30	0.8	70	1.9
clothing	19	0.5	12	0.3	6	0.2
wood, cork, furniture	71	1.9	70	1.9	2	
pottery etc.	5	0.1	3	0.1	2	
iron, sheet and fabricated metal	11	0.3	11	0.3	–	
jewellery	8	0.2	8	0.2	–	
other manufacturing	54	1.5	47	1.3	6	0.2
Electricity, gas, water	10	0.3	10	0.3	–	
Construction	104	2.8	103	2.8	1	
Wholesale, retail trade etc.	344	9	320	9	23	0.6
Transport, storage, commerce	179	4.9	176	4.8	3	0.1
Finance, business	25	0.7	23	0.6	2	
Community, social, personal services	493	14	361	10	132	4
Other	314	9	267	7	47	1.3

Source: Census of Population 1971, Vol. II, Part II, Department of Census and Statistics, Colombo, 1976.

cent respectively. Manufacturing industry was relatively poorly developed with 9 per cent of all employed. Most of these were in textiles, the food, drink and tobacco group, and working in wood etc. Metal and mechanical industries were quite small employers. Wholesaling and retailing engaged as many as did manufacturing. This is not surprising in view of the great numbers of tiny 'boutiques' along the roads, many with quite miniscule stock and turnover. The service industries employed 14 per cent of the total, more than a quarter being women, mainly servants in urban households.

Unemployment is high and underemployment also is rife. In the 1971 Census 437,400 were registered as seeking employment, compared with the census total of 3.6 million employed. By the end of 1977 the official figure had increased to over 580,000, although these numbers included those seeking to change their jobs as well as those out of work. Of the 1977 total, 29 per cent were in the technical, clerical and skilled categories, a fact which helps to explain the increasing

search by such people for employment in the financially wealthy, but technologically and educationally poorer, oil-producing countries of the Persian Gulf. An even more alarming figure of 1.3 million unemployed, of whom 80 per cent are in the 19–28 age group, is given in the *Quarterly Economic Review, Annual Supplement, 1977**. In some measure this reflects at least two features of social life. One is the tradition that parents continue to support even adult children still living with them; another is the problem, widespread in the developing world, of youths being educated beyond their parents' station in life and so becoming unwilling to work except at a level of employment which they consider befits their perceived new status.

Underemployment is a common characteristic of an underdeveloped economic system in which available work may be shared among part-time employees. The 1968 Labour Force Survey cal-

* *Quarterly Economic Review of Sri Lanka (Ceylon), Annual Supplement 1977*, London, 1977.

culated that 4.3 per cent (2.4 urban and 4.6 rural) of employed persons worked less than 15 hours weekly, and 28 per cent (19 urban and 29 rural) worked between 15 and 39 hours.* The map showing the distribution of unemployment as a percentage of the total labour force by Districts (Fig. 2.2) suggests the greater severity of unemployment in the more urbanised southwest to which many have migrated presumably in the hope of finding non-agricultural work. Colombo District, with 26.6 per cent unemployed, heads the list; Kalutara and Galle both have 26.2 per cent. At the time of writing unemployment is probably as low as it has been for several years. Government development works such as the Mahaweli Project, industrial growth and the availability of work for skilled labour in the Middle East have reduced the problem.

*Wilson, P. *Economic Implications of Population Growth– Sri Lanka Labour Force, 1946–81,* Australian National University, Canberra, 1975, p. 147.

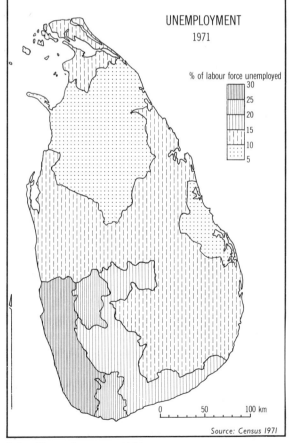

UNEMPLOYMENT
1971

% of labour force unemployed
30
25
20
15
10
5

0   50   100 km

Source: Census 1971

2.2 Unemployment, 1971

Gross National Product (GNP)

Table 2.2 shows the sectoral composition of GNP in 1978 and three earlier years to illustrate the trend of change.

Table 2.2 Gross National Product (percentage)

Sector	1953[1]	1959[2]	1970[2]	1978[3]
Agriculture, forestry, hunting, fishing	49.9	39.1	34.2	31.8
Mining and quarrying	0.1	0.5	0.7	1.8
Manufacturing	4.7	11.6	12.3	20.7
Construction	8.6	4.8	6.4	4.9
Electricity, gas, water, sanitation	0.5	0.2	0.2	0.6
Transport, storage, communications	4.9	9.2	10.0	8.1
Wholesale, retail trade	8.8	13.6	15.5	17.4
Banking, insurance, real estate	0.4	0.9	1.3	2.1
Ownership of dwellings	7.0	3.4	3.5	1.3
Public administration, defence	5.7	5.1	4.5	3.8
Services	10.2	12.3	12.6	8.1

Sources:
[1] data from Balakrishnan, N. and Gunasekera, H. M. Statistical Appendix in de Silva, K.M. *op. cit.,* p. 258.
[2] data from Central Bank of Ceylon, *Review of the Economy,* Colombo, 1976.
[3] data from Central Bank of Ceylon, *Annual Report for the Year,* Colombo, 1979.
Note: That totals exceed 100 per cent is due to the exclusion from the tables of an adjusting net factor for income from abroad which in the years concerned was a negative quantity.

GNP per head of population was RS 2,543 in 1978 approximating to US$ 164, when the total value was Rs 36,139 million at current cost. This represents a 50 per cent increase since 1959. If population growth had been half the rate in this period the increase would have been 78 per cent. The sectoral values differ somewhat from the proportions of the work force employed therein. Thus mining, manufacturing, and transport and communications show a relatively higher contribution to GNP than their workforce would suggest, presumably because of greater capital investment permitting higher per capita productivity. In the agricultural sector, domestic agriculture accounted for more than 73 per cent of the total (mainly paddy production) in 1977 with the plantation sector providing the remaining 27 per cent. The latter figure may give a misleading impression of the importance of the estate sector. How vital it is to the economy is clearly seen in the export trade statistics for 1977 and 1978 set out in Table 2.3, and for a number of past years in Table 2.4.

It is clear that in GNP the primary sector is becoming less dominant as manufacturing and the tertiary sector become stronger. At 1959 costs, total GNP more than doubled between 1959 and 1978, rising from Rs 5,893 million to Rs 13,002 million. Population rose from 9.6 million to perhaps 14 million in the same period to give a change in per capita income from Rs 612 to Rs 917 at 1959 prices.

Table 2.3   Composition of exports, 1977 and 1978 (current value and percentage of total)

Product	Rs million		Per cent	
	1977	1978	1977	1978
Tea	3,503	6,401	53	48
Rubber	931	2,021	14	15
Coconut products*	489	1,259	7	10
Minor crops	184	371	3	3
Gemstones	298	531	4	4
Industrial products	866	1,891	13	14
Others	345	733	5	6
Total	6,616	13,207	99	100

Source: Central Bank of Ceylon, *Bulletin*, Colombo, April 1978 and February 1979.
* Kernel and coir.

Table 2.4   Composition of exports, selected years (by percentage of total value of all exports)

Product	1950	1960	1970	1978
Vegetable products				
tea	50.3	61.8	56.0	48.5
rubber	27.1	21.3	21.9	15.3
coconut products	18.3	13.3	14.2	9.5
cinnamon	0.5	0.8	1.5	1.3
cardamoms	0.2	0.2	0.6	0.3
cocoa	0.05	0.4	0.4	0.4
citronella	0.6	0.2	0.1	0.03
Fish products	–	0.02	0.3	1.8
Mineral products				
graphite	0.4	0.3	0.4	0.4
gemstones	–	0.2	0.2	4.0
Textiles and clothing	–	0.05	0.4	3.6
Total of items listed	97.45	98.57	96.0	85.13

Source: Sri Lanka/Ceylon Yearbook, Colombo, various years, and Central Bank of Ceylon, *Review of the Economy 1978,* Colombo, 1978.

Exports

The heavy dependence on plantation products for earning foreign exchange is very apparent, these making up 76 per cent of the total. Such commodities are notoriously subject to fluctuations in the world market price. Tea is a non-essential beverage for which substitutes exist, particularly coffee. Natural rubber suffers from competition from synthetic rubber and, in the vegetable-oils trade, substitutes exist for coconut oil.

Table 2.5 and Figure 2.3 show the trends in tea and rubber exports by indices of volume and value since 1967. The value of imports is also shown similarly and in Table 2.5 the terms of trade, i.e. the export price index as a percentage of the import price index. While the volume of export trade has fluctuated relatively slightly in the case of tea (between 100 and 81) and rubber (between 97 and 122) their value has increased, more or less marching with inflation in the case of tea, but more erratically in the case of rubber. The volume of imports shows more variation than that of exports, from 108 to 56, but in terms of value, imports have been rather erratic. Despite a substantial drop in volume to 1974–75, their rising value (largely due to the escalation in the price of oil and related products like fertilisers) depressed the terms of trade. The Table and Figure illustrate how difficult it is for rubber producers, for example, to foresee market trends. Since they provide less than 5 per cent of the world's natural rubber they are hardly likely to have much impact on its price. Sri Lanka's fluctuating income from rubber in the mid 1970s ran inversely to the volume of its exports, rising as exports fell, and *vice-versa*.

The terms of trade index is a critical indicator of the quantum of imports that can be paid for with a given quantum of exports. As the index falls so the terms of trade are said to deteriorate. It can be seen that early 1970s saw a progressive deterioration in the terms of trade which had serious repercussions on real national income and, through that, ultimately on the political situation.

After tea and rubber, coconut products constitute 10 per cent of the total exports and 'minor export crops' 3 per cent. The item 'coconuts' covers a range of products made from the fruit of that valuable palm. From the kernel of the fresh nut is made

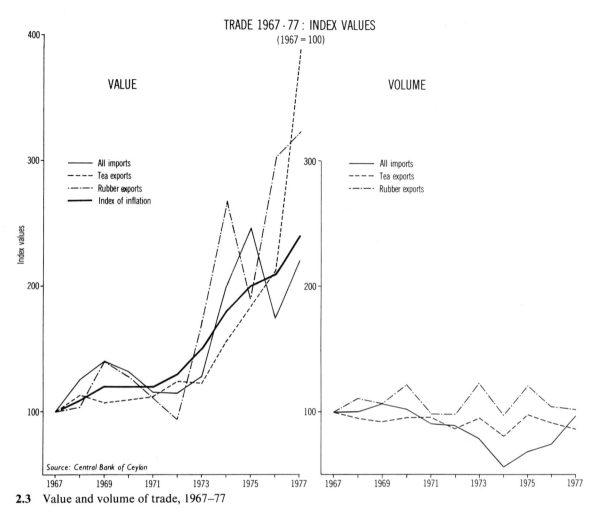

2.3 Value and volume of trade, 1967–77

Table 2.5 Indices of export and import volumes and values, 1967–78 (1967 = 100)

	Tea			Rubber			All imports (price index)	All exports (price index)	Terms of trade
	Export volume (kg million)	*Export volume (index)*	*Export prices (index)*	*Export volume (kg million)*	*Export volume (index)*	*Export prices (index)*	*All imports (price index)*	*All exports (price index)*	*Terms of trade*
1967	218	100	100	132	100	100	100	100	100
1968	209	96	114	150	113	104	126	117	93
1969	202	93	108	143	108	141	134	117	88
1970	208	96	110	161	122	128	140	118	84
1971	208	96	113	129	98	111	150	117	78
1972	190	87	125	130	98	96	158	118	75
1973	206	95	124	161	122	172	209	137	65
1974	175	81	158	128	97	269	370	213	58
1975	213	98	185	161	121	191	433	199	46
1976	200	92	214	137	104	304	383	239	62
1977	186	86	389	136	102	324	471	382	81
1978	193	89	680	138	104	686	877	698	80

Source: Central Bank of Ceylon, *Bulletin*, Colombo, February 1979.

desiccated coconut, and its export value is generally somewhat less than that of coconut oil, extracted by pressing the dried kernel, or copra. About a fifth of the export value is from the coir fibre from the husk. The minor export crops include cinnamon, cardamoms, cocoa, citronella, pepper, cloves, etc.

Fish products are a small but increasingly valuable item of exports, accounting for 1.2 per cent of the total in 1977 and 1.8 per cent in 1978. Prawns and lobsters made up 90 per cent of the value of this item in 1978.

Gemstones (precious and semi-precious) have in recent years made up 5.5 per cent of exports on occasion, a very great increase on negligible levels in the 1950s and 1960s. The mining of gemstones requires little capital so production can expand quickly to meet increases in demand. In 1976 Hong Kong took 38 per cent of the gems exported, followed by Japan (33 per cent) and Switzerland (10 per cent). Smaller buyers included the USA, West Germany, Singapore and France.

Graphite (plumbago) mining is a more heavily capitalised industry. In war time, exports of this valuable lubricating medium (99 per cent carbon) have exceeded 33,500 tonnes per annum, but normally the level is in the range of 7–11,000 tonnes. Petroleum technology has developed alternative heavy lubricants which explains the progressive decline in exports from 302,533 and 262,442 tonnes over the decades 1900–09 and 1910–19 to 98,270 and 93,372 tonnes during the periods 1950–59 and 1960–69. Most production goes to the USA, the UK and Japan (see below, Chapter 6).

Manufactured goods are an increasingly important export item, notably textiles and articles of clothing. Sri Lanka has developed a high reputation for *batik*. It should be noted, however, that in 1978 52 per cent of the value of exports of industrial products (14 per cent of total exports) was made up of bunker oil and petroleum refinery products.

An 'invisible export' not recorded in Table 2.5 is the earnings from tourists visiting Sri Lanka which were estimated to have been worth Rs 870 million of foreign exchange in 1978. Tourism has been increasing steadily, the numbers rising almost two and a half times between 1973 (77,883) and 1978 (192,592). Western Europe accounts for 67 per cent, the majority of the visitors originating in Western Germany, France and the UK. The northern hemisphere winter from November to March is the popular season to visit the island, but no month had less than 3.7 per cent of the total in 1978. During the southwest monsoon the east coast beaches are dry and sunny. Most hotels are air-conditioned. Room availability by regions in 1975 and 1978 is set out in Table 2.6, with the percentage occupancy in 1975.

Table 2.6   Tourism, 1975 and 1978

Region	Rooms available 1975	1978	Percentage occupancy 1975
Colombo city	1,059	1,321	48
Colombo region	669	1,009	39
South coast	790	1,402	33
East coast	230	345	24
High country	212	244	16
Historic cities*	514	969	33
Northern region	58	57	18
Total	3,532	5,347	37

Source: de Silva, G.M.P. 'Level of utilisation of capacity and estimate of room requirements in the hotel industry in Sri Lanka 1977–82', Central Bank of Ceylon, *Staff Studies* 7 (1), 1977, p. 21; *Statistical Pocket Book* 1979, Colombo.
*Kandy, Anuradhapura, Polonnaruwa, Dambulla, Sigiriya.

Imports

The composition of Sri Lanka's imports in 1977 and 1978 is shown in Table 2.7, while Table 2.8– using data for four selected years – reveals some significant trends over the 1950–78 period.

The continuing high proportion of total imports made up of basic foodstuffs underlines the major problem of the economy of Sri Lanka. The question of Sri Lanka's capacity to achieve self-sufficiency in food production is examined further in Chapter 4.

In common with all petroleum importing countries, the rise in oil prices fixed by the OPEC group since 1974 has made savage inroads into foreign exchange earnings. Petroleum's share of imports more than doubled between 1970 and 1976.

On the optimistic side may be noted the progressive decline in the import of textiles, yarn and clothing, a range of manufactured goods in which Sri Lanka has become a substantial exporter.

Table 2.7 Composition of imports, 1977 and 1978 (current value and percentage of total)

| | *Rs million* | | | *Per cent* | | |
	1977		*1978*	*1977*		*1978*
Foodstuffs	2,403		4,249	40	29	
flour and wheat		871	2,095	14		14
rice		917	689	15		5
sugar		197	553	3		4
other foodstuffs		418	912	7		6
Textiles, clothing	461		1,228	8	8	
Petroleum	1,490		2,499	25	17	
Chemicals, fertilisers etc.	418		1,292	7	9	
Base metals	265		928	4	6	
Other intermediate goods	134		496	2	3	
Machinery	420		1,800	7	12	
Transport equipment	287		1,682	5	12	
Other	135		376	2	3	
Total	6,013		14,550	100	99	

Source: Central Bank of Ceylon, *Bulletin*, Colombo, February 1979.

Table 2.8 Composition of imports, selected years (by percentage of total value)

	1950		*1960*		*1970*		*1978*	
Foodgrains	30.6		15.7		24.1		19.1	
rice		23.8		12.4		13.0		4.7
flour and wheat		6.8		3.3		11.1		14.4
Petroleum and products	2.3		7.4		8.4		17.2	
Chemicals etc.	1.6		6.6		7.0		8.9	
Paper and products	1.3		2.0		2.0		2.0	
Textiles, yarn, clothing	14.3		11.9		8.6		8.4	
Metals and articles	3.8		6.2		6.4		6.4	
Machinery	3.1		7.0		11.0		12.4	
Transport equipment	2.8		7.9		5.7		11.6	
Total	59.8		64.7		73.2		86.0	

Source: Central Bank of Ceylon, *Bulletin*, Colombo, February 1979.

Fluctuations in the imports of machinery and transport equipment indicate the impact of varying import restrictions rather than changes in real demand – a view which a casual inspection of the age of the motor vehicles still in use confirms. Following a change of government in 1977, some important restrictions have been relaxed in order to rehabilitate machinery on the estates and transport equipment generally, the consequences of which may be seen in Table 2.7. Compared with 1977, more than twice as many private cars and almost five times as many goods vehicles were newly registered in 1978.

10　The western basin of Colombo Harbour looking north. The sailing boats beyond the warehouses in the foreground ply between Sri Lanka and the Maldive Islands; lighters just beyond them move cargoes around the harbour

The Balance of Trade

After a run of ten years (1966–75) with a negative balance of trade, the years 1976 and 1977 showed a return to a trade surplus, only to be followed in 1978 by another deficit year (Table 2.9).

The balance of trade describes only a part of the country's financial position *vis-à-vis* the outside world. The government's budgetary account provides another aspect. In 1976 and 1977 the account was in deficit by Rs 2,914 and Rs 2,127 million respectively. In 1978 foreign finance contributed Rs 3,798 million net towards meeting the deficit. Rs 3,215 million came from loans, and Rs 583 million from outright grants, part of the loans funds going to repayments.

Direction of Trade

Since Independence there have been important changes in the relative position of Sri Lanka's trading partners. These changes reflect in part the process of 'decolonisation' and in part the growth of trade with the Communist bloc and China, often begun under bilateral agreements. The agreement with China under which Sri Lanka exchanges natural rubber for rice is a longstanding barter arrangement. In 1979 the trade protocol with China did not include any rice imports, but covered a range of industrial fuels, raw materials and manufactured goods: kerosene, diesel oil, chemicals, textiles, newsprint, metals, light industrial products, etc. to the value of US$ 55 million. China agreed to take rubber, coconut oil, cocoa and medicinal herbs in exchange.

In Table 2.10 only countries which have received 2 per cent or more of Sri Lanka's exports in one of the four years listed are included.

The changes in the pattern of export trade suggest a spreading of commercial connections across the world rather than a switch based on political considerations alone. There has been, however, a comparative reduction in trade with the British Commonwealth and with the USA. In the period since 1950 Japan has come to the fore as an industrial trading nation and Singapore and Hong Kong have developed strongly. Pakistan's improved position in 1977 is due to its having substituted

Table 2.9 Balance of trade, 1961–1978 (values in Rs million)

Year	Exports	Imports	Balance	Terms of trade index (1967 = 100)
1961	1,733	1,703	+ 30	136
1962	1,808	1,660	+ 148	142
1963	1,731	1,490	+ 241	129
1964	1,876	1,975	− 99	105
1965	1,949	1,474	+ 475	112
1966	1,700	2,028	− 328	109
1967	1,690	1,738	− 48	100
1968	2,035	2,173	− 138	93
1969	1,916	2,543	− 627	88
1970	2,033	2,313	− 280	84
1971	1,947	1,986	− 39	78
1972	2,009	2,064	− 55	75
1973	2,617	2,715	− 98	65
1974	3,471	4,554	− 1,082	58
1975	3,933	5,251	− 1,318	46
1976	4,815	4,645	+ 170	62
1977	6,638	6,007	+ 631	81
1978	13,206	14,522	− 1,316	80

Sources: Central Bank of Ceylon: *Review of the Economy,* Colombo, 1976; and *Annual Report for 1977,* Colombo, 1978; and *Bulletin,* Colombo, February 1979.

Table 2.10 Export trading partners (in order of magnitude in 1977: by per cent of total)

	1950	1960	1970	1977
Pakistan	2.6	1.2	2.1	8.7
UK	24.5	28.3	22.8	8.6
USA	22.3	9.3	7.2	8.1
China	−	6.8	12.6	7.0
Iraq	−	−	2.8	5.8
Japan	0.1	3.1	3.3	5.2
UAR/Egypt	4.4	0.2	2.8	4.9
West Germany	3.7	4.1	4.1	4.2
South Africa	3.8	4.7	4.0	3.3
Australia	7.6	6.5	3.6	3.2
Netherlands	4.0	2.4	1.7	3.0
Saudi Arabia	−	−	−	2.8
Syria	*	*	*	2.7
Hong Kong	−	0.4	0.4	2.5
Canada	6.3	4.6	2.6	2.1
USSR	−	2.2	4.1	2.0
Iran	−	−	−	2.0

Source: Sri Lanka/Ceylon Customs Returns, Colombo 1950–70; *External Trade Statistics,* December 1977.
* Included with UAR/Egypt.

Sri Lanka tea for its supplies from Bangladesh, cut off when the latter seceded in 1971. The Middle Eastern countries have come out of their relatively closed economies to buy abroad the goods that used formerly to be luxuries but are now well within the reach of the petroleum owning states. With the rise in the cost of Middle East oil there also has been some attempt by the OPEC countries to ease the strain on the economies of the less developed countries by purchasing from them and in some degree balancing their trading accounts with them. (See Table 2.10.)

The import picture is rather simpler, the reason being that a few oil and food grain producers and industrial nations can meet Sri Lanka's needs, while tea, on the other hand, finds a market in very many lands irrespective of the structure of their economies. (Table 2.11)

That two petroleum exporting countries headed the 1977 list requires no comment. Then follow suppliers of industrial goods (USA, Japan, India, UK) and foodstuffs (USA, India, Australia, Thailand, China, Pakistan).

Table 2.11 Import trading partners
(In order of magnitude in 1977: by per cent of total)

	1950	1960	1970	1977
Saudi Arabia	–	–	–	12.6
Iran	4.0	3.9	6.2	9.9
USA	3.0	3.6	5.4	9.1
Japan	2.7	8.4	8.0	6.7
India	15.5	13.7	9.2	6.0
UK	19.7	22.1	13.5	5.5
Australia	6.9	4.9	4.6	4.9
Thailand	4.9	1.0	1.2	4.8
China	0.2	6.8	11.8	4.8
Pakistan	1.2	1.4	2.4	4.6
France	0.6	1.6	2.5	3.9
West Germany	0.8	4.0	5.7	3.7
Burma	19.6	6.3	3.6	2.8
Italy	1.3	1.0	1.2	2.3
USSR	–	0.3	1.7	2.2
Singapore	0.6*	0.5	1.3	2.1

Source: as Table 2.10.
* with Malaya

Living Standards

With 36 per cent of the population in the groups earning less than Rs 200 per month and 40 per cent earning Rs 200–399, there is a considerable number of people living on sub-marginal diets. The worst off are the urban poor (with under Rs 200 monthly in 1969–70) for whom the market is the only source of food. They were averaging an intake of 1,901 calories and 44g of protein. The rural poor fared marginally better, with 2,099 calories and 47g of protein, since many of them could probably obtain some foodstuffs from their own gardens. Among the poor at that time the best provided for were those on estates who had 2,255 calories and 54g of protein.

The determination of a country's standard of living is fraught with difficulty. Average values, such as GNP per capita, can be misleading since they give no impression of how equitably the total is spread among the population. A better measure, particularly used to complement per capita income, is the concept of 'physical quality of life'. While this suffers from similar limitations, it covers factors other than income which, together, may tell us as much about real living conditions (and possibly human happiness) as any monetary value. A recent study uses infant mortality, life expectancy at age one and literacy to arrive at an index of the physical quality of life.*

While Sri Lanka, with a GNP per capita of $200, ranks among the world's Low-Income Group of countries (averaging $166), in respect of the Physical Quality of Life Index, Sri Lanka (with a value of 82) stands between the Upper-Middle (68) and High-Income (93) Groups. Table 2.12 shows Sri Lanka's position relative to its near neighbours and to some countries representative of other Income Groups. It is interesting to speculate what monetary value might be placed upon the fact of living in a continually warm, moist climate as enjoyed by most of Sri Lanka's population.

* McLaughlin, Martin M., *et al.* 'The Measurement of Development Process: A Note on the Physical Quality of Life Index (PQLI) and the Disparity Reduction Rate (DRR)', in McLaughlin *et al.*, *The United States and World Development Agenda 1979*, Praeger Publishers, New York, 1979, pp. 129–44.

The authors' thanks are due to Mr E. F. Dias Abeyesinghe, High Commissioner for Sri Lanka in Australia, for drawing our attention to this paper.

Table 2.12   Per capita GNP and physical quality of life

	Per capita GNP 1976 $		Physical quality of life index*	
SRI LANKA	200		82	
Low-income countries				
(per capita GNP <$300)	166		40	
Bangladesh		110		32
Burma		120		50
India		150		41
Pakistan		170		36
Lower middle-income countries				
(per capita GNP $300–699)	429		67	
Thailand		380		71
Upper middle-income countries				
(per capita GNP $700–1999)	1,215		68	
Brazil		1,140		66
Malaysia		860		73
High-income countries				
(per capita GNP > $2000)	4,976		93	
UK		4,020		94
Australia		6,100		94
USA		7,890		95

Source: McLaughlin, Martin M. *et al, loc. cit.* Table A-4.
*The 'physical quality of life' index is derived by averaging the three indices of infant mortality, life expectancy at age one, and literacy, giving equal weight to each.

The condition of the poorer sector of the population in Sri Lanka has been the subject of several surveys, from which the following comments have been derived.

Average food availability suggests an adequate diet in that it provides about 2,200 calories and 45 g of protein daily, but there is an excessive dependence on starchy foods which provide three-quarters of the calories, rice alone giving 45 per cent. More than 60 per cent of the protein is from cereals, 14 per cent from fish, 10 per cent from pulses and only 5 per cent from meat and milk.

Averages of course obscure extremes, and it is certainly true that the poor consume less than the wealthy, particularly of the more expensive protein-rich items.

As is common in the Third World, it is malnutrition rather than undernourishment that presents the greater threat to health especially among children. Studies of protein-calorie malnutrition (PCM) in school children in 1974 found it to be severe among 14 per cent, the highest incidence being in Matara-Hambantota (26 per cent), Kandy-Nuwara Eliya (18 per cent) and Colombo (16 per cent). Altogether, half the island's population suffered from 'moderate' to 'more severe' malnutrition.*

It is difficult for the Westerner to visualize what it means to be poor in Sri Lanka with reference to food intake alone. A study by the Marga Institute in 1973 provides a range of criteria against which to judge the conditions of life of the mass of the urban people. The study used four income groups, as follows.

Among those households with less than Rs 200 per month the household head, who may be unemployed or at best a casual labourer, has four dependents. The household occupies a slum tenement or a shanty, actually owned by only 40 per cent of such dwellers. Saving money is out of the question for 95 per cent. Per hundred householders, 17 have a radio, 14 a sewing machine and eight a bicycle.

In the next higher income range, Rs 200–399 per month, the breadwinners are manual workers. Saving is beyond 80 per cent of householders; 38 per cent own their house; 29 per cent have a radio; 22 per cent a sewing machine, and 16 per cent a bicycle. The home is small, providing little privacy, and has a bucket toilet.

At Rs 400–600 per month, home ownership is still only 38 per cent, but saving is possible for 27 per cent. Per hundred households, there are 54 radios, 51 sewing machines, 29 bicycles, two refrigerators and one motorcycle! Of those with incomes over Rs 600 per month, 43 per cent can save, 32 per cent own their home, and there are more plentiful consumer durables per hundred households: 82 radios, 13 motor cars or vans, 25 bicycles, but fewer sewing machines (21) since more can afford to have their dresses made for them.

The proportion of income spent on food and drink ranges from 66 per cent among the poorest to 54 per cent by those earning over Rs 600 per month. Housing ranges between 10 and 12 per cent

*ESCAP, *Population of Sri Lanka,* Country Monograph Series No. 4, Bangkok, 1976, p. 308, quoting three sample surveys.

of income, clothing 7 to 8 per cent. Differentiation is greater in respect of education (3 to 8 per cent), and most in consumer durables (0.13 per cent to 2.6 per cent).

11   Unloading cargo, mostly flour, from ships anchored offshore at Kankesanturai, Jaffna District, on the northernmost coast of Sri Lanka

Chapter 3

Traditional Subsistence Agriculture

Introduction

This chapter serves to establish the patterns of traditional agriculture, the various ways in which the pre-industrial cultivators utilised the environments they occupied in order to support themselves, and the land-holding systems they evolved. Agriculture in the Dry Zone is discussed first, as it occupies the largest area and has been the cradle of agricultural practices in the island. Wet Zone and Jaffna agriculture are reviewed to point out the main ways in which they differ from that of the Dry Zone. In Chapter 4 we examine the processes of modernisation in agriculture, and the extent to which traditional methods and social attitudes are still significant influences and constraints upon development.

The cultivator looks to his land to provide rice and other grains, pulses, oilseeds, vegetables, spices and perhaps sugar and tobacco. For extra protein in the diet, fish is the main source except among the Muslims who also favour goats' meat and occasionally beef. By and large the Buddhists are not greatly interested in livestock rearing, since their beliefs prevent them from taking life deliberately. They keep buffaloes as work animals and some cattle for draught purposes. The Hindu Tamils tend to favour cattle for work and as milch animals. Their particular religious prejudice is against cattle-slaughter, though they rear goats for sacrificial purposes.

Traditional Agriculture in the Dry Zone

Two studies by M.U.A. Tennakoon and a paper by B. H. Farmer provide the skeleton for sketching a model of Dry Zone agriculture.* These studies incorporate a cropping calendar upon which most of Figure 3.4 is based and diagrams used in constructing Figure 3.2.

The landscape of the Dry Zone is characterised by wide, gently rolling interfluves separating generally shallow valleys containing a relatively narrow spread of alluvium (see Fig. 3.1 of generalised (soils). In those valleys where maximum river flow is sufficiently moderate to permit control by dams of earth and stone, tanks could be constructed to hold back part of the discharge in reservoirs which could be released as required to supply the paddy

12 A team of men using mamotties cultivating a paddy field in Galle District in preparation for the yala crop. A rubber holding is in the background on the right

*Tennakoon, M. U. A. (i) 'A note on some Social and Economic Problems of Subsistence Farming in Rural Settlements of the Dry Zone of Ceylon,' *Staff Studies*, Central Bank of Ceylon, 2, (1), 1972. (ii) 'Spatial Organisation of Agriculture in the Traditional Rural Settlements in the Mahaweli Development Areas: Problems and Prospects,' *Staff Studies*, Central Bank of Ceylon, 4, 1974, p. 89–110.

Farmer, B. H. 'Problems of Land Use in the Dry Zone of Ceylon', *Geographical Journal*, CXX(1), 1954, p. 21–31 is the basis for part of Figure 3.2.

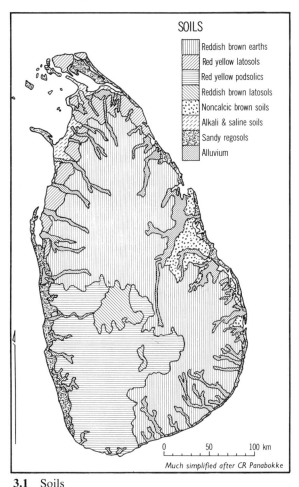

SOILS

	Reddish brown earths
	Red yellow latosols
	Red yellow podsolics
	Reddish brown latosols
	Noncalcic brown soils
	Alkali & saline soils
	Sandy regosols
	Alluvium

0   50   100 km

Much simplified after CR Panabokke

3.1 Soils

13 Teams of roped buffaloes 'mudding' paddy fields for a yala crop at Hungama in Hambantota District, an activity accompanied by much shouting and splashing. In the background is the Hungama Lime Factory

fields. An alternative method of maintaining a supply of water to storage tanks, or direct to the fields, was by means of *anicuts*.

In the situation depicted in Figure 3.2 the village community makes use of three categories of land: the paddy lands under the irrigation command of the tank; the *gangoda* lands upon which the village is built, where each homestead stands in a productive garden of trees, shrubs and annual plants; and the interfluve areas of forest in which *chena* or shifting cultivation can be practised. Figure 3.3 shows the land use pattern of a typical section of the Dry Zone near Anuradhapura within which

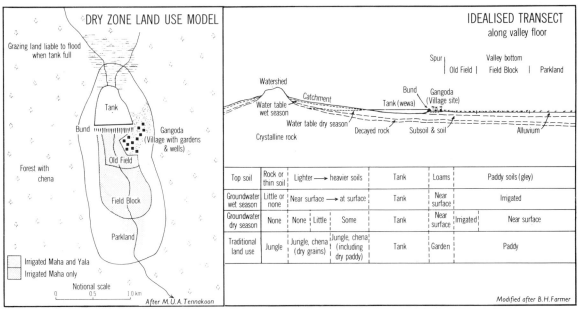

DRY ZONE LAND USE MODEL

Grazing land liable to flood when tank full

Tank

Bund — Gangoda (Village with gardens & wells)

Old Field

Forest with chena

Field Block

Parkland

☐ Irrigated Maha and Yala
▨ Irrigated Maha only

Notional scale
0   0.5   1.0 km

After M.U.A. Tennakoon

IDEALISED TRANSECT
along valley floor

Spur | Valley bottom
Old Field | Field Block | Parkland

Watershed
Catchment
Water table wet season
Bund Gangoda (Village site)
Tank (wewa)
Water table dry season
Decayed rock   Subsoil & soil   Alluvium
Crystalline rock

	Rock or thin soil	Lighter → heavier soils		Tank	Loams	Paddy soils (gley)
Top soil	Rock or thin soil	Lighter → heavier soils		Tank	Loams	Paddy soils (gley)
Groundwater wet season	Little or none	Near surface → at surface		Tank	Near surface	Irrigated
Groundwater dry season	None	None	Little	Some	Tank	Near surface	Irrigated	Near surface
Traditional land use	Jungle	Jungle, chena (dry grains)	Jungle, chena (including dry paddy)	Tank	Garden	Paddy

Modified after B.H. Farmer

3.2 Land use model: Dry Zone

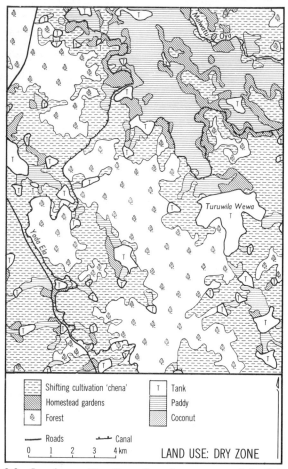

Shifting cultivation 'chena'
Homestead gardens
Forest
Roads
Canal
0   1   2   3   4 km
Tank
Paddy
Coconut
LAND USE: DRY ZONE

3.3 Land use: Dry Zone (based on a map of the Sri Lanka Survey Department with the sanction of the Surveyor General)

the model situation of Figure 3.2 is repeated beside almost every tank.

With the paddy lands intensity of utilisation decreases away from the tank (Fig. 3.2). Closest to the tank bund and adjacent to the village is the Old Field which is most likely to carry both *maha* and *yala* crops during an average year. Yields here may be lower than elsewhere despite the opportunities for more careful cultivation close to home, because the soil is in constant use. However, ownership of at least a part of the Old Field is socially very important and a qualification for village leadership. Consequently, the Old Field tends to become excessively subdivided among all the children on the death of a parent, and holdings are often appreciably smaller than those in the Field Block. In two villages studied, Tennakoon found the contrast to be thus: in village *B*, 97 holdings

on the Old Field averaged 0.22 ha, compared with 25 holdings averaging 0.29 ha on the Field Block; and in Village *D*, 484 holdings on the Old Field averaged 0.15 ha compared with 173 averaging 0.57 ha on the Field Block.

The Field Block lies adjacent to the Old Field but further downstream from the tank. It was developed later than the Old Field and although it is less certain of being supplied with irrigation water for two crops in a year, it is regarded as being of higher monetary (though not social) value. Farmers with land in the Field Block are in a good situation to expand their holdings into the Parkland; since pressures to subdivide on the grounds of prestige are absent, larger properties may be built up.

Much of the Parkland lies too far from the tank to benefit from irrigation. In the good alluvium of the valley floor beyond the reach of irrigation, rain-fed paddy may be grown when rains are adequate. Land values in the Parkland are at best about 30 per cent of those in the Field Block, and at worst 6 per cent.

In addition to the subdivision of holdings that normally occurs under the traditional practice of succession, a common feature of holdings is their fragmentation into several parcels, sometimes in more than one village in the case of parents who have come from different villages. For example a 7.2 ha holding was found to be scattered over 34 parcels, 26 in the Old Field and 8 in the Field Block (one of these ten kilometres distant); another of 4.4 ha was in 24 parcels with some up to 14 km away; a third farmer with 5.3 ha owned 50 parcels distributed under the command of seven tanks.

A common means of overcoming the obvious inconvenience of such fragmented holdings is to let out distant parcels under sharecropping or *ande* agreements, and to rent other lands closer to the main parcels owned. Under *ande*, land is let out to tenants in return for a fixed share of the crop grown. The share of the crop paid to the landlord varies, in part because his level of inputs into the enterprise varies. The Paddy Lands Act of 1958 tried to legislate for fixed rents and security of tenure, but in practice traditional share-cropping arrangements persist. In Polonnaruwa 50 per cent of the crop goes to the landlord, in Anuradhapura 48 per cent, in Kurunegala 42 per cent, in Puttalam 37 per cent, in Hambantota 27 per cent, in Vavuniya

22 per cent and in Trincomalee 18 per cent. There is a full range of land tenancy situations, from that of the absentee landlord renting his land to tenants or letting it out on *ande* terms (often to relatives and friends), to the cultivation of *ande* land by landless people in a traditionally neo-feudal situation. Some owner farmers use only family labour, others hire labour on long term or seasonal contracts.*

Even today agricultural techniques are relatively primitive on most farms. The land is prepared for sowing in a variety of ways. Buffalo or bullock drawn ploughs may be employed to work the un-flooded fields, or teams of buffaloes roped together in twos or threes may be driven round and round a flooded field 'mudding' or 'puddling' the soil with their hooves. Hand cultivation using the traditional *mamotties* (hoes) persists in some areas. Harrowing and levelling are done by draught animals pulling a light wooden board. The *mamotty* is used to mark out shallow channels in the paddy field to stimulate the movement of water through the crop. Pre-germinated paddy seed is then broadcast onto the wet mud. Meanwhile the bunds marking out individual fields and maintaining the level of water therein have been repaired, again with the *mamotty*.

Traditionally, paddy is not fertilised and, apart from a little weeding, the crop is neglected until harvest except for necessary maintenance of the irrigation channels. The water supply from the tank to the Old Field is controlled by the irrigation headman and the channels are a communal responsibility. In the Field Block and beyond, channels are generally privately owned and may become points of dispute among neighbours.

Using small sickles, the harvest is cut by hand, men and women joining in this task. The sheaves are neatly stacked in the fields until the time comes for threshing. The stacks are then pulled apart and the grain is trodden out by cattle or men. It is winnowed by shaking from baskets in the breeze. The straw is stacked near the cattle stalls beside the homestead and the grain is stored nearby in basket-work *bissas*, mounted on stumps to protect it from rats and damp.

The annual round of agricultural activity is set out in the cropping calendar (Fig. 3.4). In this Figure the rainfall graph, characteristic of the cen-

*Wickremeratne, L. A. in de Silva, K. M. (ed.) *op. cit.*, pp. 248–251.

14 Buffalo plough teams preparing a wet paddy at Gabbala in Kegalle District. Homestead gardens of mixed trees in the background

15 Making a palmyra leaf fence north of Jaffna. The first row of leaves are placed upright side by side and are sewn in place with coir twine using a needle 30 cms long (propped against the fence behind the worker). The supporting structure is a 'live' fence of saplings whose leaves are used as green manure and fodder

16 Ploughing a dry field with a bullock team on the grey soils: northwest of Jaffna at the beginning of the hot dry season, before the clay hardens. The flanks of the bullocks have been scored in a Hindu religious ceremony said to keep them docile. Upper left; a crop of salt-tolerant beetroots and on the horizon palmyra palms

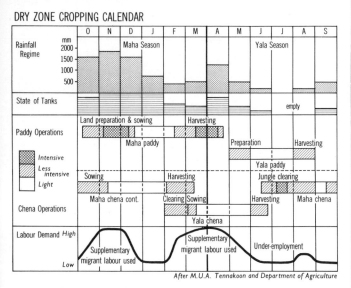

DRY ZONE CROPPING CALENDAR

		O	N	D	J	F	M	A	M	J	J	A	S
Rainfall Regime	mm 2000 1500 1000 500		Maha Season						Yala Season				
State of Tanks									empty				
Paddy Operations		Land preparation & sowing				Harvesting			Preparation		Harvesting		
Intensive / Less intensive / Light			Maha paddy							Yala paddy			
Chena Operations		Sowing			Harvesting			Jungle clearing					
		Maha chena cont.			Clearing Sowing				Harvesting		Maha chena		
					Yala chena								
Labour Demand High / Low		Supplementary migrant labour used			Supplementary migrant labour used			Under-employment					

After M.U.A. Tennakoon and Department of Agriculture

3.4 Dry Zone cropping calendar

tral Dry Zone, is based on 'Agro-Ecological Regions of Sri Lanka' – a chart published by the Department of Agriculture, Peradeniya, 1976. In the Dry Zone, as the calendar shows, the rains of the *maha* season (October to March) are heavier than those of the *yala* season (April to September), and the *maha* paddy crop is the major objective of cultivation. Although some rains may fall in September and early October, sowing of the *maha* crop is generally delayed until the tanks are full enough to guarantee a crop. Land preparation for sowing is at its height in November and December and local labour may have to be supplemented by migrant seasonal workers from the Wet Zone. A similar manpower crisis occurs at harvest time in March and April. For several months of the year,

17 This young girl is planting out yala paddy seedlings in tiny fields in the Ella Gorge in Badulla District

18 This toddy tapper is bringing his morning's sweet toddy to the tavern in pots lined with lime to arrest fermentation. His basket holds the tools of his trade. Near Kalmunai, Batticaloa District

particularly in mid-*yala* season, there is severe underemployment which may be mitigated somewhat by *chena* cultivation. The *yala* season opens with at best the moderate rainfall of April, which is unlikely to refill the tanks depleted during *maha*. Consequently much less land can be irrigated in *yala*, and it may in fact be necessary to ration the supply by practising *bethma* on the Old Field. This involves restricting the area sown to paddy to a block of fields nearest the tank outlet. Fragmentation of holdings probably ensures that each family with Old Field lands has a direct share of the available water. Alternatively, the water may be shared by apportioning the harvest among all landholders. During the months when the area of the tank is much reduced, the lush pasture growing in the tank bed as the water recedes provides valuable fodder for livestock. A third paddy crop *meda*, taken between *maha* and *yala*, may be mentioned in passing. It is sown in situations when the maha crop has failed through irregularity in the rains.

The *gangoda* (village site) in a traditional settlement is usually close to one end of (and a little below) the tank bund where the water table is always reasonably close to the surface. Here, wells can easily be dug to provide a domestic water supply, and the roots of the most essential fruit trees like coconuts, mangoes, and jak can find enough moisture. The homestead gardens of the *gangoda* are a valuable source of nuts, fruits, leaf and root vegetables and spices for the family pot. Where population pressure has forced the spread of the *gangoda* area up on to the interfluve, the homestead gardens are less luxuriant and year-round supplies of well water are generally not available.

Chena

The forest lands of the Dry Zone, although of low productivity in terms of timber other than firewood and local constructional materials, have represented an economic reserve from time immemorial. They have been an insurance against natural disaster striking the paddy lands or against times when population outran the capacity of the paddy lands to support it. The family with too little paddy land could take up an area of forest to clear for *chena* cultivation of subsidiary food crops. In common with shifting cultivation elsewhere in Asia, *chena* cultivation involves the cutting down of trees and scrub jungle during a dry period, the burning of the debris and the planting of crops in the ash-enriched soil. Such crops are entirely rain-fed and so the risk of failure or low yields is high. Traditionally, most commonly sown are the food grains *kurakkan* (*Eleusine coracana*) and maize, manioc (cassava or tapioca), the oilseed *gingelly* (*Sesamum indicum*) and mustard, chillies, bananas, pulses, beans and various vegetables, notably of the pumpkin and gourd type. (Some of these crops are discussed further in Chapter 4.) Traditional *chenas* carried a mixture of crops for one or maybe two years before reverting to jungle when weed growth choked the cultigens. Over a 15 to 20 year period a moderately tall forest could develop before being cleared once more.

It is possible to obtain a good *chena* crop, but compared to paddy cultivation the enterprise is fraught with more uncertainty. Among the five sample villages in Tennakoon's study, many farmers practiced *chena* cultivation on areas varying from half to one hectare per family.

19 Winnowing rice in the wind, traditional fashion, in Hambantota District

20 Terraced wet paddy fields near Welimada in the Uva Basin, Badulla District. The fields in the foreground have recently been transplanted. Banana plants near the drying cloths behind the loaded washerwoman

The effort and time taken to clear and burn a *chena* in readiness for the arrival of the rains, and to build a temporary hut in which to live – not only in order to be on hand to cultivate the crops but also for the purpose of scaring off marauding elephants and wild boar –, tends to affect adversely the standard of cultivation of their paddy lands. In particular, *chena* cultivators prepare and sow their Old Field fields later than others and this may upset village irrigation routines, or they may even leave some fields unused. Nonetheless, *chena* cultivation tends to utilise surplus labour in the seasons of underemployment.

Within the quite extensive area that constitutes the Dry Zone, there are variants of the threefold system of paddy, *gangoda* and *chena* described above. In some coastal areas where the villages, strung out along sandy beach ridges beneath their coconut gardens, are separated by lagoons from their extensive paddy lands, potential *chena* land is too far away to be profitable to clear and supervise, and this element in the system is absent or much reduced.

Another variant is found where tanks are absent, as in parts of lowland Badulla and Monaragala Districts. The paddy element barely exists, and *chena* has been almost the sole source of livelihood, supplemented by whatever permanent tree and garden crops can be raised around the homestead.

21 Hand harvesting paddy by sickle is universal in Sri Lanka: a maha harvest scene near Anuradhapura. The men's lungis (skirts) may be worn short or ankle length

Traditional Agriculture in the Jaffna Peninsula

Climatically, the Jaffna Peninsula suffers typical Dry Zone characteristics at their most extreme. As Figure 3.6 indicates, the brief heavy rains that signal the start of the *maha* season between October and December tail away to low and unreliable levels in the relatively cool dry season of January to March. At the start of the *yala* season there are modest falls in April, but from June to August there is a high probability of total drought.

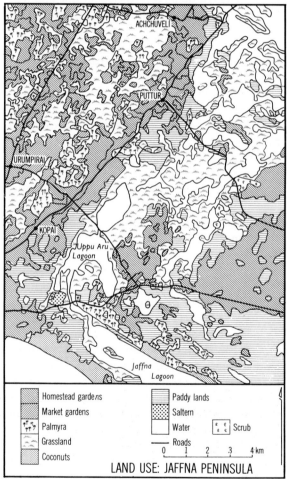

3.5 Land use: Jaffna Peninsula (based on a map of the Sri Lanka Survey Department with the sanction of the Surveyor General)

The chief distinguishing feature of the Peninsula is its complete lack of rivers, and the area is only saved from resembling the driest interfluves of Vavuniya or Mannar Districts by being underlain by an excellent aquifer of Miocene limestone.

Wells in this limestone provide irrigation water for the intensive garden-like cultivation of the red soil areas. The grey loamy soils of the lower ground are used for rain-fed paddy in *maha*, and may carry a *yala* crop (but not of paddy) if irrigation is available. As a rule most of such land lies fallow in *yala*.

Land use in a typical portion of the area immediately northeast of the town of Jaffna is shown in Figure 3.5. The open sea lies three kilometres north of the area. The lagoons are mainly saline, most of them being connected to the sea. They provide valuable fishing grounds, particularly in the season of the northeast monsoon when those inland expand to cover much of the grassland. Where the Miocene limestone outcrops and soils are very thin, poor grassland and thorny scrub is the only ground cover, with occasional palmyra palms in better pockets of soil. Palmyra plantations occupy land of intermediate quality with coconuts on sandier sites. As with coconuts, the palmyra palms are a source of the refreshing drink *toddy* and of sugar, as well as providing a variety of building material. On areas of thicker red soils the homestead and market gardens are in marked contrast, the former heavily shaded by fruit trees, palmyra and coconut palms, the latter very intensively and carefully tilled for multiple crops and dependent for most of the year on well irrigation. Much effort has been expended to increase the area of cultivation by clearing rock and redistributing red soil.

Productivity in the market gardens is carefully maintained by penning cattle on the fields between crops, sometimes in portable thatched shelters, and by digging in green leaves cut from living fence trees and sunn hemp (*Crotalaria*) grown for the purpose. Household rubbish is also used, and manure is now brought in from as far away as Anuradhapura District. What is seen now in Jaffna is a highly commercialised adaptation of the traditional agriculture of the region. The basic patterns of cultivation are set out in the cropping calendar (Fig. 3.6). A clear distinction is seen between the utilisation of the red soils mainly given over to intensive vegetable production, and the lower grey soils of the paddy lands. Early during the rainy season green manures such as sunn hemp are grown on part of the red soils, while the remainder is prepared in readiness for planting in the drier half of the *maha* season when minimum tempera-

22 Bullocks treading out the maha rice grain on woven reed mats, Colombo District

CROPPING CALENDAR: JAFFNA PENINSULA

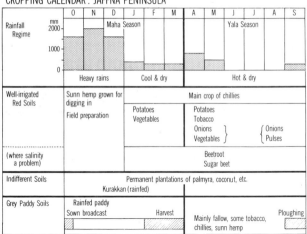

		O	N	D	J	F	M	A	M	J	J	A	S
Rainfall Regime	mm 2000 / 1000 / 0	Maha Season						Yala Season					
		Heavy rains		Cool & dry			Hot & dry						
Well-irrigated Red Soils		Sunn hemp grown for digging in / Field preparation			Main crop of chillies								
					Potatoes Vegetables			Potatoes Tobacco Onions Vegetables }			{ Onions Pulses		
(where salinity a problem)					Beetroot Sugar beet								
Indifferent Soils					Permanent plantations of palmyra, coconut, etc.								
		Kurakkan (rainfed)											
Grey Paddy Soils		Rainfed paddy Sown broadcast				Harvest		Mainly fallow, some tobacco, chillies, sunn hemp					Ploughing

3.6 Cropping calendar: Jaffna Peninsula

23 Where man power is cheaper than beast, rice may be threshed underfoot as here near Madampe, in Ratnapura District. Note temporary sunshade

24 Jaffna women planting out onions in a puddled field, a scene typifying the intensive cultivation of the red soils in the northern peninsula. Onions are a hot season crop following potatoes during the cool dry season. A patch of chillies behind

25 Sheltered from the northeast monsoon rain in a moveable byre in Jaffna Peninsula, these cattle are tethered in a banana patch to provide manure. A scene in December

tures average 18°C. Short season temperate vegetables such as potatoes, cabbage, cauliflower, tomatoes and string beans do well at this time of year, as do brinjals and snake gourds. Chillies, probably the major cash crop of the Peninsula, are sown from January onwards, maturing at the end of the hot, dry *yala* season. During the latter, potatoes and vegetables continue to be planted as well as the major crops, tobacco and onions. Time may allow two onion crops, each of 60 to 65 days duration. Pulses, such as *mung* beans, may be sown to add nitrogen to the soil while producing a saleable crop.

The main constraint on farming on the red soils is the water supply. Towards the end of *yala*, from July to September, there is a risk of well water becoming brackish, and on ground close to lagoons salinity may come to the surface. It has been found that beetroot and sugar-beet can tolerate a fair degree of salinity and chillies and onions a modest amount, up to 2000 ppm of salt.

On the grey soils, rain-fed broadcast paddy is all-important in *maha*, to be followed in *yala* by some sunn hemp (for seed to be used on the red soils in *maha*) and perhaps with tobacco and chillies where well water is assured. In the open fields water now appears to be raised mainly by small petrol pumps, although some homesteads still use the manually operated *picottah* for domestic supplies.

Apart from the red and grey soils there is a third category of land less easy to define, too stony or infertile for vegetables or paddy, but capable of supporting palmyra and coconut palms or a rain-fed crop of the millet *kurakkan*.

26 The typical vegetative confusion of a homestead garden in Kandy District. Coconut palms, banana plants, kapok trees (with pods that hold the fibre), a jak fruit tree on the right, and pepper vines climbing the trunks can all be seen. The farmer is returning home from the well with drinking water

Pressure on the land is acute in the Jaffna Peninsula. This is reflected in the generally small size of holdings of paddy lands, 81 per cent being less than 0.8 ha (in 1946) and they are probably much smaller now. Most holdings are managed by their owners using hired labour, often low caste Hindus, who form part of the large number of landless and underemployed labour.

Traditional Agriculture in the Wet Zone

In contrast to the Dry Zone with its relatively unproductive interfluves between pockets of paddy land beneath tanks, the uplands tend to be economically more significant in the Wet Zone. They are occupied by homestead gardens, smallholdings and, more recently, by plantations of perennial crops. Notwithstanding, paddy farming is still the mainstay of many a Wet Zone village.

It may be argued that cultivating plantation crops is hardly a traditional activity. However, we are not concerned here with the large scale sector of that industry. It is impossible to separate completely commercially-oriented cultivation of perennial tree crops on smallholdings from subsistence paddy agriculture, since the same farmer may practise both. In any case, much of the former has been so long established as to have become part of the local tradition.

The sample land use map of a part of the Wet Zone lowlands (Fig. 3.7) illustrates the intimate juxtaposition of the several land use elements. While the detail varies from place to place, the general principle holds. An important variable in more rugged areas, in Ratnapura District for example, is the addition of forest and grassland on steep slopes. Traditionally, the higher country was unoccupied.

Paddy lands, homestead gardens and smallholdings of perennial crops, i.e. those usually managed by resident owners using family labour, may be identified as the traditional land use elements. Paddy farmers normally have homestead gardens, as do smallholders of 'highland', i.e. land other than valley bottom paddy. Some households extend their enterprise over all three. *Chenas* are rare in the Wet Zone today, largely because the forests have been cleared to make way for perennial crops which make profitable use of the land. The lack of a sufficiently marked dry season for

clearing and burning the plots may have been a contributory factor. Traditionally, the forests were also a source of fruit and firewood. In the hills of Ratnapura District, however, *chenas* are still common on some steep slopes, and in the drier parts of the central hill country they used to form an element in the traditional pattern of land use which incorporated terraced paddy lands and homestead gardens in the valleys, *chenas* on the slopes and upland pastures on the hill tops. Alienation of land to estates effectively put an end to this system, relic survivals of which have been described at Ella in the Dry Zone transition.*

* Wikkramatileke R., 'Ella Village', *Economic Geography* (28), 1952, pp. 355–63.

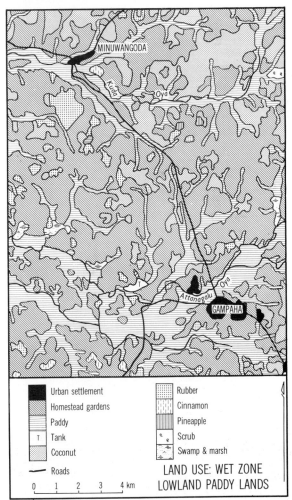

3.7   Land use: Wet Zone lowlands (based on a map of the Sri Lanka Survey Department with the sanction of the Surveyor General)

27 The limestone rock of the Jaffna Peninsula is a valuable aquifer from which the Tamil villagers obtain water for household purposes and to irrigate cash crops. This woman is operating a *picottah*. The pole is attached to a crossbar supported by a structure 6 m high and counter weighted at one end to make the work easier

28 A maha season chena near Punewa about 10 miles south of Vavuniya: sweet potatoes in the foreground, maize beyond, grow amid the stumps of the burned-off Dry Zone jungle. A pumpkin is climbing the tree. In the left background is a temporary shelter for the cultivators who owned some paddy land elsewhere

Since the coming of Europeans, many Wet Zone village families have found sources of income additional to those obtained directly from their lands. Wages may be earned on estates, in gem mines, or in service or craft industries in urban centres. This marks a major contrast to conditions in the isolated and economically less diverse Dry Zone villages.

With rainfall generally abundant and well distributed, irrigation is not essential and in large part the paddy crop is rain-fed. Supplementary irrigation, valuable to protect the *maha* crop against the risk of drought in December and January, is provided by diversion works on the streams. Tank storage of water is exceptional, becoming evident only near the boundary of the Dry Zone.

An excess rather than a shortage of water is the more common complaint of the Wet Zone cultivators. From their middle courses the many short but occasionally vigorous rivers have prematurely flattened long profiles. Consequently, lagoons and marshes are common in their lower reaches, and the river mouths are usually obstructed by sand bars built up by waves driven by the dominant southwesterly winds. Flooding is a regular occurrence, tending to affect not only the plain of the main river but also those of its tributaries which become ponded back. It is the tendency for such areas to become water-logged in the *yala* season, particularly when the southwest monsoon is active.

This is also a period of heavy cloud and low sunshine. Together, these factors lead to the *yala* crop being rather less important than the *maha* (see Chapter 4). Comparative figures for average daily sunshine for Colombo and Kandy in the Wet Zone, and Maha Illuppallama near Anuradhapura in the Dry Zone are given in Table 3.1.

Paddy holdings are small as a rule. For example, the median size is 0.4 ha in a sample from Colombo District and 0.6 ha in Kandy District. In Colombo District (where of course urban pressures are greatest) 71 per cent of the paddy area is in holdings of less than 1 ha, and in Kandy 37 per cent. In general, the owner cultivates his own land; this is the case on 67 per cent of the Colombo sample and 59 per cent in Kandy. *Ande* sharecropping arrangements apply to the majority of the remainder. Ratnapura and Kegalle however showed a very high incidence of *thattumaru* (applying to 25 and 36

Table 3.1 Average daily sunshine, in hours

	Maha			Yala						Maha		
	J	F	M	A	M	J	J	A	S	O	N	D
Colombo	6.2	7.5	8.2	8.6	8.3	6.2	6.6	6.1	6.4	6.1	6.1	6.3
Kandy	4.8	5.9	7.4	7.6	7.2	6.6	6.1	5.7	6.1	6.1	5.7	5.1
Maha Illuppallama	5.1	6.8	8.5	8.8	9.0	8.4	8.6	7.7	8.4	7.8	6.8	6.2

Source: Domros, M. *The Agroclimate of Ceylon*, Steiner, Wiesbaden, 1974, p. 174.

per cent of holdings in the 1946 census). In this system, land owned jointly is cultivated in turn by each owner.*

Cropping methods are much the same as in the Dry Zone though fewer ploughs seem to be used, more land being prepared by teams of men wielding *mamotties* or by buffaloes 'mudding' the paddies. Threshing is often done by cattle hoofs or human feet.

Homestead gardens here are less constrained in their location by soil moisture conditions than in the Dry Zone *gangodas*. Settlement is consequently more dispersed, notably at the margins of the paddy fields and along roads. The climate allows a wide range of plants to be grown and at first impression a homestead garden is a confused, luxuriant, green, multi-storeyed jungle. Most plants in the garden contribute to the diet of the household or the decoration of the house, and some provide a small surplus to sell in the local market. Almost every garden grows coconuts, mangoes, papaws, bread fruit, jak fruit and bananas; many grow *areca* nuts and pepper, and some grow cloves and nutmegs. Among annuals, chillies are very important and many vegetables are grown: yams, onions, brinjals, green gram. There may well be a betel vine for its aromatic leaf for chewing, and a few pineapples. Tea, cocoa, coffee, rubber and kapok more properly belong to the smallholder sector, but may be found mingling in the homestead gardens also.

While there is much variation in the nature of smallholdings they are mainly distinguishable from homestead gardens by having fewer species

and by growing them on a commercial basis. Monocultural smallholdings are common and are usual in the case of cinnamon, but undercropping, as of cocoa or coffee beneath rubber, or of bananas or pineapples beneath coconuts is also practised.

29 Near Monaragala the chena cultivators build tree houses from which to protect their crops from wild pigs and the occasional elephant. Crops in the foreground include several manioc (tapioca) plants, a young banana, a yam, and a tall papaw (papaya). Sugar cane can be seen in the background

*Agrarian Research and Training Institute (ARTI), *The Agrarian Situation Relating to Paddy Cultivation in Five Selected Districts of Sri Lanka: Part 2 Kandy District, 1974; Part 5 Colombo District, 1975.*

With a more or less continually moist climate the farming calendar in the Wet Zone (Fig. 3.8) is less marked by seasonal extremes in labour demand than in the Dry Zone, and in any case the wider range of occupations in the Wet Zone means that families are better able to recruit the help of their relatives and friends locally in an emergency. Furthermore those underemployed in the slack season in the paddy fields can hope to find temporary work on small holdings and there is always something to be done in the homestead garden. Picking and processing cocoa beans coincides with the period of least work in the paddy fields, as does part of the major cinnamon cutting and peeling season.

CROPPING CALENDAR for the WET ZONE LOWLANDS

3.8   Wet Zone cropping calendar

30   Chenas on the hill slopes above homestead gardens of areca palms (betel nuts), jak trees and others at the hill foot, and hill paddy in the foreground. Near Bibile, Monaragala District

31   A villager's house near Monaragala showing the light wooden frame infilled with mud balls. The roof is of palm fronds and grass

Chapter 4

The Quest for Food Self-Sufficiency

Introduction

In the previous chapter we noted the major characteristics of peasant agriculture in its traditional forms, and saw it as a system concerned mainly with supporting the village economy at a subsistence level. Under British rule the island economy was developed almost exclusively for the export of plantation crops to the neglect of the peasant paddy producing sector. Certainly the British from time to time showed their concern (for the Dry Zone particularly) and some rehabilitation of the ancient irrigation systems was accomplished. The colonial rulers began to realise the problems of land shortage created by alienation to plantations (under the Crown Lands Encroachment Ordinance of 1840) and the concentration of investment in this commercial sector. Government sponsored colonisation of lands in the Dry Zone was seen as a step toward solving these problems. Irrigation works there could extend the paddy area and provide some relief for the economic hardships of the Wet Zone population, contributing at the same time to the nation's welfare by increasing the indigenous food supply.

Following Independence, it has been a deliberate aim of policy to dismantle the dual economy established under the British and to create a fully integrated economy run "for the people, by the people" of Sri Lanka. The role of peasant farming has been revolutionised from its local self-sufficiency to become the key to national economic wellbeing. Development of the physical infrastructure needed to promote peasant agriculture has proceeded apace and will reach its climax when the water resources of the Mahaweli Ganga are brought to optimum utilisation in the near future. In parallel with this physical engineering there has been a huge programme of social engineering whereby great numbers of colonists from crowded parts of the island have been established as paddy farmers in the Dry Zone. By 1968 about 60,000 families representing a population of some 400,000 had been settled in colonisation schemes. The process continues.

With increasing momentum and effect, modernisation of agricultural technology has been taking place over the past two decades as Sri Lanka adopted and adapted to local conditions many of the practices and inputs of what is now generally called the 'Green Revolution'. While the paddy cultivator has been the principal beneficiary from modernisation, its effects have spilled over beyond the paddies into the realm of *chena* and other non-irrigated agriculture. Improved communications to urban markets with their increasing purchasing power have helped transform the non-paddy sector in many areas.

32 Working a paddy field in ill-drained land with a tractor is increasingly common as here near Matara. Generally the work is done under contract, and the tractor owner is becoming a wealthy and influential member of his community

Paddy Production Since Independence

Sri Lanka's basic agricultural problem was indicated in the tables of exports and imports: as an agricultural country, how is it to reduce the need to import foodstuffs and so leave more of the earned foreign exchange for the purchase of manufactured goods and, at the same time, how is it to maximise at low cost the production of exportable plantation commodities? The struggle for self-sufficiency in foodgrains continues. As more rice becomes available locally under new schemes and using better technology, the import of food may eventually be substantially reduced. Current data indicate a rise in food imports in 1977 when rice and wheat flour imports topped 1.07 million tons, to fall to 0.8 million tonnes in 1978 however.

The basic facts of the situation are shown in Figure 4.1 which reveals the fluctuating but substantially upward trend in rice production for the period since Independence, marching in parallel with population and with the quantum of food grain and flour imports needed to sustain the nation. The proportional contribution of local production towards total supply has increased from between 34 and 40 per cent in the late 1940s and early 1950s, to between 50 and 60 per cent in the late 1970s, a quite considerable achievement

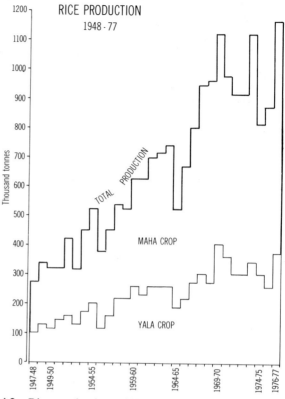

4.2   Rice production, 1948–77

when it is noted that it has meant almost tripling production from an average around 340,000 tonnes in the first six years of independence to 950,000 tonnes in the six years to 1976–77.

The seasonal make-up of the total Sri Lanka rice production since Independence is shown in Figure 4.2. As already indicated, two cropping seasons are recognised traditionally in Sri Lanka: the *maha* season from October to March and the *yala* season from April to September. The maps showing the distribution of rainfall in these two seasons (Fig. 1.7) indicate *maha* as the more generally wet season, while in *yala* the distinction between a wet Wet Zone and a dry Dry Zone is quite marked.

Figure 4.2 indicates the *maha* crop as being the greater, and also that year to year fluctuations in rice production are mainly attributable to variations in the *maha* crop, which in any case normally accounts for about two-thirds of the total, a proportion that has risen from around 60 per cent at the time of Independence. As the larger area of *maha* paddy is in the Dry Zone its yields are much affected by that region's highly variable rainfall

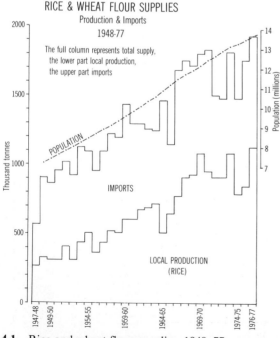

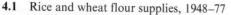

4.1   Rice and wheat flour supplies, 1948–77

upon which the all-essential irrigation tanks depend for replenishment.

The main trends in paddy cultivation are summarised in the maps in Figure 4.3 showing by Districts the area harvested in each season in the fairly normal years 1949–50 and 1977–78. The circles representing the total area harvested by Districts are divided proportionately for *yala* and *maha* crops. The sector representing the *yala* area is oriented to the southwest whence the rainfall comes, and *maha* to the northeast. These sectors are shaded to indicate the percentage irrigated. As three of the 1949–50 Districts, i.e. Anuradhapura, Batticaloa and Badulla, were each subsequently subdivided into two, the 1977–78 data are shown for former comparable areas. The great increase in paddy growing in the Dry Zone since Independence is immediately obvious. Table 4.1 sets out the salient facts in terms of the Wet and Dry Zones and the country as a whole, and Figure 4.4 shows the distribution of lands actually used for paddy according to latest available maps.

Since 1949–50 the total paddy area harvested has increased by 434,000 ha, or 110 per cent (Table 4.1a). Most of this increment is in the Dry Zone where the increase has been 359,000 ha, or 194 per cent, with only 35 per cent increase in the Wet Zone. It follows that more of the increase has been in the area harvested in *maha* (124 per cent) than in *yala* (86 per cent). *Maha* now accounts for two-thirds of the total rice area (Table 4.1b). Much of the increase has been made possible by the extension of irrigation.

In the Dry Zone, 281,000 ha or 230 per cent more land was irrigated than in 1949–50, and in the Wet Zone 124 per cent (Table 4.1c).

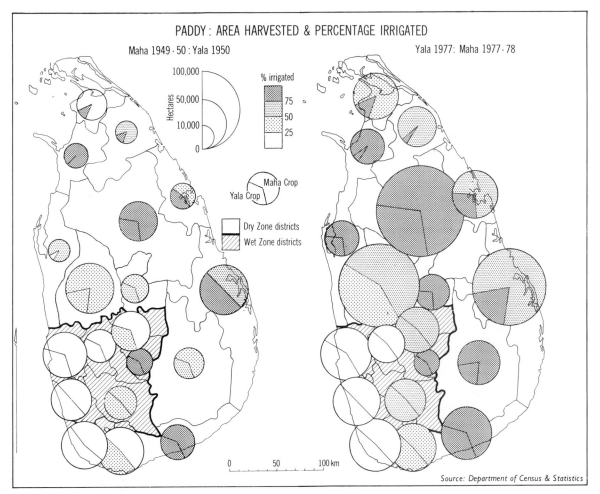

4.3 Paddy, area harvested and irrigation, 1949–50 and 1977–78

Table 4.1   Paddy area harvested and irrigated, 1949–50 and 1977–78

| | *Sri Lanka* | | | *Wet Zone* | | | *Dry Zone* | | |
	1949–50[1]	1977–78[2]	*Per cent increase*	1949–50[1]	1977–78[2]	*Per cent increase*	1949–50[1]	1977–78[2]	*Per cent increase*
(a) Paddy: Area harvested (thousand hectares and percentage increase)									
Maha crop	247	553	*124*	117	157	*34*	130	396	*205*
Yala crop	149	227	*86*	95	129	*36*	54	148	*174*
Total	396	830	*110*	212	286	*35*	185	544	*194*
(b) Paddy: Maha and Yala crops as percentage of total by Zone									
Maha crop	62	67		55	55		71	73	
Yala crop	38	33		45	45		29	27	
Total	100	100		100	100		100	100	
(c) Paddy: area irrigated (thousand hectares and percentage increase)									
Maha crop	100	342	*242*	24	58	*142*	76	284	*274*
Yala crop	67	162	*142*	21	43	*105*	47	119	*153*
Total	167	504	*202*	45	101	*124*	122	403	*230*
(d) Paddy: area irrigated as percentage of Maha, Yala and total									
Maha crop	41	62		21	37		58	72	
Yala crop	45	59		22	33		87	80	
Total	42	61		21	35		66	74	
(e) Paddy: Wet and Dry Zone crops as percentage of Sri Lanka total by season									
Maha crop	100	100		47	28		53	72	
Yala crop	100	100		64	47		36	53	
Total	100	100		53	34		47	66	

Sources:
[1] *Statistical Abstract*, Department of Census and Statistics, Colombo, 1951;
[2] Department of Census and Statistics, unpublished mimeographed tables; courtesy Mr H. Jayasinghe.
Notes: The data refer to the crop seasons (i) *maha* 1949–50 and *yala* 1950 and (ii) yala 1977 and *maha* 1977–78.
Rounding off accounts for some apparent errors in addition.
The allocation of Districts to Wet or Dry Zones follows the practice of the Central Bank of Ceylon. The following are Wet Zone Districts: Colombo, Kalutara, Galle, Matara, Kegalle, Ratnapura, Kandy, Nuwara, Eliya and Badulla.

33   Winnowing, modern fashion, with a muscle-driven fan to provide the breeze, in Colombo District. Reed mats keep the grain clean

The percentage irrigated in the Dry Zone is about double that in the Wet Zone, even during *maha*, the most generally wet season (Table 4.1d). In the Dry Zone the proportion irrigated ranges from 72 per cent in *maha* to 80 per cent in *yala*, compared with 37 and 33 per cent respectively in the Wet Zone. In the driest Districts of the Dry Zone, i.e. Jaffna, Vavuniya and Mannar, the whole *yala* crop has to be irrigated if any harvest is to be reaped, and in these same Districts 80, 96 and 94 per cent respectively are irrigated in *maha*, and over 80 per cent in Batticaloa, Monaragala and Amparai. In the Wet Zone, on the other hand, irrigation is often a more casual procedure, valuable as a standby when rains are erratic, but rarely absolutely essential to the harvesting of a crop.

PADDY LANDS

0   50   100 km

4.4   Paddy lands

34 Epitomising the 'green revolution' the contents of this farm suppliers shop in Kandy include a wide range of insecticides and sprays

The basic contrasts in paddy cultivation are between Wet Zone and Dry Zone: the Wet Zone has abundant moisture but a shortage of land, while in the Dry Zone the position is reversed, there being unreliable rainfall, a shortage of water, but available land. The map (Fig. 4.5) showing the percentage of the total land area used for agriculture by Districts, points to the greater problem of land availability in the Wet Zone.

The concentration of water in tanks from a wider catchment, in order to support a paddy crop over a smaller area, is fundamental to agricultural settlement in the Dry Zone. Because of their shallowness, exposing a large area of water to evaporation in relation to their total volume, tanks are inefficient reservoirs. Yet for centuries they have been the major water resource in the Dry Zone.

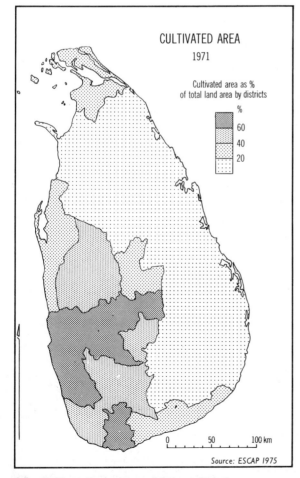

4.5 Cultivated area as percentage of total

Water Resources and Paddy in the Dry Zone

Almost everywhere in the Dry Zone annual rainfall is less than 2,000 mm, and extensive areas receive less than 1,500 mm. The marked seasonality in rainfall distribution has been noted (Fig. 1.10) and its notorious variability from year to year is indicated in the rainfall dispersion diagrams (Fig. 1.9). When seasonal rainfall fails over whole districts, as during *maha* 1974–75, tanks fail to fill and harvests are seriously reduced. Figure 4.6 shows how widespread was the shortfall in harvest throughout northern Sri Lanka compared with an average year – from three-quarters to effectively total failure in the four districts from Anuradhapura northwards. In Figure 4.7 it can be seen that in the ten months up to February 1975 rainfall at Anuradhapura had been below normal, and during the crucial period (October to January) the deficiency was extreme. With little or no water in the tanks, cultivation of irrigated paddy was negligible in many areas, and the rain-fed crop stood no chance of maturing.

At the opposite extreme, excessive rainfall can cause disastrous floods, threatening tanks and drowning growing crops. The floods of December 1957 exemplify the damage that may result when

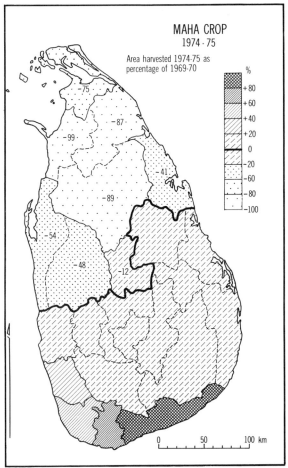

MAHA CROP
1974 - 75

Area harvested 1974-75 as
percentage of 1969-70

	%
	+80
	+60
	+40
	+20
	0
	-20
	-60
	-80
	-100

-75
-87
-99
-41
-89
-54
-48 -12

0   50   100 km

4.6   *Maha* crop, 1974–75

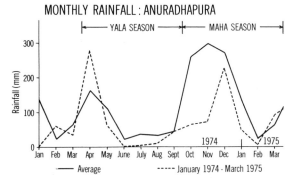

4.7   Monthly rainfall, Anuradhapura

Table 4.2   December rainfall, average and in
1957
(in millimetres)

	Average	*1957*
Jaffna	267	757
Mannar	213	620
Anuradhapura	242	927
Puttalam	168	699
Colombo	175	546
Kandy	211	830
Ratnapura	214	483
Vavuniya	343	927
Trincomalee	373	757
Batticaloa	490	1,181
Badulla	315	777
Nuwara Eliya	190	803
Hambantota	121	480
Galle	224	399

Source: based on data obtained in the Sri Lanka
Meteorological Department, Colombo; Courtesy
Mr I. D. T. de Mel.

an intense cyclonic depression hovers over the island for several days. Average December rainfall
and that experienced in 1957 for 14 stations are
listed in Table 4.2.

It is clear that December 1957 was exceptionally
wet throughout Sri Lanka, several stations record-
ing four times their average precipitation. From
reports in the *Ceylon Daily News* between 23 and 30
December 1957 the worst of the damage can be
assessed. Several large and many small tanks were
breached by flood surges, among them Giant's
Tank, Hurulu Wewa and Parakrama Samudra
(Fig. 4.17). The Gal Oya Left Bank channel was
breached (with dire consequences for the *maha*
crop dependent on its irrigation). The Hambantota
salterns were submerged, ruining the salt harvest.
Altogether, 250,000 people were rendered home-
less and at least 125 were drowned. Even elephants
were reported washed away down the Aruvi Aru.

35   A farmer near Dambulla, Matale District, is spraying
his paddy with insecticide

River Regimes

Most of the rivers with courses in the Dry Zone have regimes which are seasonally unbalanced as well as being highly variable. The general pattern of seasonality can be gauged from Figure 4.8 from which it can be seen that most Dry Zone rivers discharge more than 80 per cent of their flow in the *maha* season, and six of them over 90 per cent. The Wet Zone rivers generally show a balance only slightly in favour of the *yala* season, on average 46 per cent in *maha*, 54 per cent in *yala*.

Figure 4.9 shows the regimes of three characteristic rivers. The location of the gauging points is shown on Figure 4.8.

The Kelani Ganga is a Wet Zone river with minimum flow during the *maha* season, a peak in May, June or July during the southwest monsoon, and a secondary peak in September–October. The three years chosen illustrate a dry, an average and a

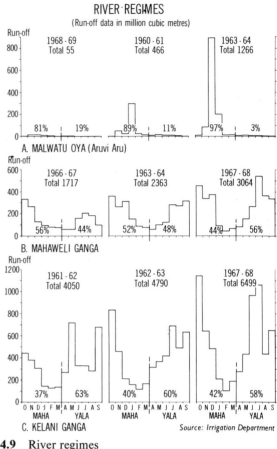

RIVER·REGIMES
(Run-off data in million cubic metres)

A. MALWATU OYA (Aruvi Aru)

B. MAHAWELI GANGA

C. KELANI GANGA

Source: Irrigation Department

4.9   River regimes

wet year. Over 27 years the Kelani Ganga's average flow was 4627 × 10⁶m³, compared with 6499 × 10⁶m³ in a year of heavy flood (1967–68). The Malwatu Oya, known better perhaps as the Aruvi Aru, is entirely a Dry Zone river, and shows great extremes of flood and drought. In a dry year when the *maha* rains failed (1968–69) and the river scarcely flowed at all, the total discharge amounted to only 54.5 × 10⁶ m³ compared with 1266.1 × 10⁶m³ in a year of heavy flood (1963–64). The average is 414 × 10⁶m³. The dry season is always dry in the north.

Fortunately for Sri Lanka, the Mahaweli Ganga, the country's longest river, has its headwaters in the Wet Zone highlands and flows across the Dry Zone. Near Kandy it has an intermediate type of regime, two-thirds of its flow being in *maha* and one-third in *yala*. Its average flow here, 2462 × 10⁶ m³ from a catchment of 1417 km², is little more than half of that of the Kelani Ganga from an area of similar size. The flow is well in excess of the

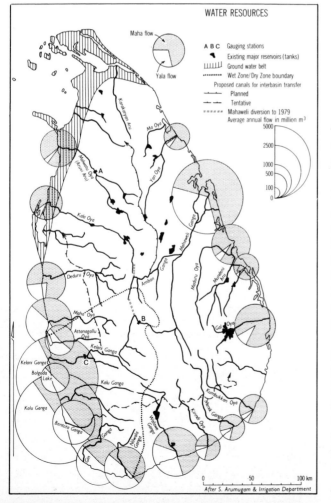

WATER RESOURCES

A B C   Gauging stations

Existing major reservoirs (tanks)

Ground water belt

Wet Zone/Dry Zone boundary

Proposed canals for interbasin transfer
   ———   Planned
   —·—   Tentative
   ------   Mahaweli diversion to 1979

Average annual flow in million m³

After S. Arumugam & Irrigation Department

4.8   Water resources

capacity of the lowlands within the Mahaweli basin to utilise. It is the challenge of putting this surplus to work in other parts of the Dry Zone that has produced the Mahaweli Development Scheme, discussed further below.

Groundwater in the Dry Zone

Since the few rivers in the northernmost parts of Sri Lanka have extremely seasonal regimes, it is fortunate that groundwater underlies some of this area (Fig. 4.8).

The exploration of Sri Lanka's groundwater resources is still in its early stages. Lacking extensive alluvial plains, and with much country underlain by impermeable crystalline rocks, Sri Lanka has only modest prospects of finding productive aquifers. The Miocene limestone formation of the coastal belt extending from south of Puttalam through Mannar and Jaffna Districts has some potential, all the more important in view of the comparatively low rainfall of this region. A number of tube wells are operating, most of them non-artesian and requiring power pumps to raise the water. In some cases fresh water is known to overlie salt water, indicating a risk that over-pumping could lead to saline contamination. It seems unlikely that groundwater will prove of more than local and small scale importance compared with surface water resources, but its use is already enabling some paddy farmers in the Malwatu Oya (Aruvi Aru) delta to obtain a *yala* crop in the dry season while relying upon rainfall and irrigation from Giant's Tank for the main *maha* crop. The great hopes held for groundwater development in Mannar District are epitomised in the cover picture of its Agricultural Implementation Programme, 1978 (Fig. 4.10), on which the dry soil and the misery of hungry cattle confronting the weeping couple beside their *mamotty* on the left, contrasts with the happy harvesting group on the right whose paddy is watered from the tube well. It is questionable whether paddy cultivation is the optimum use for groundwater. The traditional and now highly commercialised intensive agriculture of the Jaffna Peninsula, based upon groundwater which has been described in Chapter 3 can perhaps better repay the capital costs of well sinking and the purchase and maintenance of pumps.

After 'Wimalan'

4.10   Cartoon: Mannar

36   Between Puttalam and Anuradhapura tobacco is becoming an important cash crop on permanent farms where there was formerly chena. The remains of the burnt-over jungle can be seen in the dead trees

Colonisation of the Dry Zone

It has been largely to relieve the pressures on land in the Wet Zone as well as to increase Sri Lanka's food supply that governments have promoted colonisation of the Dry Zone.* Discussion of colonisation – the settling of families on land alienated to them by the Crown in areas away from their homes – cannot be divorced from that of the restoration and further development of the water resources of the Dry Zone. This section concentrates on the question of colonisation, while the importance of water resources to paddy production is examined subsequently. (See Fig. 4.11.)

* Along with numerous students of Sri Lanka in many fields we are greatly indebted to B. H. Farmer for his classic study, *Pioneer Peasant Colonisation in Ceylon,* Oxford University Press, London, 1957.

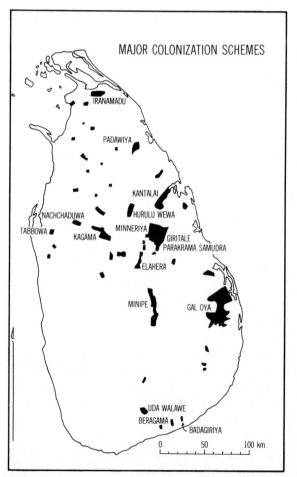

MAJOR COLONIZATION SCHEMES

IRANAMADU
PADAWIYA
KANTALAI
NACHCHADUWA
HURULU WEWA
TABBOWA
MINNERIYA
KAGAMA
GIRITALE
PARAKRAMA SAMUDRA
ELAHERA
MINIPE
GAL OYA
UDA WALAWE
BERAGAMA
BADAGIRIYA

0   50   100 km

4.11 Major colonisation schemes

Prior to World War I the British, who recognised from the ruins the splendour and complexity of the ancient irrigation systems of the Dry Zone, and who were learning in their Indian Empire the possibilities for profitable investment in irrigation, made some attempts to restore derelict tanks and channels. By 1900 they had restored several tanks and *anicuts* supplying the coastal paddy fields in Batticaloa and Amparai Districts, the huge reservoir at Kala Wewa with its Yoda Ela leading to Anuradhapura, and the large tank at Kantalai in Trincomalee District. Up to 1914 Minneriya, Giritale, Nachchaduwa and Giant's Tank were restored (Fig. 4.17). These were all works in irrigation engineering of benefit to the local residents and to any individuals with the means and initiative to settle on their own account.

The early 1920s saw several large scale efforts by companies and individual entrepreneurs to grow rice in the Dry Zone when prices were high. Their failure was due in part to poor communications and the devastating effects of malaria on the work force. Government sponsorship of colonisation by peasant cultivators to use the unoccupied land commanded by restored irrigation works began effectively in 1920 in the Nachchaduwa Scheme near Anuradhapura. Here, colonists drawn initially from Colombo, Kandy and Galle Districts, but eventually almost half coming from nearer the scheme, were given 2 ha of paddy land and some non-irrigable 'high land' for homestead and garden (which they had to clear themselves), a temporary house, free meals until they became self-supporting, free irrigation water, paddy seed and buffaloes on credit, free tools and coconut and jak plants. The scheme failed and was abandoned in 1924 having been dogged by malaria, as were many that followed.

At Tabbowa, a tank was restored in 1926 to assure the town water supply of Puttalam, and in addition to enable a colony to be established to grow irrigated coconuts on 2020 ha. At first, paddy cultivation was prohibited, but in 1932, by which time the vulnerability of a peasant economy based on the monoculture of an export commodity was all too evident, the colonists were allowed to grow rice as well. It was here that a social constraint that for a time reduced the popularity of colonisation appeared. Holdings were designed to support the colonist and his immediate family. Only one heir could inherit the holding, the intention being that other sons should in due course take up new holdings in the area, a system quite at odds with Sri Lanka tradition.

Another special case of colonisation was at Beragama in Hambantota District where a colony of economically depressed Malays, formerly fisher-folk and saltpanners from the coast, was established in 1930 on the Walawe Ganga Left Bank Scheme, each colonist having 1.2 – 1.6 ha of paddy land and 0.4 ha of 'high land'.

Britain's conscience as a colonial power became increasingly tender and by the 1930s the need to develop agricultural colonies as a means to social betterment as well as for the island's economic wellbeing had been recognised. Government, in which the Ceylonese population was now better represented, began to take more initiative. For example, under D. S. Senanayake who in 1932 became Minister of Agriculture and Lands, the Land Development Ordinance of 1935 was introduced, making it possible for government to promote colonisation and to give more direct assistance to the colonists by clearing the land for the settlers, building roads and providing a range of welfare facilities such as hospitals, schools and anti-malarial measures. Although predominantly for small and landless peasants with agricultural backgrounds, middle class settlers were encouraged on some schemes. However, the prime consideration had now become the actual colonisation of the Dry Zone by peasant farmers.

The principles upon which aided peasant colonisation was to proceed, at least until 1953, were worked out and 31 Dry Zone colonies were established in all, 27 of them between 1939 and 1953. Up to 1953 the largest in terms of settlers were Gal Oya (3565 allottees) and Parakrama Samudra, near Polonnaruwa (2780 allottees). The policy adopted from 1939 was in effect to bring the colonist into a ready-made farm of 2 ha of paddy and 1.2 ha of 'high land' complete with house, and to subsidise him till his first harvest. A considerable infrastructure of domestic water supply, irrigation channels, roads, schools, social amenities and a marketing organisation was provided.

By 1939–40, when World War II intervened, the popularity of colonisation schemes had increased, despite the persistence of malaria.

In the Minipe Scheme (1940) lying on the left

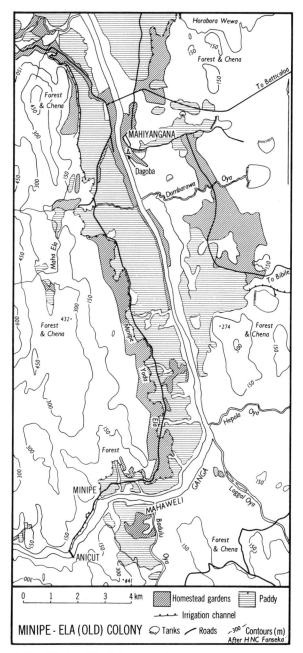

4.12   Minipe-Ela Colony

bank of the Mahaweli (see Fig. 4.12) each of the 571 allottees was given 2 ha of irrigated land and 1.2 ha of 'high land', allocations that were generous compared with those of more recent schemes, and are now considered too large for a colonist to handle efficiently.

Following the introduction of DDT spraying in 1945, malaria was effectively eradicated, and the

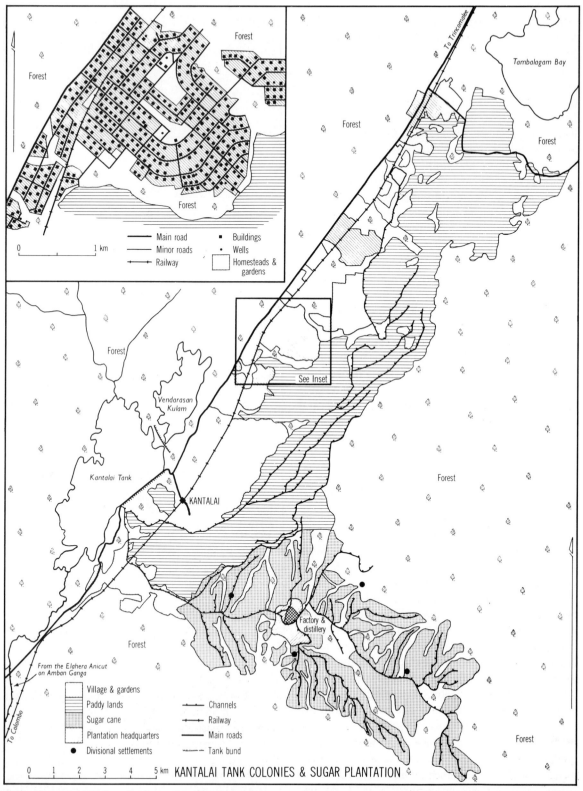

Forest

Forest

Forest

Tambalagam Bay

Forest

To Trincomalee

Forest

See Inset

Vendarasan Kulam

Forest

Kantalai Tank

KANTALAI

Forest

Factory & distillery

Forest

From the Elahera Anicut on Amban Ganga

To Colombo

Forest

Main road   Buildings
Minor roads   Wells
Railway   Homesteads &
                         gardens

0   1 km

Village & gardens
Paddy lands   Channels
Sugar cane   Railway
Plantation headquarters   Main roads
Divisional settlements   Tank bund

0   1   2   3   4   5 km   KANTALAI TANK COLONIES & SUGAR PLANTATION

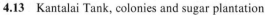

4.13   Kantalai Tank, colonies and sugar plantation

number of applicants to become colonists increased despite the reduced scale of aid then being offered.

In 1953 the area allotted was reduced to 1.2 ha of paddy and 0.4 – 0.8 ha of 'high land'. This enabled the same level of government investment to settle many more colonists, while not reducing paddy production seriously. While the smallest holdings might provide only minimal subsistence needs, on the larger holdings, rather than exert themselves to produce a big surplus and to create wealth and savings for personal investment, the colonists tended to work their land more extensively in order to produce only as much as they needed for present health and happiness within the norms of their cultural milieu.

The colonies based on the reconstructed Kantalai Tank (1959) (Fig. 4.13) are fed by a channel deriving from the Amban Ganga. A large area set aside for cultivating sugar cane supplies the sugar refinery and distillery established there. The layout of a typical colony settlement is shown in the inset.

Badagiriya, a small colony near Hambantota, is laid out rather like a garden suburb, each house standing in a little plot, behind a thorn scrub hedge lining the road. Figure 4.14 is based on air photographs and field investigations. In the dry climate of that district the gardens appear sparse and shrivelled in comparison with most homestead gardens, and for some months when the wells dry up water has to be carted in from Hambantota by tractor and trailer for domestic purposes. Some families fetch drinking water 2 km by bicycle, and take their clothes to the irrigation channel to wash. Clearly, hand irrigation of garden crops and trees is out of the question. Kapok, cashew, mango, *murunga*, lime and coconuts were among the useful trees, bougainvillea, frangipani and neem among the decorative trees noted in the gardens. To supplement the income from their 1.2 ha plots of paddy, many families cultivate *chenas* in the forest, up to eight kilometres distant. There, a temporary hut is built and a range of crops are planted in *maha* in the ashes of the burnt trees: cotton, cowpea, green gram, peanut, *kurakkan*, chillies, manioc, maize, gourds (climbing the tree stumps), pumpkins (trailing on the ground), *gingelly,* papaw, and *tal* (a palm whose juice is made into a honey-

37   The shed (in the centre of the previous photograph) is used for drying tobacco leaves before they are sent to market. Note the cadjan roof

like sugar). The forest produces wood which is sold in bundles by the roadside.

Badagiriya Tank (restored in 1956–57), covering 42 ha behind its two kilometre bund when full, commands 324 ha of paddy land. It is almost dry by August so it is possible to grow only a *maha* paddy crop, sown broadcast in January to be harvested in May. Fishing in the tank yields a little protein. Life in the colony appears to be fairly hard, a view supported by the fact that several homesteads have been abandoned. The neat little school and a bus service to Hambantota are insufficient compensation for a hard, dry, dusty existence.

By 1963 the area granted to colonists had been reduced to 0.8 ha of paddy land and 0.4 ha of 'high land' holdings, now accepted as too small to furnish a reasonable standard of living and the capacity to repay the government's investment.

38   Market gardening for exotic vegetables is a thriving business in Nuwara Eliya District. Crops of cabbage and onions, leeks, beetroots and carrots can be seen and a patch limed on the left in preparation for planting. In the distance the slopes are under tea, and a plantation of eucalypts. The cluster of buildings in the background is a fresh water fisheries centre

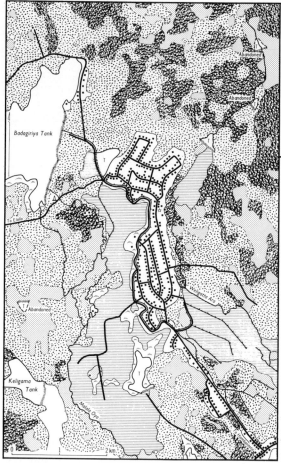

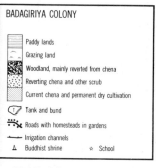

4.14   Badagiriya Colony

Table 4.3   Families settled and areas colonised.
Cumulative totals

Year: up to	Families settled	Paddy land (ha)	'High land' (ha)	Total (ha)
1953(a)	16,532	28,934*	11,818*	47,752
1958	32,091	42,661	25,609	68,272
1960	37,908	46,872	27,632	74,503
1968	60,000	73,247	45,729*	118,976*

Sources:
(a) Farmer B. H., *op. cit.*, p. 164;
Remainder, *Ceylon Year Book, 1959, 1961* and *1969*;
Colombo, 1960, 1962 and 1970.
*rough estimates

39   In the Gal Oya irrigation area, Amparai District, sugar cultivation is a large scale undertaking of the Sugar Corporation. These women are planting cuttings in furrows

Achievements of Colonisation

Colonisation has achieved much in a relatively short time and has certainly contributed to the settlement and population pattern of the Dry Zone.

Table 4.3 gives an indication of the rapidity of progress.

It must be recognised, however, that a process of settlement less dramatic because more dispersed (but really more extensive *in toto*) than the Colonisation Schemes was proceeding contemporaneously. Settlement under Village Expansion Schemes designed to settle their landless people locally accounted for 62 per cent of the land alienated under the Land Development Ordinance (up to 1953) compared with 24 per cent under colonisa-

40   The juice from the cane crusher is boiled down over a fire fuelled with waste cane in this small scale jaggery plant in Badulla District

tion schemes.* In crowded areas villagers could obtain 0.2 to 0.8 ha of Crown Land, and 0.8 to 2.0 ha where land was plentiful.

The population supported by colonisation schemes included more than just the cultivating families. For 1953, Farmer suggests a total of 95,000 or 1.1 per cent of Sri Lanka's population, and for 1968 the *Year Book* estimates 400,000 or 3.3 per cent of the total. In the latter year the irrigable area of major colonisation schemes amounted to half the national total of irrigated land. All the figures in Table 4.3 exclude the Gal Oya and Uda Walawe projects which, although in effect colonisation schemes, were administered separately.

Colonisation in the late 1950s was slowed down following the disastrous floods of December 1957 which caused extensive damage to tank bunds, the repair of which (27 major works and 1100 village tanks) absorbed the Irrigation Department's energies for two years.

Figure 4.11 shows the location of major colonisation schemes in the Dry Zone. Those in the Wet Zone were smaller and of a quite different kind, being concerned with perennial plantation crops, and are discussed in Chapter 5.

*Farmer, B. H. *op cit.*, p. 176.

Planning Problems

The strong feelings of family and village cohesion, and the links between land ownership and prestige in the traditional village, have made it sometimes difficult to find volunteers to migrate to a remote scheme. Until its eradication in the late 1940s malaria was a formidable deterrent to settlement in the Dry Zone, as also were lack of communications and the hard work needed to open up the land for cultivation in the earlier colonies. Over the years there has been plenty of debate concerning government policies and practice in colonisation. The selection of colonists has sometimes raised strong criticism, colonisation officers complaining that town dwellers with no agricultural experience, or men lacking physical stamina or motivation have sometimes been chosen.

There have been criticisms of a communal nature also. Some Sri Lanka Tamils see a further threat to their disadvantageous position as a minority in the progressive peopling by southwestern Sinhalese of the Dry Zone areas formerly regarded as Tamil districts. Criticism has also focused on the social and physical planning of colonisation schemes. The projects now being developed under the Mahaweli Ganga Scheme are likely to benefit from a great deal of research into the defects of early colonies. Among the problems has been the dispersion of homesteads along the road in a colony, which adds to the feelings of isolation that any migrant group is apt to suffer in new surroundings. In some schemes, e.g. Badagiriya, the water supply to homesteads has been insufficient to allow the colonists to create the kind of homestead garden (to which they were previously accustomed) that gives not only shade and privacy, but also a fair range of food crops to supplement the basic diet of rice.

Despite all these adverse aspects there now seems to be no dearth of volunteers seeking to obtain land in the new colonies being developed.

A more modern planning approach is seen in a colonisation scheme currently being developed under the Kala Wewa reservoir, now supplemented by water from the Mahaweli Ganga. As Figure 4.15 shows, a hierarchy of settlements is planned, ranging from residential hamlets, villages providing retailing and community amenities, to townships for higher order functions.

Water Resource Development since Independence

The Gal Oya Scheme
Since Independence, the reconditioning of Dry Zone tanks has been greatly accelerated and, with foreign aid in finance and modern technology,

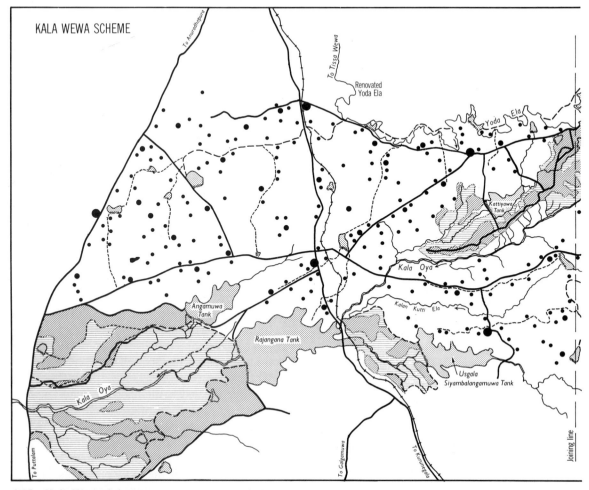

4.15   Kala Wewa Scheme

much more ambitious schemes for regional water management have been designed and are in the process of implementation. The first to be completed was the Gal Oya Scheme which created a 1000 km² reservoir, the Senanayake Samudra, on the boundary of Monaragala and Amparai Districts, to command a potential irrigated area of 48,560 ha and to form the basis for settling a large number of colonists in formerly jungle country. A 10 MW power station was incorporated to utilise the 33 m head of water provided by the dam. The Gal Oya basin lies wholly within the Dry Zone, and the river's regime is strongly seasonal, 91 per cent of the flow being in *maha* (Fig. 4.8). In Figure 4.16 some impression can be gained of the change brought about by this project. Its headworks were completed in 1951 and the first colonists were settled in 1950–51.

The Gal Oya Scheme was the first major project conceived in the heady atmosphere of the brave new world of independence. It was to be another Tennessee Valley multipurpose river basin project, producing power, controlling floods and providing a stored supply of irrigation water. In the event, while all these objectives were achieved, it was a very expensive experiment, the benefit – cost ratio being calculated as 0.5:1.0 by the Project Evaluation Committee set up in 1966.*

* B. H. Farmer was appointed chairman of the Committee whose report was published as *Sessional Paper No. 1*, Colombo, 1970. The one profitable part of the project was the supply of water to the *purana* lands, the old established areas already settled before the dam was built.

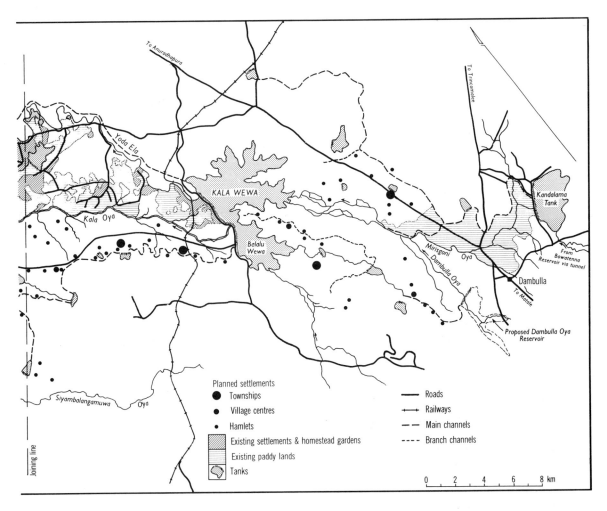

Planned settlements
● Townships
● Village centres
· Hamlets

Existing settlements & homestead gardens
Existing paddy lands
Tanks

— Roads
↔ Railways
– — Main channels
---- Branch channels

0   2   4   6   8 km

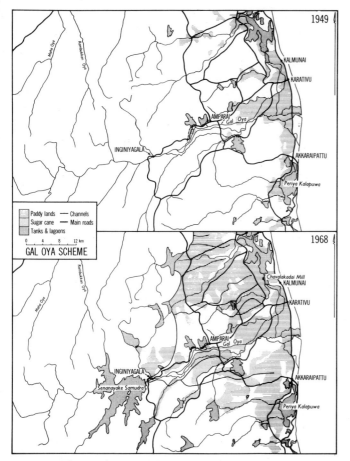

GAL OYA SCHEME

Paddy lands — Channels
Sugar cane — Main roads
Tanks & lagoons

1949

1968

The major criticisms of the project were by no means unique to the Gal Oya Scheme, and were replicated in many parts of the developing tropical world immediately after World War II, when heavy land engineering technology became available along with an excess of enthusiastic optimism that nature could now be bent to man's needs. Without adequate survey of the soils into which the irrigation water was to be spread, the Gal

41 The raw sugar (jaggery) being poured into the tray from which it will be transferred to moulds

4.16 Gal Oya Scheme

Oya Scheme went ahead at full speed and with little regard for costs. Land was cleared of jungle using heavy machinery, at contract costs running to ten times those normally regarded as reasonable when local labour and 'low technology' were applied.

The major work in the project was the damming of the Gal Oya to create the Senanayake Samudra at Inginiyagala, now a beautiful lake in a nature reserve, and a tourist attraction. From the dam two major canals lead water to the left and right banks of the Gal Oya's course. The Left Bank Main Channel commands lands up to 30 km distant to the northeast towards Kalmunai and Batticaloa, while the Right Bank Main Channel leads more directly east to irrigate the sugar plantation and the paddy lands towards the coast. Some of these latter areas were already under cultivation before the scheme was inaugurated and totalled some 13,400 ha (10,500 ha of paddy), under restored tank schemes.

The Gal Oya Scheme was to provide better irrigation to these areas and to make new land capable of double cropping available for colonisation. The first settlers established in 1950–51 were 292 families displaced from the site of the Senanayake Samudra, and over the next 15 years they were followed by 12,000 more, both local peasants and newcomers from the Wet Zone. At first the colonists were given 1.6 ha of paddy and 1.2 ha of 'high land', but these levels were reduced in 1953 (as happened on other colonisation schemes) to 1.2 ha of paddy and 0.8 ha of 'high land', and later to 0.8 ha paddy and 0.4 ha of 'high land'.

As in many irrigation schemes, the control of water is a major problem. Farmers closer to the source may be able to manipulate channels to ensure their own supply at the expense of the 'tail-enders' at the extremity of the system. This happens particularly in the dry *yala* season. When cultivators happen to be different ethnic groups and traditionally antipathetic, such problems can become magnified to the extent of forcing the tail-end farmers off their land altogether. Another difficulty has been the defective planning which located some settlers' fields above the level commanded by the irrigation channels.

Some encouragement was given to farmers to grow tobacco as a cash crop in the *yala* season, as a less thirsty crop in rotation with paddy in *maha*, when the northeast monsoon brings additional moisture. Tobacco has not proved very successful, but the need persists to find alternatives to the double cropping of rice. Without a break from flood irrigation, pests and diseases are difficult to eradicate in the paddies, but the problem is made more difficult by the need to keep water flowing in the channels to meet domestic requirements.

On the 'high lands', some rain-fed paddy may be grown in *maha*, but the more usual crops are vegetables, chillies, onions, manioc, maize, cowpeas and *gingelly*, grown on *chenas* by settlers accustomed to *chena* clearing. The favoured tree crops are coconuts, oranges and (by some) *murunga*. While four-wheel tractors may be seen working the heavy soils, cattle and buffaloes are still much in evidence.

Apart from paddy cultivation, a major innovation is an irrigated sugar cane plantation of 4050 ha, not all of it on the site originally intended, where soils were of variable quality. Its large modern crushing mill has an associated distillery to manufacture alcohol from molasses and to produce rum, brandy and whisky by adding imported flavouring. These plants ran at a loss for many years. Other industries introduced were a tile works to use local clays, a sawmill and wood working plant, an engineering school and workshop, and a large rice mill at Chavalakadai across the lagoon behind Kalmunai. Fish tanks have been built below the dam, and seedling teak is being grown for distribution to reafforestation areas.

Uda Walawe Reservoir Project
The seasonal regime of the Walawe Ganga, which

has some tributaries within the Wet Zone, is better balanced between *maha* (63 per cent) and *yala* (37 per cent) than is that of the Gal Oya (Fig. 4.8). The Uda Walawe Project was Sri Lanka's second venture into river valley development. It is only part of a scheme to develop the water resources of the whole Walawe basin and it is still under construction. The main elements in the project are the completed Uda Walawe Dam with its 6 MW power station and an irrigation command of 32,000 ha, and the Samanalawewa Dam, planned to generate 120 MW and command a further 8,090 ha. Sizeable pre-existing tank and *anicut* systems within the basin are now given supplementary supplies of water. As in the Gal Oya Scheme and at Kantalai, a sugar plantation is included in the plan and already 486 ha of sugar cane are cultivated to supply a mill making syrup. Ultimately, a refined sugar plant is envisaged. Other alternatives to irrigated paddy are favoured for parts of the area in order to make more effective use of the water. Cotton, which requires much less water than paddy, and subsidiary food crops in the paddy fields and 'high lands' are being encouraged. By 1976 the areas planted were 9,000 ha of paddy, 3,640 ha of subsidiary crops and 405 ha of cotton. In the second phase (1977–81) there are to be 6,000 ha each of sugar and cotton, and 1,200 ha of paddy under the left bank channel. Among the problems being experienced in developing this scheme are water distribution difficulties in the right bank area, and the premature occupation by squatters of areas of high land on the left bank earmarked for ultimate irrigation, thus 'jumping the queue' for allocation of land to colonists.

43 Polgolla Diversion Barrage near Kandy, diverts water from the Mahaweli Ganga into the channel in the foreground leading to a tunnel through mountains to the north. (Fig. 4.17)

42 Pouring jaggery into moulds from which the final saleable product will be taken

Mahaweli Ganga Project

In essence, the Mahaweli Development Scheme is designed to harness the resources of the Mahaweli and its tributaries for hydro-electric power generation to develop to the full the irrigation possibilities within the basin and that of the adjacent Maduru Oya, and to transfer surplus water into the upper reaches of the Kala Oya, Malwatu Oya (Aruvi Aru), Yan Oya, Ma Oya, Karakar-yan Aru, Parangi Aru and Pali Aru – all Dry Zone rivers. Existing tanks and new reservoirs will be used to store water locally, thus modernising and enlarging the ancient systems of irrigation and making possible double cropping of rice and the cultivation of other crops over large areas of land, both presently used and yet to be cleared. Ultimately, 364,200 ha (26,500 ha of it new land) will be commanded, and 507 MW of hydro-electric

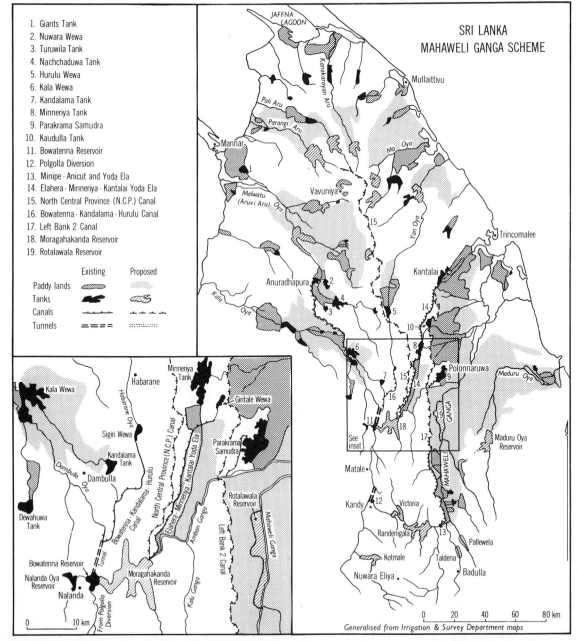

1. Giants Tank
2. Nuwara Wewa
3. Turuwila Tank
4. Nachchaduwa Tank
5. Hurulu Wewa
6. Kala Wewa
7. Kandalama Tank
8. Minneriya Tank
9. Parakrama Samudra
10. Kaudulla Tank
11. Bowatenna Reservoir
12. Polgolla Diversion
13. Minipe - Anicut and Yoda Ela
14. Elahera - Minneriya - Kantalai Yoda Ela
15. North Central Province (N.C.P.) Canal
16. Bowatenna - Kandalama - Hurulu Canal
17. Left Bank 2 Canal
18. Moragahakanda Reservoir
19. Rotalawala Reservoir

	Existing	Proposed
Paddy lands		
Tanks		
Canals		
Tunnels		

SRI LANKA
MAHAWELI GANGA SCHEME

Generalised from Irrigation & Survey Department maps

4.17　Mahaweli Ganga Scheme

power installed – hopefully by 1982. Of the total area irrigated, 174,000 ha are outside the Mahaweli-Maduru Oya basins, in the north-central region. The principal features of the project are mapped in Figure 4.17. In Phase I, Project I, completed in 1978, a barrage across the Mahaweli at Polgolla (12 on Figure 4.17) near Kandy, diverts up to 56.6 m^3 per second of water through an 8 km tunnel to a power station (40 MW) on a tributary of the Amban Ganga. It should be noted that in periods of low flow (see Fig. 4.9) it is not possible to divert this amount of water, and the power station then operates during hours of peak demand only. A reservoir at Bowatenna diverts up to 28.3 m^3 per second through a 6.4 km tunnel, and canals then lead it into branches of the Kala Oya (and thus into existing tanks like the Kala Wewa and Kandalama Tank), into the Habarane Oya, and so to the Hurulu Wewa. Downstream of Bowatenna Reservoir, established canals, forming the Elahera-Minneriya-Kantalai Canals, carry the increased flow to improve supplies to the irrigated tract west of the Mahaweli between Polonnaruwa and Trincomalee. Further developments are under construction, notably the Kotmale Multipurpose Complex near Nuwara Eliya, which will provide storage to smooth the seasonal supply curve at the Polgolla diversion, and the Maduru Oya Reservoir east of the Mahaweli Ganga's middle course. Preparatory work on the Victoria, Randenigala and Moragahakanda Projects is in hand.

The Mahaweli Development Scheme and others of lesser scale will go far to change the face of the Dry Zone as a relatively empty region, as represented in Figure 4.5. Quite apart from the irrigation engineering works described, the fulfilment of the scheme involves establishing colonies of farmers and the infrastructure of services to support them – a considerable exercise in social engineering, but one in which the authorities now have long experience upon which to draw.

The radical concept of inter-basin transfer of water, now a reality in the Mahaweli Scheme, is spawning ambitious proposals elsewhere for 'transbasin' conveyance of surplus from other Wet Zone rivers into the Dry Zone. The adequate resources of the Kelani Ganga may some day be diverted to irrigate dry areas in Puttalam District, while the Kalu Ganga headwaters may be chan-

44 Minipe Anicut on the Mahaweli Ganga diverts water into the channel (left background) to irrigate paddies in the Minipe Scheme (Fig. 4.12). Chenas have been cleared in the hills beyond

nelled eastwards beyond the Kumbukkan Oya basin. These tentative plans are shown in Figure 4.8.

Jaffna Lagoon Scheme

Water-resource development of a very different kind from that involving the manipulation of drainage systems is a possibility for the Jaffna lagoons. The debate about the relative merits of the lagoons as salt and brackish water fishing-grounds and as potential fresh water reservoirs has been going on for many decades, and from time to time engineering works to exclude salt water have been constructed at various points but have fallen into disrepair. It is still considered quite feasible to convert the Elephant Pass Lagoon into a fresh water lake as the first stage in a progressive freshening of the inland lagoons of the Peninsula. Reclamation of 4,450 ha of saline (and thus currently non-cultivable) land is claimed as possible, and in addition irrigation water could be made available for a further 8,000 ha.

Chena: from Shifting to Permanent Dry-land Cultivation?

The value of *chena* cultivation as an insurance in the traditional agricultural economy has been discussed in Chapter 3. The period allowed for the regrowth of natural vegetation, formerly 15–20 years (which allowed forest to redevelop) has been falling progressively under the pressures on the land of an increasing population. It has been observed in the wetter parts of the Dry Zone, e.g. Western Monaragala District, that clearing for *chenas* now takes place after only five years, by which time a cover of low trees and shrubs has developed. In a steep-sided narrow valley about 20 km west of Monaragala, a village schoolmaster described the *chena* cropping succession as maize, *kurakkan* and beans, often in monocultural patches, in *maha*; and in *yala* gingelly, the latter more in hope than in expectation of a return. The *chena* cultivator selects his own plot on Crown Land and is charged a small fee by a village official. More than half the *chena* farmers here are dependent solely on *chenas*, the remainder having other sources of income such as paddy land or wage labouring. A family needs at least 0.6 ha of *chena* for its support but cannot cope with more than 1.2 ha because of the labour involved in weeding, in which the whole family assists, often to the detriment of children's schooling. Sometimes a group of 20 or so villagers will clear a more remote *chena* collectively, dividing it into plots for family cultivation.

This situation approximates to the traditional *chena* system and takes place legally on Crown Land. In some areas, as seen east of the Uda Walawe Reservoir, land designated for sugar cane and other permanent uses when the Left Bank Canal is developed is currently being occupied more or less illegally by *chena* cultivators whose families reside elsewhere. *Illuk* grass rather than scrub jungle has become firmly established here as the secondary growth following *chena* cultivation. The cultivator has to burn off the grass and dig out the larger clumps of roots in order to sow crops for a couple of seasons: maize, manioc, cow-peas, chillies, pumpkins etc. in *maha*, gingelly and groundnuts in *yala*. Bananas, manioc and papaw are grown as year-long crops which may continue being productive as the *illuk* springs up to choke lower plants. The minimum period under *illuk* fallow appears to be three years, but where land is more plentiful a resting period of five or six years may occur. A similar pattern is found in the Dry Zone west of the Walawe Ganga.

Further west again, in the Wet Zone in southern Ratnapura District, a form of *chena* occupance is practised on some estate lands where estate labourers are allowed to clear patches of unused ground to sow upland rice for a season. Such lands are usually on the upper slopes and are allowed to revert to bush fallow for five to six years.

Without an up-to-date air and ground survey it is impossible to estimate accurately how much of the island is used for *chena* cultivation. Figure 4.18 is based in part on the land use maps produced in the 1960s from aerial surveys carried out under Colombo Plan auspices, and in part on personal observations in 1978 and 1980. At best, the map gives an idea of the areas within which *chena* may still be practised, but undoubtedly in many regions the areas available for *chena* are being reduced for various reasons. Much traditional *chena* land in the Dry Zone has been absorbed by village expansion and colonisation schemes. In parts of the Wet Zone and its borders with the Dry Zone, landless villagers have been allotted small plots of

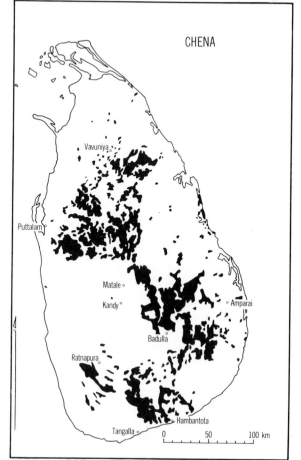

4.18   *Chena*

'high land' in recent years. These areas are too small to allow bush or grass fallowing under a *chena* type system, and appropriate permanent tree crops like coconuts are planted on them. Government policy regarding soil conservation in the watershed areas of reservoirs is to prevent *chena* cultivation, thus further reducing the land which might be used.

Over recent years several changes which have affected *chena* cultivation have been taking place in the demographic, economic and technological environment of peasant agriculture in Sri Lanka. In general, *chena* has been changing from a source of supplementary subsistence crops to become one producing a cash income.

The longstanding constraint upon the continuous cropping of *chenas*, especially in the Dry Zone, has been the growth of weeds, particularly *illuk (Imperata cylindrica)* which choke the cultigens. When the cultivated plants can be fertilised artificially, weeded and perhaps watered, it may be possible to achieve a second (and maybe further) crops off the same land. This is easier in the Wet Zone. However, market factors play the key role. Good prices for tobacco, and subsidised inputs, change the farmers view of traditional practices.

45 Water is being pumped from a well by this small motor to irrigate a crop of chillies on grey soils in Jaffna. Note the palmyra palms on the horizon. Rows of beans and gourds line the path. Fallow paddies beyond

Similarly, a demand for papain, an extract from papaw used medicinally and as a meat tenderizer, or a guaranteed price for chillies or some other crop, can stimulate the producer in search of a profitable adventure, be he a village farmer or an urban entrepreneur. Higher returns stimulate expenditure on modern inputs like fertiliser and the purchase or hire of small pumps to enable streams to be tapped to support the crops.

The range of and area under the major subsidiary food crops grown in *yala* 1976 and *maha* 1976–77 are indicated in Table 4.4. It is impossible to say how much of this area is from *chena*, and how much from permanent cropping.

Most of these crops are seasonal, but *manioc*

Table 4.4 Major subsidiary crops, 1976–77 (by season harvested, thousand ha)

Crop	Maha 1976–77	Yala 1976	Total
Manioc	68		68
Chillies	36	19	55
Kurakkan	30	11	41
Sweet potatoes	19	21	40
Maize	26	8	34
Pulses	17	10	27
Gingelly	10	15	25
Sugar cane	25		25
Tobacco	8	5	13
Brinjals	7	5	12
Groundnuts	6	4	10
Red onions	5	4	9
Red pumpkin	5	3	8
Bandakka (Lady's Fingers)	4	3	7
Turmeric	3	3	6
Beans	2	2	4

Source: Personal communication of Mr H. Jayasinghe, Department of Census and Statistics.
Note: The growing period of manioc and sugarcane extends into the *Yala* season.

46 Pump house and sluice gates at one of the control points in the Madu Ganga Scheme (Fig. 4.28) in Galle District. The sluices protect the area to the left from any inflow of salt water. The pump helps maintain a manageable level of fresh water in the cultivated area to the left

and *sugar cane* remain in the ground for a full year or more (Fig. 4.19). Manioc is a hardy tuber that produces an abundance of starch with the minimum of effort. As the distribution map shows, it is widely grown in the Wet Zone and the moister parts of the Dry Zone. The cultivation of sugar cane by temporary occupiers of cleared *illuk* and scrub is also an example of opportunist enterprise. It is also becoming popular as a soil-rehabilitating crop before replanting tea. When the price is favourable, sugar cane is a profitable crop which can be ratooned (grown without replanting) for several years in succession in quite rough country. It is crushed and the juice is boiled down to jaggery in small plants requiring little capital. Refined white sugar is produced by State owned factories from cane grown in large irrigated monocultural plantations at Kantalai in Trincomalee District (Fig. 4.13) and near Amparai under the Gal Oya Scheme (Fig. 4.16).

Chillies (Fig. 4.20) are a very popular dry-land crop, particularly when restriction on their import increases their price. Another advantage of chillies on *chenas* is that wild pigs and other animals do not eat them. They are mainly grown in *maha*, and more in the Dry Zone than the Wet.

The traditional *chena* grain, *kurakkan*, is grown mainly in *maha*, over the north-central and south-eastern Dry Zone, although some is also cultivated in *yala* (Fig. 4.21). Some upland paddy is also grown in the Wet Zone.

Sweet potatoes (Fig. 4.22) are predominantly a Wet Zone crop although they are found too in the moister parts of the Dry Zone. Maize (Fig. 4.23), due to its drought tolerance and productivity, is a popular *chena* crop in *maha* in the wetter Dry Zone.

Gingelly (Fig. 4.24) as a source of vegetable oil is commonly grown in *chenas* in *yala*. In Dry Zone *chenas* it is almost the only crop grown then. Its distribution is very similar to that of the several crops included under the heading of pulses: green gram, cow-pea and dhal.

Cigarette *tobacco* has become a major *maha* cash crop in Nuwara Eliya and the hilly wetter regions of the Dry Zone. As a *yala* crop it is also significant on paddy lands where irrigation cannot support a second rice crop. The Ceylon Tobacco Company Limited (a branch of British American Tobacco) has a monopoly of the market, controlling every stage of production. It provides free seed and plants it on the farmers' land, advancing fertilisers and chemicals against the value of the harvest.

In the wetter areas where some 5,200 ha are grown, the farmer has to flue-dry the leaf, a process demanding a considerable amount of firewood. For this reason, and because the crop is clean weeded, thus leaving bare soil exposed, the industry has come under attack for causing soil erosion in the watersheds of planned hydroelectric power reservoirs. In drier areas, responsible for about 800 ha, tobacco can be air-dried.

Farmers may grow tobacco for two years on the same land, after which maize, *kurakkan*, mustard or gram will be grown for a year. Small areas of cigar, *bidi* (cheap local 'smokes') and chewing

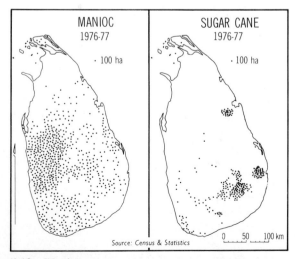

4.19   Manioc, sugar cane

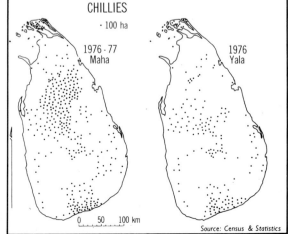

4.20   Chillies

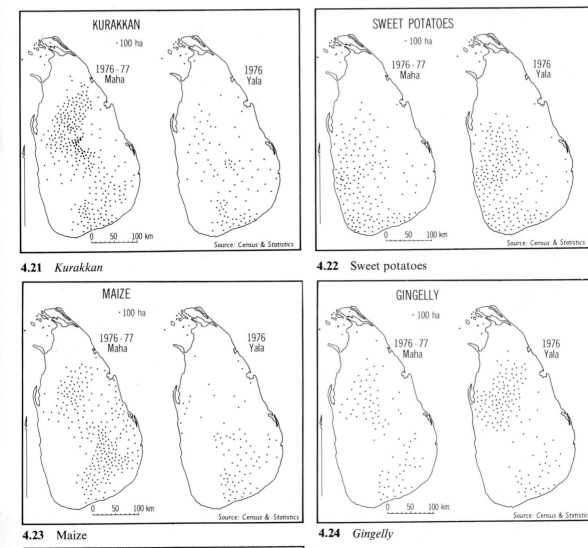

4.21 *Kurakkan*

4.22 Sweet potatoes

4.23 Maize

4.24 *Gingelly*

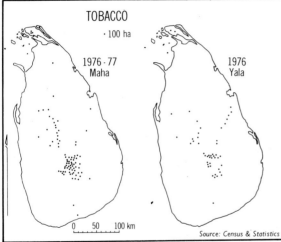

4.25 Tobacco

tobacco are also grown: cigar quality particularly in Jaffna and Kurunegala.

Bananas are almost ubiquitous throughout the island, most commonly in homestead gardens but also as a commercial crop on Dry Zone *chenas* and on the fringe of the Wet Zone. Cotton is also grown as a highland crop on *chenas* and on permanently cultivated uplands.

The search for a satisfactory way of permanently farming the 'dry lands' beyond the reach of large scale irrigation – and consequently unsuited to paddy – has been going on for many years at the Maha Illuppallama Research Station near Anuradhapura. Reliable economic methods of farming the Dry Zone using rain-fed crops alone have eluded the researchers. With unpredictable rainfall, dry-land farming seems possible only if a modicum of irrigation water is available as an insurance. A promising application of this principle is being tried in the Kurundankulama Scheme on the outskirts of Anuradhapura.

The Kurundankulama Dry Farming Settlement, started in 1938, has been through numerous vicissitudes. It began as a group of individual farmers with 4 ha each in a total settlement of 40 ha. In an extension in 1948 new settlers had 0.8 ha for their own use and worked the rest co-operatively until, in 1950, the whole scheme became a co-operative farm. This failed, and the land reverted to individual ownership in 1957. A recent report found 266 ha occupied by a population of 416. Most holdings were between 3.2 ha and 5.7 ha. Only 40 per cent of the land was cultivated in *maha* and 25 per cent in *yala*. Furthermore, a few farmers also cultivated *chena*, or took up paddy lands outside the settlement. The holdings in this scheme are considered rather too large for a family to work, 2 to 2.4 ha being thought more appropriate.

One 2.4 ha farm in this scheme, visited in 1978, had a well and a small petrol pump. The seasonal cropping pattern is as follows. In *maha*, when the rains come, the main cash crop, chillies, is grown

47   Senanayake Samudra on the Gal Oya, the first major multipurpose river development project in Sri Lanka. The catchment area is now a National Park. The lake is named after D. S. Senanayake first Sinhalese Minister of Agriculture and Lands and later Prime Minister at the time of Independence

yala, *gingelly* is sown on most of the land. On this farm, fertiliser is applied only to the chillies.

Rain-fed agriculture is the basis of the Dry Farming Settlement although, with the possibility of purchasing small pumps with the proceeds from selling high value chillies, irrigation from wells is being introduced where possible. The major crops are chillies in *maha* and *gingelly* in *yala*, as shown in Table 4.5.

Tractors are largely used in land preparation. Fertilisers are applied, particularly to chillies, and some chemical control of pests and disease is practised. In *toto*, these dry farms provide somewhat better living conditions than traditional village agriculture. Farms like this were said to be in serious difficulty if there were two successive failures in the *maha* rainfall, causing the well water to fail.

It is possible that *chena* will some day give way to permanent cultivation on lines similar to these, but greater government interest and encouragement will be needed to bring dry-land crops to parity with paddy when it comes to issuing subsidies and setting up supporting services.

Where supplementary irrigation is not available, as on some steeply sloping areas that grow tobacco or papaws in the Wet Zone – Dry Zone transition of Matale, Kandy and Ratnapura, *chena* might become a system of periodic fallowing to rest the land for a year every two or three years, the rain-fed crops being assisted by fertilisers. Whatever happens, the State is unlikely to tolerate much longer the wasteful exploitation of its forests that *chena* has meant in years past.

Table 4.5   Crops grown at Kurundankulama, 1975–76

	Percentage of maha area (total 106 ha)	Percentage of yala area (total 67 ha)
Gingelly	–	93
Chillies	44	2
Paddy	8	2
Kurakkan	7	1
Maize	3	–
Cow-pea	16	–
Green gram	5	–
Yams	10	–
Vegetables	5	2
Others	2	–

Source: Gooneratne, W. *et al. Kurundankulama Dry Farming Settlement*, Research Study Series No. 17., Agrarian Research and Training Institute, Colombo, 1977.

on half the holding and cow-pea, green gram, kurakkan and maize on the other half. In the subsequent year the use of the two halves is reversed. A small strip of 0.4 ha on the lowest land grows rain-fed paddy in *maha* and lies fallow in *yala*. In

In the context of supplementary crops this is an appropriate point to mention the Youth Employment Schemes that were inaugurated in 1966 to try to find a meaningful occupation for some of the many thousands of educated but unemployed and frustrated youths of the nation. In the mid 1960s maybe 200,000 youths aged between 19 and 25 were unemployed, of whom 40 per cent were educated to GCE O level. That some young people were given purposeful and healthy work to do, learning thereby something of the ways and problems of the cultivator who is the mainstay of the country, probably matters more than success in strictly economic terms.

There are five kinds of Youth Scheme: two relate to the plantation crops – tea and coconuts; one deals with animal husbandry and subsidiary crops; and two specifically involve crops other than paddy raised with the help of lift or reservoir irrigation. One Youth Scheme visited in Mannar District

had a well in the limestone with water at 15 m, requiring the motor pump to operate halfway down the shaft. On 12 ha, 20 young men were growing chillies and black gram on the *terra rossa* soils. Success or failure depends entirely on the water supply.

Each youth received a subsistence allowance for up to two years, and a contribution towards removing stumps, building a temporary hut and a latrine on his plot, purchasing seed etc. Most of the youths were Tamils from Jaffna Peninsula, only 80–100 km from their homes. They have tended not to settle permanently on the project site but to remain only during the cultivation period.

The *Sri Lanka Yearbook*, 1977, reported that 4127 youths were resident in 48 Youth Schemes covering 7480 ha. Of 43 schemes in 1973, 23 were for subsidiary food crops in the Dry Zone.

A much larger scheme at Visuvamadu Kulam* (Fig. 4.26) just south of Elephant Pass Lagoon in Jaffna District was begun in 1966 with 60 youths in the first stage, using gravity-flow irrigation from a tank to cultivate chillies, at that time starting to fetch high prices. In the second stage, lift irrigation opened up a higher block, and in the third stage wells were dug to groundwater, downslope of the areas already developed. By 1973, 315 ha of chillies and 177 ha of paddy were being cultivated by 600 youths. Incidentally, there were 960 families in the adjacent Village Expansion Scheme.

While each youth got individual possession of 1.2 ha of land, the capital equipment of the scheme was managed co-operatively. So profitable was the cultivation of chillies (even on this small scale) that 25 tractors were purchased from individual profits and these young men became contract tractor ploughers outside the area of the scheme! As in many co-operative projects, it has proved difficult to recover loans advanced, since the project does not handle the sale of the product.

Problems for Paddy Development in the Wet Zone

About 34 per cent of the total area under paddy is in Wet Zone districts. As can be seen in Figure 4.3 and Table 4.1 there is a much closer correspond-

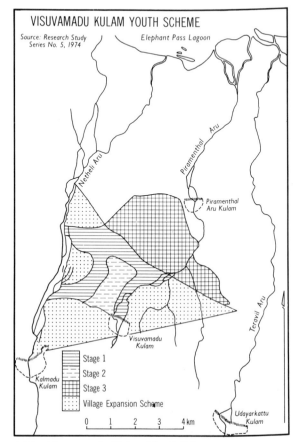

4.26 Visuvamadu Kulam Youth Scheme

*Ellman, A. O. and Ratnaweera D. de S. *New Settlement Schemes in Sri Lanka*, ARTI, Research Study No. 5., Colombo, 1974.

ence of the *maha* with the *yala* paddy area in the
Wet Zone than in the Dry Zone, the *maha* crop
accounting for 55 per cent of the annual total here,
as against 73 per cent in the Dry Zone. Despite
maha being the drier season in the Dry Zone, yields
are higher then (Table 4.6). The higher rainfall
of the *yala* season, often producing floods, and the
cloudier weather associated with it which pro-
motes the development of plant diseases and pests,
combine to make it a less favourable period for
paddy cultivation. Sown in April, the *yala* crop
comes to maturity in July or August when
conditions are seldom ideal for ripening, cutting,
threshing, drying and storing the grain.

Paddy here relies largely on rainfall supplemented by water led from the streams in *elas*.
Although the rainfall is over 2000 mm per annum,
and is normally well distributed throughout the
year, occasional dry spells occur, more often in
January and February but sometimes also in
August, which make the maintenance of the *elas* a
worth-while insurance. (Note the incidence of low
totals in the rainfall dispersion diagrams for Wet
Zone towns in Figure 1.9). Apart from the environmental difficulties, part of the blame for low yields
in the Wet Zone must be placed on the field practices which are not intensive. Transplantation is
exceptional, to some extent because the high
organic content of the marsh soils renders them too
weak to support transplanted seedlings. Normally
pre-germinated seed is broadcast on to the puddled
land.

The problem of flooding differs between the
flood plains along the major rivers and the areas
around the coastal lagoons. In the case of rivers
like the Bentota Ganga, Gin Ganga and Nilwala
Ganga, flood protection involves building
levees to restrict the flood current to the main
channel, thus expediting its discharge to the sea
and preventing its flood water entering the tributary basins. Sluices allow the tributary drainage to
enter the main river when its level is low.

The coast from Chilaw to Matara consists of a
system of beach ridges 100–600 m wide, enclosing
lagoons and interrupted by occasional rocky
headlands. Longshore drift of sand under the
impelling force of the dominant southwest
monsoon maintains these ridges and constantly
extends sandspits northwards at each river
mouth. The flow of the smaller rivers, however, is

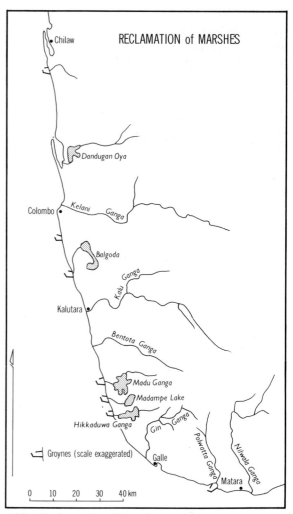

4.27   Reclamation of marshes

often inadequate to keep the channel through the
sand bars open. Behind the coastal ridges the
lagoons, of varying salinity, are surrounded by
marshlands at 0.3 m below to 1.0 m above
mean sea-level (MSL) (Fig. 4.27). During periods
of intense rainfall the lagoon levels rise until the
sand bar is breached and seaward flow relieves the
flood. Although the tidal range is small (+ 0.46 m
to − 0.3 m MSL at maximum spring tides), should
these tides coincide with floods the problem is
accentuated. Tides are also responsible for salt
water intruding into sea-connected lagoons in
dry periods. Building groynes at river mouths is
one measure that is being taken to keep the river
channels open for the free flow of flood waters
from the lagoons, but sluice gates may also be
necessary to prevent the inflow of salt water.

One such scheme, the Madu Ganga Salt Water Exclusion Scheme (Fig. 4.28) illustrates in more detail the approach to the problem of the coastal lagoons. The Madu Ganga, in Galle District, forms a lake 8 km² in extent which drains to the sea about a kilometre distant at Balapitiya through a natural channel, the depth of which is restricted by rock and whose mouth is constrained by a longshore drift of beach sand building up a bar. This effectively dams the river during dry periods and while the lake deepens when the river is in spate there is some delay before the river waters breach the bar to release the impounded floodwaters. Much of the 810 ha of paddy land in the tributary valleys draining into the lake is low-lying; one-third of it lies between – 0.3 and +0.6 m MSL, and another third between +0.6 and 1.5 m MSL. To reduce the frequency of flooding of the paddy lands the following works have been undertaken. First, rock groynes were built 140 m out to sea at the mouth of the river, to reduce longshore drift, but a sand bar still forms occasionally, and villagers clear it from time to time with the help of the Irrigation Department. Subsequently, several of the tributary valleys were separated from the lake by embankments incorporating sluices and (in three cases) pumps to enable excess water to be evacuated. The embankments also serve to prevent salt water intruding under tidal flow during dry weather. An additional exit for the lake was cut at Galkanda, five kilometres north of Balapitiya, discharging into the sea through a channel cut in the rock. The drainage channels entering the lake have been cleared and some of them shored up with revetments of bamboo or coconut logs, to prevent blockage by slumping of the banks, while the river bed under the railway and road bridges has been deepened by blasting.

There seems to be no solution in the foreseeable future to one serious constraint in paddy cultivation in the marshy tracts, even when the water level and salinity can be better controlled. Below 0.6 m the soils change from mixed alluvial to bog soils, which are soft and incohesive with insufficient body to hold the roots of paddy plants which may consequently float away given the slightest encouragement.

Up to 1977, eight reclamation schemes involving 7263 ha had been completed and another on the Gin Ganga was under construction to improve drainage of 4856 ha there. A further four schemes for 4000 ha were expected to be begun shortly. The Polwatta Ganga Drainage and Reclamation Scheme (1500 ha) was inaugurated in 1978.

The Wet Zone Districts hold over 65 per cent of the population of Sri Lanka but contain only 34 per cent of the paddy area, with yields considerably lower than those in the Dry Zone. This suggests that paddy cultivation here plays a subsidiary role to other agricultural enterprises. Homestead gardens, smallholdings and particularly plantations, together with economic activities in fields outside agriculture, are more important here than in the Dry Zone.

Market Gardening in the Wet Zone

In World War II, Sri Lanka was the headquarters of the South East Asia Command during the Allies' struggle against the Japanese. The cool, healthy climate of the hill country made Nuwara Eliya an ideal location for military hospitals and recreation centres. To supply these (and the troops garrisoned in the low country) with fresh temperate climate vegetables, the local farmers were given seed and fertiliser. From these beginnings an intensive vegetable-growing industry

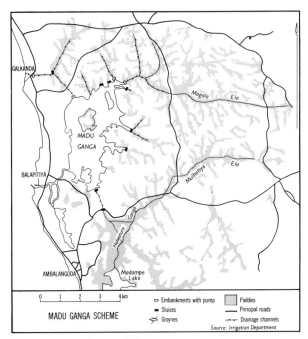

4.28 Madu Ganga Scheme

has developed in the hill country especially around Nuwara Eliya, but also in parts of Badulla and Kandy Districts close to communications. Besides vegetables for the Colombo market, a speciality is the cultivation of seed potatoes for use in the low country, even as far afield as the market gardens of the Jaffna Peninsula. Of the area under potatoes (3023 ha) 79 per cent is in Nuwara Eliya and Badulla which together produce 84 per cent of the total of 27,700 tonnes. These two districts, with Kandy, account for 95 per cent of the cabbages, 86 per cent of the carrots, 85 per cent of the *kuol khol*, and 90 per cent of the leeks. Radishes, beans and beetroots have a wider distribution but are still important in the hills.

Around Nuwara Eliya, market-garden crops are grown in rapid succession, much care, fertiliser and many waterings being lavished upon them. In the mid-country where one paddy crop is possible in the wet season, a vegetable crop may be taken in the dry season, where there is insufficient water for a second paddy crop.

Modernisation in Agriculture

The traveller is soon struck by the signs of modernisation in field agriculture, even though traditional methods of cultivation, processing and transport remain more common. There is convincing evidence in the rise in paddy productivity per unit area between 1949 and 1977 that changes have been taking place.

Yields of paddy per ha by seasons and zones are given in Table 4.6. Rice yields would be 68 per cent of the figure for paddy, i.e. unhusked rice.

The very considerable improvement in yields is attributed to the introduction of high yielding varieties (HYV) and the better methods of cultivation that have been associated with the 'Green Revolution': water control, fertiliser use, the chemical control of pests and diseases, etc. The Dry Zone paddy, especially that irrigated in *maha*, shows the highest yields of all, at 2780 kg/ha. Overall, it is the irrigated crops that are generally better yielding since they are most likely to benefit from the 'Green Revolution package'.

In the year 1975–76, 77 per cent of the paddy sown was of improved varieties. In Sri Lanka a distinction is made between 'old' high yielding varieties (OHYV), like H-4, which were in use in the early 1960s, and the new HYV (NHYV) which were developed in the 1970s, in part from genetic material evolved at the International Rice Research Institute at Los Baños in the Philippines. By 1970 about 70 per cent of the paddy area was in OHYV. Most popular today are the locally bred NHYV Bg 11–11 (taking four months to mature) and Bg 34–6, Bg 34–8 and Bg 33–2 which take between three and three and a half months. In Hambantota, H–4 occupied 25 per cent of the paddy area in *maha* 1976–77, the NHYV 63 per cent. The latter dominated in Polonnaruwa accounting for 93 per cent of the area sown. Kandy has 54 per cent OHYV and 30 per cent NHYV while Colombo cultivated traditional

Table 4.6 Paddy Yields, 1949–50 and 1977–78: National and zonal averages (Kilograms per hectare)

	Maha 1949–50	Yala 1950	Maha 1977–78	Yala 1977	Percent increase Maha	Percent increase Yala
Sri Lanka	796	710	2,321	1,909	191	168
rain-fed	730	599	1,728	1,537	137	157
irrigated	894	845	2,678	2,167	200	156
Wet Zone	736	605	1,839	1,675	150	177
rain-fed	721	584	1,636	1,459	126	150
irrigated	788	680	2,179	2,112	177	211
Dry Zone	850	891	2,513	2,113	196	137
rain-fed	742	741	1,811	1,783	144	140
irrigated	928	917	2,780	2,186	200	138

Source: as for Table 4.1.

indigenous varieties on 69 per cent of the paddy land with NHYV on only 26 per cent.*

Generally, HYV are adopted more in *maha* than in *yala*, owing to the greater uncertainty of irrigation water in the latter season. Fertiliser is widely used, the quantity consumed by paddy farmers in 1978 running at 136,127 tonnes compared with 128,043 tonnes in 1973, before the price rose due to the world petroleum crisis, causing consumption to fall to 49,714 tonnes in 1975. In 1954, before the introduction of HYV only 9,550 tonnes were used.† There is a subsidy of fertilisers amounting to 50 per cent of the landed cost.

As already mentioned, the practice of transplanting paddy seedlings is by no means universal. The percentage of the total paddy area transplanted in 1972–73 ranged from 11 per cent in Colombo District through 37 per cent in Hambantota, to 77 per cent in Polonnaruwa and 89 per cent in Kandy. In the near swampy conditions of much of the Wet Zone coastal lowlands, transplantation is hardly possible in the bog soils. The clayey soils of the terraced hillsides of Kandy are by contrast an excellent medium for transplantation. One reason sometimes argued for transplanting is that the rows of paddy plants can subsequently be more effectively weeded, but with the introduction of weedicides this is no longer so important.

Mechanised cultivation with tractors, four-wheel or two-wheel, is becoming popular. For the heavier and wetter lands a four-wheel tractor is needed. Farmers using tractors generally hire them to plough or to thresh the paddy, and the tractor owner is becoming the richest and even the most influential man in the village. For much of the time tractors of both types are used to pull trailers carrying passengers and goods from place to place. The number of agricultural tractors and engines has risen from 7646 (tractors and trailers) in 1963, to 28,642 in 1973 and 38,321 in 1978.

Modernisation inevitably requires capital for which agents or branches of the Bank of Ceylon are found even at the village level to help handle the cultivation loans of the Comprehensive Rural Credit Scheme. The Peoples Bank also operates

48 Colonist's house at Badagiriya in Hambantota District. The occupants have added a mud walled lean-to and cadjan verandah to the structure provided by government. Cotton from the colonist's chena 5 miles away is drying in the foreground. The dry climate makes it difficult to grow a homestead garden

in this field, through co-operative rural banks and multi-purpose co-operative societies. During nine crop years from 1967–68 to 1975–76, Rs 510.6 million was lent out in paddy loans and Rs 298.6 million was repaid, the rate of default standing at 40 per cent. In some years the rate of default was as much as 58 per cent while in good years it was as little as 13 per cent. The distribution of loan advances for specific uses in 1976 is recorded in Table 4.7.

Sri Lanka leads South Asia in having set up a system of agricultural insurance. In 1977–78 40 per cent of the *maha* crop was insured (though

Table 4.7 Agricultural loans, 1978

Purpose	Percentage of total (total Rs 326.1 million)
Production: paddy	56.1
Production: subsidiary food crops	18.7
Production: sugar cane and cotton	4.8
Crop diversification	0.1
Animal husbandry	0.7
Small industry	0.6
Machinery and equipment	9.3
Housing, electrification and digging wells	5.0
Debt redemption	1.3
Consumption	0.5
Trade and others	2.9

Source: Central Bank of Ceylon, *Review of the Economy*, Colombo, 1978.

*Rantunga, A. S. and Abeysekera, W. A. T. *Profitability and Resource Characteristics of Paddy Farming,* ARTI, Research Study No. 2, Colombo, 1977.

†Central Bank of Ceylon, *Economic and Social Statistics of Sri Lanka*, Vol. 1, No. 2, 1978.

less than half of the premia due had been collected) and Rs 5.75 million were paid out in indemnities. For the *yala* crop of 1977 8 per cent was insured, the indemnities paid exceeding the 8 per cent of the premia collected. Cattle insurance is also available, and when a government loan is used to purchase stock there is a compulsory rate of 3 per cent of the value of the animal.

Other aspects of institutional change that have affected the farmer since Independence are embodied in three pieces of legislation. The Paddy Lands Act of 1958 gave sharecroppers (in theory at any rate) security of tenure and reduced their rent from one-half to one-quarter of the crop, as a general rule. Security meant the tenant could raise credit more easily and, furthermore, gave him a longer-term interest in the productivity of the land, encouraging investment in inputs. Unfortunately, the landlords have been able to circumvent effectively the intentions of the Paddy Lands Act. In 1972 the Land Reform Law set a ceiling of about 10 ha on the amount of paddy land an individual could hold, and the Agricultural Productivity Law reconstituted the Cultivation Committees (originally set up under the Paddy Lands Act) to oversee all kinds of agriculture at the village level.*

Among the impediments that prevent the full benefits of appropriate modern technology being achieved, traditional landholding systems are the most resistant to change. *Ande* or sharecropping is widespread. It is often encouraged by fragmentation of holdings into many small parcels, resulting from the system of property succession. Operational holdings may be consolidated by taking and giving of plots under *ande*. Such practice may well contribute to higher productivity or at least to operational efficiency. When, however,

49   The neat house of a colonist on the dry farming settlement near Anuradhapura. The garden includes papaw in the foreground and some betel leaf vines on the frame

*This summary is based on Weerekon, Bradman, 'Role of Administrators in a Changing Agrarian Situation: the Sri Lanka Experience', *Journal of Administration Overseas*, London, 1977, pp. 148–161.

landless cultivators take land under *ande* and face the prospect of paying half of their crop to the landlord, they are unlikely to invest more than the minimum of inputs, like fertiliser; or of labour. Consequently, productivity is far from the optimum.

Investment on long-term improvements in paddy production is also inhibited by the common landholding practice of *thattumaru*, under which the partition of ownership of land is achieved by sharing its use over time rather than by subdividing the fields. While this avoids the reduction of holdings to uneconomic levels, the man who uses the land for one year in five, for example, will limit his inputs to those giving immediate returns. Under a further system, *kattimaru*, several joint owners may rotate their occupance of plots of comparable size. Again, this is a practice unlikely to encourage investment in increased productivity.

Fragmentation of property presents problems for mechanisation. Ownership of even a tiny parcel in the heart of the Old Field carries prestige, and an owner will be most reluctant to sell such a plot even to achieve a consolidated holding. Since each plot is marked out by a bund, it becomes well nigh impossible to use tractors or even buffalo without risk of damage to crops and bunds.

Finally, mention may be made of a negative aspect of irrigation practice that results in much wastage of water. 'Staggered cropping' is the term used to describe how cultivators of plots under the irrigation command of a single tank often carry out their farming operations at different times in an unco-ordinated fashion. The water delivery system is designed for the convenience of the community as a whole, simultaneously providing water to all the fields in one section. If some fields are uncultivated the water available is in part wasted. The needs of HYV for precise watering calls for a stronger water administration than is traditional in the village.

Livestock

Livestock play a secondary role in the agricultural economy of Sri Lanka. Cattle and buffaloes are used for ploughing, to draw carts and to thresh paddy, and buffaloes, – because of their strength and anatomical adaptation to wallowing in swamps – are also used to muddy the paddy fields. Cows of both species are important for milk production. In 1978, cattle totalled 1,541,513 and buffaloes 814,407.* Sheep totalled 23,000, goats 450,000 and pigs 41,000. The sale of milk by farmers through co-operatives is well established, and the National Milk Board alone collected 43.7 million litres in 1976 out of a total production of 248 million litres. Of the Milk Board's total, 57 per cent was converted into milk powder, 21 per cent pasteurised or sterilised, and 18 per cent processed into condensed milk. As population increases and affluence rises, the demand for milk products will rise, so there are good prospects for developing more integrated dairy herds in conjunction with coconut plantations and agriculture generally.

Neither the Buddhist Sinhalese nor the Hindu Tamils are great meat eaters. The majority are in fact, probably fish-eating vegetarians. The Muslims and many of the urban middle class, of all ethnic groups, eat meat to some extent. In 1978 the number of animals slaughtered was as follows: cattle, 189,000; buffaloes, 3,000; goats and sheep, 127,000; and pigs, 18,000. Jaffna, where the Hindus use them in ritual slaughter, has about one third of the goats and four fifths of the sheep population.

*There is a clear cultural factor accounting for the distribution of cattle and buffaloes. Jaffna, Mannar and Nuwara Eliya with predominantly Hindu Tamil populations favour cattle.

Chapter 5

Perennial Crops

Introduction

The perennial, so-called plantation crops, which have been the basis of Sri Lanka's prosperity for a century, and which accounted for 76 per cent of the value of exports in 1978, are mainly produced in the Wet Zone. These perennial crops, which occupy almost twice the area used for paddy, have not altered significantly in their distribution over the past 50 years. The area under the principal perennial crops is shown in Table 5.1. There has been little change in the area under tea and rubber since Independence. In 1946, 224,000 ha were under tea, 257,000 under rubber. That coconuts have increased from 372,000 ha to 451,472 ha is a reminder that unlike the other crops listed above, which are mainly produced for export, there is a strong local demand for coconuts amounting to about 60 per cent of production.

A distinction used to be made in the plantation industry between indigenous smallholdings and mainly foreign-owned estates. Two pieces of legislation have radically changed the situation. The Land Reform Act No. 1 of 1972 set a ceiling of 20 ha on the area any private individual could own,

Table 5.1 Area under principal perennial crops, 1978

Crop	hectares
Coconut	451,472
Tea	242,903
Rubber	226,328
Cinnamon	21,926
Cocoa	8,567
Pepper	7,449
Coffee	6,438*
Cardamoms	4,509
Citronella	4,259

Source: Department of Census and Statistics, *Statistical Pocket Book,* Colombo, 1979, and Central Bank of Ceylon, *Economic and Social Statistics of Sri Lanka* Vol. 1, No. 2, 1978.
* 1976

50 Tea factory, near Wategoda, in Nuwara Eliya District (Fig. 5.8). VP tea on the right contrasts with older less homogeneous bushes on the left. Note the old tea was planted in vertical rows while the VP tea is in horizontal rows to conserve soil and moisture. This is Up-country tea at an altitude of 1300 m. The cliffs rise to almost 2000 m

51 Factory on a tea estate in the Low-country at 100 m, east of Galle, distinguished by paddy fields and coconut palms alongside the tea, and low dadap shade trees

and the Land Reform Amendment Law of 1975 provided for the takeover of lands owned by public companies, both indigenous and foreign. The tea and rubber industries, for example, which had been dominated by British capital and management and were becoming progressively owned by indigenous interests after Independence, were taken over by Sri Lanka government corporations. Another aspect of land reform was the breaking up of parts of some estates into miniscule holdings of 0.2 – 0.4 ha, in response to the political pressures for redistribution of property among the landless. It is unlikely that this process will proceed far in view of the government's declaration that the 'integrity of the economically viable large units ... will be preserved.'* Peiris further comments that 'probably a major share of the smallholding acreage is in units owned by persons whose main occupations lie outside subsistence farming. Smallholdings of cash crops often represent in Sri Lanka the savings and investment of business and professional classes or acquisitions and inherited property of a wealthy minority of the rural population'.

Since Independence the smallholders' share of the area under tea and rubber has increased appreciably. In coconuts it was always very important. Cardamoms are usually grown as a subsidiary enterprise on large tea estates. Cocoa is associated with both smallholder and estate enterprises but seldom on its own, since it requires shade which may be economically provided by rubber, coconuts or some other productive tree. Cinnamon, citronella and cashew nuts, on the other hand, are products of monocultural enterprises generally of small to medium scale. Pepper vines require supporting trees and, in conjunction with other crops, are grown on estates using shade trees, as well as on smallholdings and homestead plots. The very minor crops, coffee, cloves and nutmegs are grown on a small scale.

The extent to which smallholders can prosper in growing plantation crops depends to some extent on their ability to process the product for export economically and efficiently. Economies of scale compel smallholders to have their tea processed in a large factory, which in some places is now a co-operative venture. Rubber may be made into smoked sheet in small plants or large, but the

*Peiris, G. in de Silva, K. M. (ed.) *op. cit.*, p. 234 and p. 216–7.

52 On Newburgh Estate, near Ella in Badulla District, the planted grasses have been slashed and holes are being dug in readiness for tea seedlings to be bedded in. Down slope beyond the road the tea plants are almost hidden beneath the grevillea shade trees. In the background can be seen terraced paddy fields

better quality-control attainable in scientifically well-managed factories and the resultant higher price is tending to centralise processing. Coconuts are the raw material of two quite separate industries. The processing of the husk into coir fibre can be done manually by the cultivator's family or in small plants as can the drying of the kernel to produce copra. However, oil extraction from copra is a factory industry, as is the production of desiccated coconut from fresh kernels.

Processing to make the rest of the plantation products non-perishable and transportable is a relatively simple domestic industry, although for high export quality, in cardamoms for example, greater scientific handling is often needed.

Since forestry is a large-scale, long-term public industry it is convenient to discuss it in this chapter.

53 On Yuillefield Estate near Hatton (Fig. 5.8) a superintendent's bungalow stands at the top of the slope in its shaded setting. Below, the steep hill-side has been newly laid out with drains prior to planting with grass. Part has previously been planted with VP tea. The near horizontal drains prevent erosion and encourage water to sink into the sub-soil to the benefit of the tea growing down slope. Towards the valley bottom are the labourers' 'lines'

Tea

It is estimated that perhaps two million of the population of Sri Lanka depend on tea directly or indirectly for their livelihood, and for nearly a century it has provided the island with its main source of foreign exchange. The tea industry is so firmly embedded in the Sri Lanka mind, and so long associated with the nation's prosperity, that it has been difficult to persuade politicians that its future is by no means guaranteed. A recent study pointed out that in *real* terms (judged against the imports they would purchase) the prices obtained

54 On Yuillefield Estate near Hatton, the tea nursery is conveniently sited near water in the valley bottom close to a slope undergoing replanting. Seedling tea is being raised in plastic bags, for part of the time under the shelter of sackcloth. The slope beyond has been 'holed' in readiness for planting

for tea on the world market between 1960–62 and 1972–74 had fallen by 50 per cent compared with those of the 1950s.*

The depressed state of the world market is in part due to oversupply resulting from the entry of new producers in East Africa. Table 5.2 shows how Sri Lanka's share of the market has declined from 36 per cent in 1947 to 20 per cent in 1978.

Tea output in the major countries is shown in

Table 5.2 Share in world tea exports
(percentage of total)

Year	Sri Lanka	India	East Africa*
1947	36	53	4
1950	34	46	4
1960	35	37	8
1970	33	31	18
1973	30	27	21
1976	25	30	16
1977	18	29	23
1978 (est.)	20	22	26

Source: Central Bank of Ceylon, *Bulletin*, Colombo, April 1978; Tyler, G. P. 'Recent Developments in the World Tea Economy and the Potential of an I.T.A.', *Marga,* Vol. 3, No. 4, Marga Institute, Colombo, 1976, p. 36, and International Tea Committee *Annual Bulletin of Statistics 1979,* London.
*Kenya, Uganda, Tanzania, Malawi and Mozambique.

Table 5.3 Major tea producing countries, 1978
Estimated production
(thousand tonnes)

Country	1978
Asia	
India	573
China (estimates)	336
Sri Lanka	199
Indonesia	73
Bangladesh	37
East Africa	
Kenya	93
Malawi	32
Tanzania	17
Mozambique	15
Uganda	11

Source: International Tea Committee *Annual Bulletin of Statistics 1979,* London.

*Lakdasa Hulugalle, 'The integrated programme for commodities and its relevance to an International Tea Agreement,' *Marga,* Vol. 3, No. 4, Marga Institute, Colombo, 1976, p. 10.

Table 5.3, which also indicates the considerable capacity of the East African producers.

In one aspect of production Sri Lanka has an advantage over India. By virtue of its position nearer to the Equator, and the fact that some part of the tea-growing area is in full production at any one time, the month to month output of tea available for export varies only between 6.6 and 11.4 per cent of the annual total. (Note that one-twelfth is 8.3 per cent). As Figure 5.1 indicates, the range of fluctuation for North India is from nil (for three months) to 17.8 per cent, and between 4.4 and 13.4 per cent for East Africa; South India with a spread of 5.3 to 13.1 per cent most closely resembles Sri Lanka. As a consequence, Sri Lanka is able to maintain a nearly even flow of tea to the market throughout the year. The local conditions that bring about this situation are discussed further below.

TEA PRODUCTION 1946-78

5.2   Tea production 1946–78

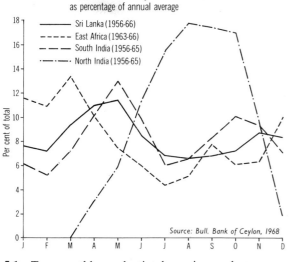

TEA. MONTHLY PRODUCTION by MAJOR PRODUCERS
as percentage of annual average

— Sri Lanka (1956-66)
---- East Africa (1963-66)
-- South India (1956-65)
-·- North India (1956-65)

Source: Bull. Bank of Ceylon, 1968

5.1   Tea, monthly production by major producers

55   Newly plucked leaf is spread out on hessian shelves or 'tats' in the factory, to wither for a few hours or a day or more depending upon weather. Newburgh Estate, Ella, Badulla District

The changing level of Sri Lanka's production since Independence is shown graphically in Figure 5.2. Production and exports have expanded by about two-thirds from the late 1940s to the all-time peak of 1965 when, of 228,236 tonnes of tea made, 224,281 tonnes were exported. These advances have taken place with very little change in area cropped. (It has increased by only 8 per cent between 1946 and 1977.) Improved yields per ha have been achieved by replanting with cuttings of better strains of tea and through a general advance in field techniques. These include the increased use of fertiliser and pest control, and changes in plucking practices and in factory processes. Some of these improvements have been encouraged by government subsidies. There is still scope for spreading the effects of the improvements throughout the smallholding sector of the industry. The latter tends to lag behind the better organised estate sector from which innovations filter down. In order to compete in the world market it is essential for Sri Lanka to keep costs to a minimum. As pressures to increase wages are difficult to resist in the long run, greater efficiency must be achieved in other ways, most important among them being the continuing replacement of old tea with plants guaranteeing both uniformity and high yields.

Table 5.4 shows the size distribution of tea holdings. Of the total area, 62 per cent is in the public sector of which 84 per cent is controlled by three organisations: the State Plantation Corporation, Janatha Estates Development Board and Udarata Cooperative Estates Development Board. The 38 per cent in the private sector is

Table 5.4   Tea holdings, 1976

Size class	No. of holdings	Total area (ha)	Percentage of total area
Smallholdings, less than 4.05 ha	122,804	47,924	20
Estates, 4.05 to 40.5 ha	3,089	32,574	14
Estates, 40.5 to 202.3 ha	536	56,386	23
Estates, 202.3 ha and over	286	103,691	43
Total	126,715	240,575	100

Source: Department of Census and Statistics, *Sri Lanka Yearbook, 1977,* Colombo 1978.

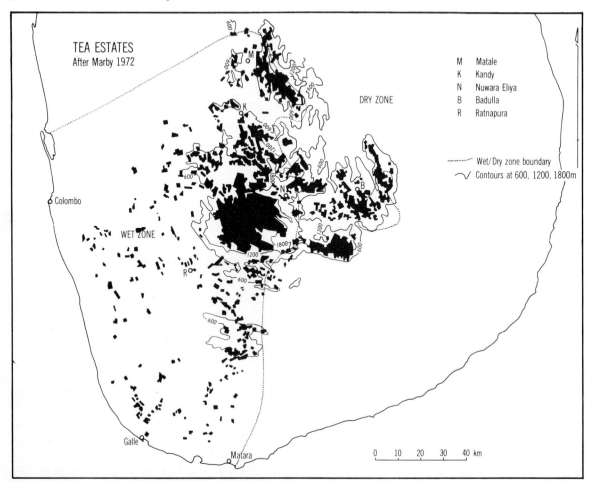

5.3   Tea estates

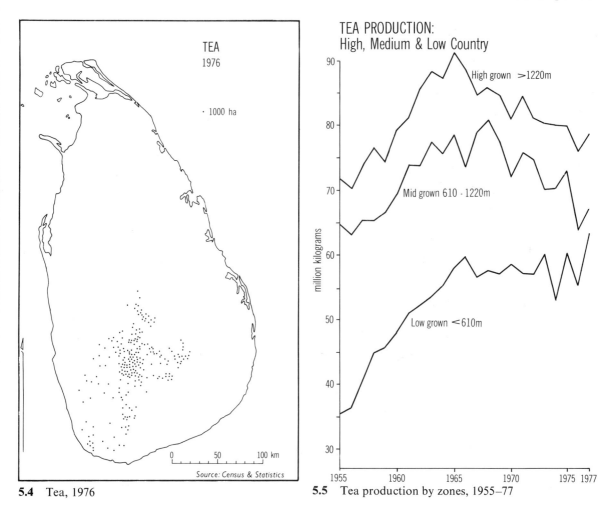

5.4 Tea, 1976

5.5 Tea production by zones, 1955–77

divided between smallholders with less than 4 ha each, and individuals with between 4 and 40 ha whom we may distinguish as small estate holders.

Economies of scale restrict the factory manufacture of tea to estates of over 40 ha and the tendency persists for small factories to close. Thus the factory side of the industry is now effectively in the hands of the nationalised corporations who process in factories on the larger estates the leaf collected from nearby smallholdings and small estates along with that plucked on their own.

Distribution of tea-growing

The distribution of tea estates is shown in Figure 5.3* and the distribution of the area actually under tea in Figure 5.4. In order to help quality control

* Figs 5.3 and 5.7 are based on maps in Marby, H. *Tea in Ceylon*, Franz Steimar Vadag GMPH, Wiesbaden, 1972, and refer to the late 1960s.

in the market, the tea trade distinguishes three types of tea by the altitudinal range in which they are grown: *high tea*, at elevations averaging 1220 m or more – these estates accounted for 41 per cent of the estate area and 39 per cent of estate production of the island in 1976 (36 per cent in 1978); *medium tea*, at heights averaging 610–1220 m – accounted for 38 per cent of the area and 33 per cent of production (31 per cent in 1978); and *low tea*, found below 610 m, and accounting for 21 per cent of the area and 29 per cent of production (33 per cent in 1978). These figures exclude smallholder tea which mainly comes from the medium and low country areas. Average total production over the five year period 1971–75 was in the ratio 38:34:27 (high:medium:low). Output by altitudinal zone for 1955–77 is shown in Figure 5.5.

Thus tea is grown in Sri Lanka through a wide range of 22 altitudes, from almost sea level up to

56 Tea factory, Rangbodde Estate, Nuwara Eliya District. This woman is feeding tea into a sifter that sorts it into size grades by shaking

57 Some tea estates have been subdivided into small-holdings such as this one near Ramboda, in Nuwara Eliya District. The tea is old and poorly maintained to judge from its open appearance. Note the smallholder's cottages

2250 m, where its yield is limited by frost. Rainfall is the major determinant of the distribution of production which is seriously affected by drought, though quality or 'flavour' teas are obtained where the plant is under slight stress rather than when regular rains are stimulating heavy leaf growth. Most of the tea region lies within the Wet Zone, but there are quite extensive medium and high estates in the centre of the Uva Basin and around its margins which lie within the Dry Zone. Figure 5.6 shows these relationships in a transect across the tea-growing area eastwards from Colombo.

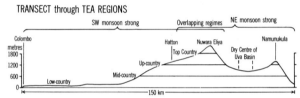

5.6 Transect through tea regions

The seasonality of rainfall controls production, there being a clear differentiation of estates receiving most rain from the northeast monsoon from those more exposed to the southwest monsoon. Because of the tendency for the 'inter-monsoonal' periods to produce convectional rainfall, it may be safer to say that the tea-growing districts are, as a rule, characterised by a dry (or at least a drier) period during one or other of the monsoons. Thus the western areas generally tend to have a drier season, if at all, early in the calendar year, while in the eastern areas the dry season comes in mid year.

Marby has grouped the tea-growing areas of Sri Lanka into seven regional types, as mapped in Figure 5.7. In the southwest Low-country, dominated by the southwest monsoon but also watered to some extent all the year round, tea-growing is quite widely distributed, and it is here that smallholders and small estates are most common. At a higher elevation, but still to the west of the hill country proper and in the Knuckles Range – under the full impact of the southwest monsoon – is the Western Mid-country. Above this is the major tea district, the Western Up-country, with many square kilometres of mono-cultural tea (Fig. 5.8). High quality teas are grown over 1800 m on several isolated mountains in what

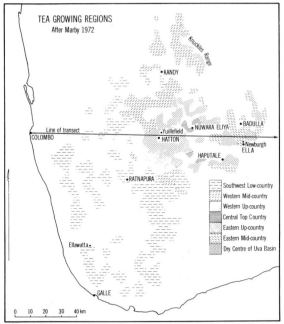

5.7   Tea-growing regions

is termed the Central Top Country which traps rain from both monsoons.

Eastwards is the realm of the northeast monsoon, a region liable to drought during the southwest monsoon. The contrast in August, for example, is remarkable over quite short distances between the rainsodden western regions and the dry sunny weather to the east of the divide. The Eastern Up-country is flanked by areas of Mid-country with a similar rainfall regime. Within these, the Dry Centre of the Uva Basin, known for its dry season 'flavour' teas, forms a distinct region. It will be noted that there is no Low-country tea on the eastern flank, conditions here being too desiccating (Fig. 5.6).

58   A tea supervisor's (foreman's) quarters on Yuillefield Estate (near Hatton, in Kandy District).
Note the simple board bed, the oil lamp, and the general appearance of sparse cleanliness

Tea Production

To illustrate some of the factors involved in tea production, aspects of three estates are analysed briefly. The estates are shown in Figure 5.7: Ellawatta Estate, in the Southwest Low-country; Yuillefield Estate in the Western Up-country near Hatton, and Newburgh Estate in the Eastern Mid-country, near Ella in Badulla District.

Ellawatta Estate has only 42 ha of tea and keeps its factory going by processing leaf from neighbouring smallholders.* In fact, only 27 per cent of the leaf used is from the estate itself.

The grades of tea made are listed in Table 5.5 which shows, for comparison, those made at

*We are grateful to Mr Mahindirdasa, factory manager at Ellawatta, for assisting us.

5.8   Land use, Up-country tea region (based on a map of the Sri Lanka Survey Department with the sanction of the Surveyor General)

59 The tea worker's kitchen is simple but clean. The woman is cooking a chapatti of unleavened flour on a girdle, using uprooted tea branches as fuel. On Yuillefield Estate, near Hatton

Yuillefield.* The following outline of the preparation and classification of manufactured tea is based mainly on a paper by Nalini Jeyapalan and A. J. Jayawardena.†

From the field, leaf is taken first to the factory to be withered either by laying out on 'tats' (close shelves of wire mesh or gunny, allowing air to move through the thinly spread leaves) or, in modernised factories, in troughs through which hot air is driven

*The data on Yuillefield was made available through the courtesy and hospitality of Mr Ernie Silva, Superintendent, and Mrs Silva. Yuillefield is a large estate which had 313 ha of productive tea in 1975. It has recently been selected for development and modernisation because of its potential.
† 'Some Aspects of the Tea Industry', *Bulletin*, Central Bank of Ceylon, Colombo, June 1967, pp. 35–36. (This was the first of four excellent articles concluding in March 1968.)

60 The tea pluckers work in gangs under a supervisor (standing on the left). At the end of each shift of about three hours they weigh-in their pick which is recorded by the tally clerk (in striped shirt). On Sutherland Estate, near Ella, Badulla District

to expedite the process. Withering softens the leaf and is essential to producing good quality.

The withered leaf is then rolled to twist and break it, thus allowing its juice to spread over the leaf particles. After a period of fermenting the leaf is fired in an oven to halt the process. The product is 'manufactured' tea, and is classified according to particle size into 'leafy' or 'leaf grades' (in which the original leaf is more or less recognisable), 'broken' and 'dust'. Sifting sorts the particles, which may be deliberately broken further by machine or by hand to produce the desired quantity of a particular grade. This is the orthodox method of tea manufacture.

'Of the Orthodox-manufactured tea, the leaf grades are further graded as Flowery Pekoes (those with a predominance of "Tips"), Orange Pekoes (with long wiry leaves and tips, with a pale liquor) Pekoes (with shorter leaves but with more colour) and Pekoe Souchongs (with broad round leaves and a pale liquor). The Broken grades are classified as Flowery Broken Orange Pekoes (consisting of small golden "tips" and possessing extraordinary quality in liquor). Broken Orange Pekoes (containing tips, with good colour and strength), Broken Pekoes (slightly larger than B.O.Ps and with less colour), Flowery Broken Orange Pekoe Fannings (possessing extraordinary quality in liquor and consisting of tips) and Broken Orange Pekoe Fannings (which are smaller than B.O.Ps and quick brewing and of good colour). The dust is referred to as "Pekoe Dust".

'It should be mentioned that these methods of grading adopted by the tea trade are "entirely artificial", though not completely arbitrary. They are mere code-names and have no uniform correlation to all the desirable properties of tea.'*

At Newburgh, an Eastern Mid-country estate of 202 ha of tea, most rainfall comes during the northeast monsoon though the maximum is in May. Production roughly follows rainfall but it seems that rainy days rather than rainfall amount may be the key factor. In 1976 a higher total rainfall produced less tea than did 1975, but the latter had a few more rainy days, i.e. days with a minimum of 2.54 mm (0.01 in.). A similar anomaly occurred in 1973 and 1974†.

*Jeyapalan, N. and Jayawardena, A. J., *op. cit.*
†The data for Newburgh Estate, and a vast amount of his knowledge and long experience in the tea industry, were made available to the authors by Mr Hubert Congreve.

61 A plucking gang at work on young VP tea (3–4 years old) on Yuillefield Estate northeast of Hatton. (Fig. 5.8) The Mana grass beyond has been planted to rehabilitate the soil prior to replanting with tea

62 Tamil tea plucker at work on Newburgh Estate, near Ella, Badulla District. As a rule, she plucks the topmost two leaves and a bud and throws them over her shoulder into the basket on her back

While monthly production fluctuates somewhat in relation to precipitation, rising after a rainy period, there is an inverse relationship to rainfall in the case of the quality of tea made. The best flavoured leaf, commanding higher prices, is obtained at Newburgh during drier spells when the amount of leaf produced is less. The Uva Basin – on the rim of which Newburgh lies – is relatively dry, and during the southwest monsoon is in a rainshadow. The airflow from the west produces a *föhn* effect, becoming warmer and drier as it descends from the Top Country. Starting in June-July and known locally as the 'Uva Blowing', the slightly desiccating wind withers the leaf on the bush, reducing yields but increasing quality and value. Figure 5.9 plots against the rainfall regime of the area the monthly prices received at the Colombo tea auctions during 1976 for BOP quality tea from an estate in the Uva Basin.* It can be seen clearly how prices soar in July-September as the Uva Blowing makes itself felt. During the northeast monsoon in the area west of Nuwara Eliya, there is a comparable but less marked effect from the 'Dimbula Blowing'.

*Data courtesy of B. Sivaratnam of Messrs. Forbes and Walker Ltd., Colombo.

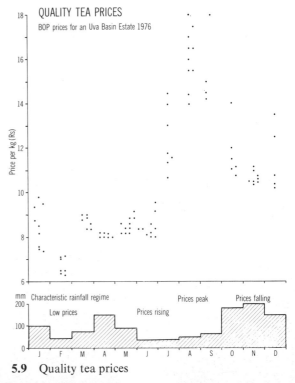

5.9 Quality tea prices

Grade	Ellawatta (total, 88,531 kg)	Yuillefield (total, 436,400 kg)
Flowery Pekoes (FP)		
Orange Pekoes (OP)	10.3	0.1
Orange Pekoes A (OPA)	8.6	
Pekoes (P)		
Pekoes Souchongs (PS)		
Flowery Broken Orange Pekoes (FBOP 1)	1.1	
Flowery Broken Orange Pekoes (FBOP)	7.2	19.4
Broken Orange Pekoes 1 (BOP 1)	15.6	
Broken Orange Pekoes (BOP)	6.0	44.6
Broken Orange Pekoes A (BOP A)	2.5	
Broken Pekoes (BP)	10.2	3.5
Flowery Broken Orange Pekoes Fannings 1 (FBOPF 1)	9.1	
Flowery Broken Orange Pekoes Fannings (FBOPF)	7.9	
Broken Orange Pekoes Fannings Special (BOPF Sp.)	0.9	
Broken Orange Pekoes Fannings (BOPF)	3.3	11.3
Broken Pekoes Fannings		8.9
Dust 1	17.4	7.9
Dust 2		4.2

Table 5.5 Tea output by grades, 1977
(percentage of total tea manufactured)
Source: Data courtesy of Mr Mahindirdasa (Ellawatta) and Mr Ernie Silva (Yuillefield)

Planting, Plucking and Pruning

A tea bush remains productive for as long as a century, but has to be pruned regularly to maintain a convenient shape for plucking. What compels replanting is less the declining productivity of the individual bush than the dying off of enough bushes in a block to produce an untidy patchy cover and a consequent waste of land, as well as a reduction in labour efficiency. The maintenance of a productive estate is no simple matter. Quite apart from plucking and processing the leaf, pruning rounds have to be organised, and replanting strategies devised and carried out. Plucking is performed by gangs of women under a male supervisor. Women are also employed on light work in the factory. Pruning and replanting are men's work.

When replanting is to take place, the old bushes are uprooted, roads are repaired, drains and terraces are redesigned if necessary, to help reduce erosion and to conserve moisture, and *Guatamala* or *Mana* grass is planted to rehabilitate the soil and to help eradicate pests and disease. Recently, it has been shown that sugar cane is effective in re-

63 Tapping rubber. The boy uses the cutting tool to re-open the bark so that latex flows to be collected in a coconut shell cup below. When the latex coagulates along the cut the flow ceases. In his left hand the tapper is holding a bundle of coagulated latex which he stripped off prior to cutting the bark

habilitation, providing a valuable cash crop at the same time.

Meanwhile, in a shaded nursery established nearby, cuttings from specially cultivated high-yielding bushes are being tended. This is known as vegetatively propagated (VP) tea. After a period of up to two years rehabilitation under grass, the block can be prepared for planting. The grass is cut at ground level for mulch or it may be uprooted. Young shade trees may have to be established. Evenly spaced holes are dug in rows along the contours to minimize soil erosion, and a young tea plant is placed in each.

Shade trees, commonly *dadap (Erythrina lithosperma)*, *Grevillea*, *Acacia* or *Gliricidia maculata* (a legume) are grown, depending partly on altitude, as much for their leaf fall or to be lopped for mulching as for the protection they may give to tea against being scorched by the sun. They may also have value in attracting birds which can reduce insect attack. There seems no conclusive evidence that shade is itself beneficial. The shade trees are ultimately a valuable source of fuel for firing the factory furnace. Spinnies of eucalypts grown for fuel may often be seen in gullies, and on exposed estates windbreaks are planted to reduce desiccation. In 1964 the Tea Research Institute recommended the removal of shade trees, but today they appear to be returning to favour.

Approximately two years after planting, depending on altitude, the tea bushes are levelled off and plucking can begin. Plucking of tea proceeds on rounds varying between 17 days on old slow growing Up-country tea and four to five days on young VP tea, but variations occur due to weather conditions, frequent public holidays, labour difficulties (including occasional strikes), and the state of the market. Fertiliser, particularly nitrogen, is applied during the rainy seasons, four to twelve applications annually being made. Pruning varies in severity and frequency according to the height and climate. Low-country tea bushes are pruned every one and a half to two years, the slower growing Top Country bushes every five.

A reliable labour force, well disciplined and skilled in the processes involved, is a tea estate's greatest asset. Some 2.5 workers per ha are needed on estates, compared with 1.2 per ha on small-holdings, which of course have no factory sector. Indian Tamil labour has for long been the mainstay

64 Fine grade crepe rubber sheets are trimmed to size before packing for export in wooden cases seen behind on right. The cuttings are then re-rolled

65 Fine crepe rubber is being rolled after drying in the racks behind in a modern factory on Dewalakande Estate, near Avissawella. (Fig. 5.12)

of the industry, particularly in Mid and Up-country districts where their 'lines' or living quarters are a striking feature of the plantation landscape. On many an estate the Tamil labour force lives quite out of contact with the Sinhalese citizenry, and their mutual integration into a single economy and society presents great problems.

In prospect, Sri Lanka has several handicaps to overcome if it is to hold or improve its position in the world's tea markets. Not the least of the nation's problems is how, within the prevailing climate of ethnic prejudice, to remove from the Indian Tamil labour force the stigma of being 'second class citizens'. The tea industry depends very heavily upon the efficiency and diligence of the Indian Tamils.

Rubber

Ranking second to tea in the list of Sri Lanka's exports, rubber is a long way behind in terms of its relative importance in the national economy and in world trade. Of total production in 1978, 89 per cent was exported and this accounted for 15 per cent of the value of total exports, a proportion that had decreased from almost 23 per cent in 1973. As Table 5.6 shows, Sri Lanka lay in fourth place in 1978 as a relatively minor world producer and exporter with 4.2 and 4.3 per cent respectively of the world totals.

Despite a reduction of 25 per cent in the area of tappable rubber, production has increased by up to 70 per cent since Independence (Fig. 5.10). This has been achieved largely by extensive replanting with high-yielding material under a subsidy scheme introduced in 1953 and periodically revised since then in line with rising costs. The rate of replanting lagged during the early 1970s but by 1978 62 per cent had been replanted and this rate is likely to improve under plans to renew 3 per cent of the existing area annually. Further contributions to the industry's efficiency have come from improved techniques of planting (with soil conservation in mind), tapping and processing, and the greater use of fertilisers and of chemicals controlling disease.

Rubber is more restricted in distribution than tea, being confined to areas of the Wet Zone below 400 m and with uniform rainfall exceeding 2,000 mm. Figure 5.11 shows the distribution, extending around the western flanks of the high-

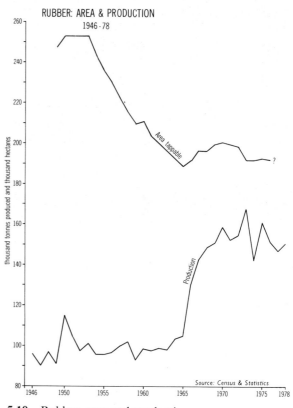

5.10   Rubber, area and production

66   Small scale processing of latex into sheet rubber can be done in a plant like this one on a 10 ha. estate in Badulla District. After coagulating the latex with acetic acid in the trays, the product is put through a mangle and dried and smoked for sale

67 Tappers bringing latex from their small holdings to be weighed in at a collecting centre for the block rubber factory in Kegalle District

lands from Matale in the north to Matara in the south. A few outliers appear around hills to the east where rainfall is adequate. In the Wet Zone lowlands it is common to find rubber and homestead gardens sharing the flat interfluves with the valley floors under paddy. The land use sample (Fig. 5.12) showing an area around Avissawella, in the east of Colombo District, is characteristic of the rubber growing region.

Holdings under rubber tend to be smaller than those under tea. Units of less than 4.05 ha accounted for a third of the total rubber area in 1976, compared with one-fifth of the tea area. Table 5.7 sets out the range of holding sizes. The larger estates have been nationalised, but the smallholdings generally remain private property, quite often of middle-class citizens on pensions or with alternative supplements to their income. Rubber, once it is established, is an easier crop for the smallholder to manage than is tea, and is less insistent in its demands on labour. Processing of latex into sheet can be done on a small scale, but quality control is important. The trend is now to encourage smallholders to deliver latex to collecting centres serving modern 'block rubber' and crepe sheet plants in which the quality of the finished product can be maintained and a better price passed on to the producer than he could get for his home rolled and smoked sheet. There are now two block rubber plants in operation at Mawanella (Kegalle District) and Avissawella. The latter specialises in making good quality block rubber

from scrap and low grade sheet. Of the total output of 146,243 tonnes in 1977 the various types produced were (as percentage of total):

Ribbed smoked sheet	58
Latex crepe	26
Scrap crepe	12
Sole crepe	3
Block rubber*	1.4
Latex	0.6

Source: Ferguson's Ceylon Directory, 1977–78.

As with tea, Sri Lanka's prospects of holding (let alone increasing) its share of the world market depends on improving the efficiency of the industry and the quality of the export product. By 1969, 45,392 ha had been taken out of rubber during periods when prices were depressed through

*In the 1978 total output of 155,662 tonnes, block rubber accounted for 3.3 per cent.

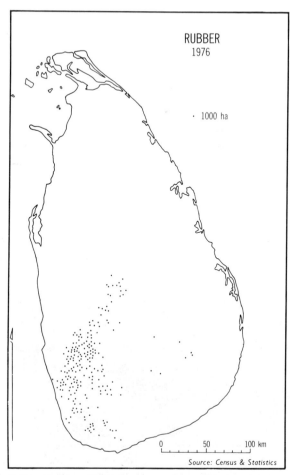

RUBBER
1976

· 1000 ha

0   50   100 km

Source: Census & Statistics

5.11 Rubber, 1976

68 A typical monocultural coconut estate, north of Negombo, in the coconut triangle. The leaves are made into cadjans for roofing material. The nuts are usually harvested by itinerant workers armed with long poles tipped with sharp knives

over-supply of natural rubber at a time when synthetic rubber was capturing an increased share of the market. Land was also lost by the urban spread of Colombo and other coastal towns into the rubber areas. There is now an urgent need to extend planting if Sri Lanka is to be ready to profit from an expanded rubber market which is likely to develop as the cost of petroleum-based synthetic rubber inevitably rises.

Over the five years 1974–78, 95 per cent of rubber production has been exported. The major local consumer is the tyre and tube industry supplying local needs but there is potential for manufacturing rubber toys and balloons for export, particularly to Japan. Producers have been perhaps over-secure with sometimes more than half the country's production assured of a market

69 Coconut husks in transit to a coir factory. Near Negombo in the 'coconut triangle'

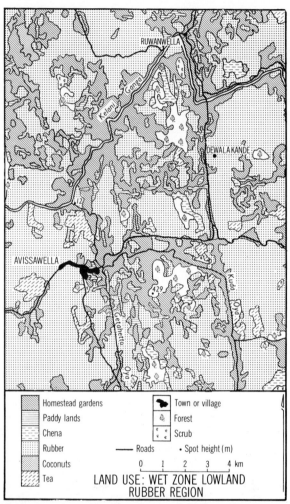

Homestead gardens — Town or village
Paddy lands — Forest
Chena — Scrub
Rubber — Roads · Spot height (m)
Coconuts — 0 1 2 3 4 km
Tea — LAND USE: WET ZONE LOWLAND RUBBER REGION

5.12 Land use, Wet Zone lowland rubber region (based on a map of the Sri Lanka Survey Department with the sanction of the Surveyor General)

Table 5.6 Major rubber producing and exporting countries, 1978 (thousand tonnes and percentage of total)

Country	Production	Per cent	Exports	Per cent
Malaysia	1,607	43	1,565	48
Indonesia	900	24	863	27
Thailand	467	13	442	14
Sri Lanka	156	4.2	138	4.3
India	133	3.6	4	0.1
Vietnam	40	1.1	35	1.1
Kampuchea, Cambodia	18	0.5	16	0.5
Others	394	11	182	5.6
World total	3,715	100.4	3,245	100.6

Source: International Rubber Study Group, *Rubber Statistical Bulletin* 33 (12), London, 1979.

Table 5.7 Size of rubber holdings, 1976

	Number	Total area	Percentage of total area
Smallholdings, less than 4.05 ha	154,445	87,721	33
Estates, 4.05– 40.5 ha	6,873	64,991	25
Estates, 40.5 ha and over	827	112,529	42
Total	162,145	265,241	100

Source: Department of Census and Statistics, *Sri Lanka Yearbook, 1977,* Colombo, 1978.

under the barter agreement with China, exchanging rubber for rice. The China–Ceylon Rubber Agreement of 1952 was of great benefit since it guaranteed a market for sheet rubber at a price above world levels, thereby giving much needed stability to the industry. The Chinese government also assisted Sri Lanka's replanting programme. China was still the main recipient of rubber in 1978 undertaking to import 49,800 tonnes, or about 32 per cent of production. In 1977 China took 44 per cent.

Coconuts

Unlike tea and rubber which are grown principally for export, coconuts play as important a role in the local economy of Sri Lanka as in its external trade. They have been grown for centuries as a domestic tree with a remarkable number of uses. The immature fruit is cut for its refreshing drink, but greater value comes from the mature nut. The husk, after retting in water, yields coir fibre which can be spun into cord, or woven loosely into bags or tightly into matting. The pulpy waste residue has so far defied man's ingenuity to put it to use, and it forms huge heaps alongside the coir factories. The coconut kernel may be shredded when fresh to make desiccated coconut, or dried to make copra which is then pressed to extract coconut oil. The shell itself can be converted into a hard charcoal.

Apart from the fruit, the fallen palm fronds are in demand as roofing and shading material, often being plaited to make *cadjans*. The trunk is used in light construction and as a water-resistant buttressing material along drainage ditches. From the

70 Splitting coconuts to separate the husk from the kernel. The workman presses the coconut onto a fixed bayonet to wrench it apart. Near Negombo in Colombo District

base of the flower stalks, toddy is collected by a particular caste, the toddy tappers, who climb the palm to obtain the juice. Unless the earthenware pots in which the toddy is collected are coated daily with fresh slaked lime, the 'sweet'

71 A coir factory northeast of Kurunegala. To the right of the factory containing the machinery, husks are piled high near to the road. In the right foreground the husks are standing in water where they ret for three weeks to facilitate the separation of the fibre from the pulpy residue. The latter is useless and is piled up in huge waste heaps seen on the left. Paddy fields beyond

toddy ferments to a cider-like beverage. By boiling the toddy a form of sugar can be obtained, and by distilling it arrack is produced.

Occupying an area second only to that under paddy, and about 9 per cent of the total cultivated area of the island, coconuts are widely grown where the soil is well drained, and where the rainfall exceeds 1,300 mm and is well-distributed throughout the year. Sunshine, high temperatures and humidity are needed for successful cultivation on a commercial scale, requirements that generally limit such planting to below 550 m. In drier areas the palm trees need access to groundwater and are commonly found near tanks, at the break of slope below foothills, along river banks and on beach ridges (where they demonstrate a tolerance of brackish conditions). As the map in Figure 5.13 shows, the optimum growing area is in the 'coconut

72   At a desiccated coconut factory near Kurunegala these men and boys break the coconut shell from the white flesh of the kernel which they put through the openings above their heads into the mill. Each may cut as many as 1,000 nuts in a day. Inside girls scrape the brown outer skin off the kernel before it is shredded.

triangle', extending on the west coast from Chilaw to the northern outskirts of Colombo and inland to Matale, an area containing 48 per cent of the total. This map also shows coconuts straddling the Wet Zone/Dry Zone boundary in the north and again in the south near the Matara-Hambantota District boundary. In Jaffna, coconuts approach their climatic limits and tend to be replaced by the palmyra palm as a source of toddy, sweetening and building material.

Table 5.8 summarises available production data. Coconut statistics are unreliable in Sri Lanka. Official sources quote the 1972 Agricultural Census for the area under coconuts (451,472 ha), while production is calculated by adding the nut equivalent of exports of oil and desiccated coconut to a figure for domestic consumption based on 7.5 nuts per person per month, i.e. 90 per year! Little change appears to have occurred since Independence.

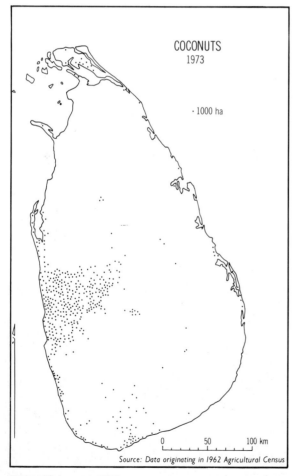

COCONUTS
1973

· 1000 ha

0   50   100 km

Source: Data originating in 1962 Agricultural Census

5.13   Coconuts, 1973

Table 5.8 Annual coconut production, 1950–78 (million nuts)

Year	Production
1950–54 (average)	2,237
1955–59 (average)	2,344
1960	2,213
1961	2,631
1962	2,842
1963	2,547
1964	2,989
1965	2,675
1966	2,459
1967	2,413
1968	2,602
1969	2,437
1970	2,445
1971	2,668
1972	2,818
1973	1,946
1974	2,030
1975	2,585
1976	2,330
1977	1,900
1978	2,207

Source: Ministry of Finance and Planning, personal communications, Colombo, 1978.

73 Coconut shell charcoal is a valuable by-product at the desiccated coconut factory. The shells are being reduced to charcoal in pits in the background. Near Kurunegala

Topping up a plastic lined paper sack with high quality desiccated coconut at a factory near Kurunegala

Fluctuations in coconut production are mainly a result of variation in rainfall; drought adversely affects the setting of nuts after flowering but it takes a year and a half to show up in a reduction in nut production. Application of fertiliser can greatly improve yield, but the practice tends to be neglected. Since little new land is likely to be available for coconut planting, and since population is increasing and with it demand, there is need to raise the level of productivity in the industry. This is difficult since coconuts do not often represent the only or even the main product on smallholdings. In one sample survey, 85 per cent of coconut landholders also cultivated paddy. Since 1956 the government has been subsidising a rehabilitation scheme to encourage smallholders and estates to replant ageing and uneconomic areas with selected seedlings and to apply adequate fertiliser. Nonetheless, the industry remains in the doldrums. Largely, this is probably because it lacks price incentives to repay the necessary inputs of capital and effort. Diversification of the coconut growers' economy is possible in moister areas by undercropping with pineapple, cocoa, coffee,

75 Girls spinning coir fibre into twine on the roadside in Galle District

76 Cooperative self-help: volunteers building a school between Puttalam and Anuradhapura. The roofing material is plaited coconut fronds, or cadjans

bananas and pepper – the latter can use the trunks as support – or by growing pasture for cattle.

Response to market changes is slow in an industry in which it takes between seven and ten years to bring the trees to fruiting, and a further eight to ten years to reach full production. However, once established, palms remain productive for 60 years, after which yields decline steeply. Replanting can be organised so that young trees begin fruiting beneath the old ones as the latter become uneconomic.

Over half the nut production is consumed domestically. How much is processed into commodities for export depends on the surplus available and the state of the world market. Table 5.9 shows the quantities of coconut products exported in a good year (1976) and a poor one (1977). Owing to the poor crop of 1977, an embargo was placed on the export of nuts and coconut oil.

Husking of nuts and the drying of the kernel flesh to make copra are often carried out by smallholders. Oil pressing and the manufacture of desiccated coconut are factory industries.

Minor Export Crops

Under this heading are grouped several crops which together account for about 3 per cent of foreign export earnings. They include cinnamon (the spice that first attracted the Portuguese to the island for trade) and coffee, which was once the

Table 5.9 Export of coconut products, 1976 and 1977

	1976		1977	
Item	Quantity (tonnes)	Percent of value	Quantity (tonnes)	Percent of value
Kernel products*				
coconut oil	58,978	36.4	2,133	2.2
desiccated	45,454	37.4	31,597	62.5
copra	1,245	1.4	276	0.4
Fresh nuts	7.2 million	1.6	–	–
Total nut equivalent	390 million		233 million	
Coir products				
mattress fibre	47,882	7.6	51,997	10.2
bristle fibre	11,528	4.2	12,379	8.8
twisted fibre	25,085	6.4	28,135	9.2
coir yarn	3,254	1.4	2,081	1.3
Shell charcoal etc.		3.8		5.4
Total value	Rs 507.9 million		Rs 517.6 million	

Source: Central Bank of Ceylon, *Bulletin*, Colombo, February 1979, and *Economic and Social Statistics* Vol. 1 (2), 1978.
*In 1978 coconut oil exports had recovered to 30,000 tonnes, desiccated coconut to 40,100 tonnes and copra to 900 tonnes.

major plantation crop. In all, these crops occupy a relatively small area. Nearly all are grown as mixed crops in the Wet Zone, some in smallholdings and homestead gardens, some on estates. The small scale plants processing and distilling the smallholders' products are a characteristic feature of the Sri Lanka countryside. In the Dry Zone, monocultural cashew nut plantations have recently been established. The government recognises the value of the minor export crops both as earners of foreign exchange, and as being capable of absorbing labour profitably. It provides incentives in the form of subsidies, loans, free planting material, pesticides and assistance in processing and marketing for cultivators of cinnamon, cocoa, cashew nuts, coffee, cardamoms, cloves, citronella, mulberry, oil palm, papaw (papaya) and pepper.

Table 5.10 shows the export quantities of a number of products for the five year period 1974–78, and their value in 1978 (or 1977 in some cases.)

The *cinnamon* tree is native to Sri Lanka which is by far the world's largest exporter of cinnamon 'quills'. Up to 20 seedlings are planted in a hole 30 cms square, giving rise to straight shoots which give the appearance of bushes two to three metres tall when ready for cutting. Replanting may not be necessary for 35 to 40 years. Shoots are cut as the bark turns brown, at which stage it can be peeled easily. Twigs and leaves are lopped to be steam-treated locally in order to distil cinnamon oil. The bark is made up into sticks or quills about a metre long, which are bundled for export. Some bark chips may be used to prepare bark oil, in demand for expensive perfumery. Leaf oil is also used in perfumes, and in flavouring and medicines. The quills and chips go to the confectionery and meat industries.

77 Citronella oil is distilled from the grass (foreground) in small plants like this one near Tangalla, in Hambantota District

Over 14,000 ha are under cinnamon, mainly in small and medium holdings. The crop is concentrated in Matara and Galle (together having 71 per cent of the area) with a further 23 per cent in the adjacent Districts of Kalutara, Hambantota and Ratnapura (Fig. 5.14). There is still a little grown as far north as Negombo, and in Colombo District one suburb in the capital retains the name Cinnamon Gardens. Cinnamon grows well on the interfluve uplands, requiring no shade, and needing about 2,500 mm of rainfall.

By contrast, *cocoa* does best under shade, especially when young, and is grown below 600 m generally as an undercrop to rubber, coconut, jak tree, etc. or with *dadap* (widely used for the same purpose in tea estates) as cover. It is grown on estates and smallholdings, but seldom as the primary crop. Ninety per cent of the cocoa is in Matale and Kandy Districts where the 'stuffy moist atmosphere' of the 'shut-in valleys of the hill country', as described by Miss Cook, provide the desirable levels of equable heat and high humidity (Fig. 5.14).* A little is also grown in Kurunegala, Monaragala, Kegalle and Badulla.† The cocoa beans are processed by the grower and bagged for despatch to middlemen who grade the product for export.

*Cook, E. K. *Ceylon*, Macmillan, London, 1951, p. 192. First published in 1930, this pioneer study is a classic for any student of Sri Lanka. It was revised and brought up to date in 1951 by the late Professor K. Kularatnam.
†The map is based on data provided by the Department of Census and Statistics relating to cocoa small holders. There is some additional hectarage on estates.

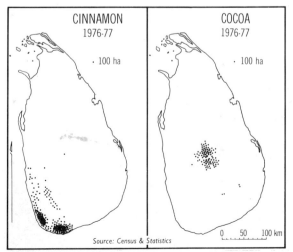

5.14 Cinnamon and cocoa

78 Cardamoms are grown as a perennial ground crop beneath a cover of natural forest as here on Doteloya Estate, above 1,000 m in the hills in Kegalle District

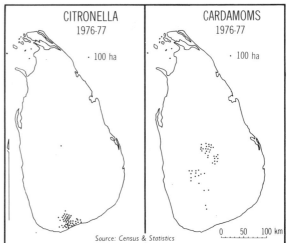

5.15 Citronella and cardamoms

Cardamoms are the fruit of a tall, shade-loving, non-woody perennial growing naturally in the humid, mist-shrouded forests of the highland Wet Zone. As a commercial crop, cardamoms are generally planted in natural forest that has been partly opened up by clearing undergrowth. It is a rewarding export crop, but if high quality is to be achieved it requires the kind of care in cultivation, harvesting and processing that is given to tea. The fruit capsules appear on flowering stalks growing from the base of the plant. The capsules should be 'green cured' in hot air barns and rigorously graded. The area under cardamoms in 1976 (4400 ha) is concentrated in Matale (41 per cent) Kandy (36 per cent) and Kegalle (12 per cent) which together account for 89 per cent of the total (Fig. 5.15). Nuwara Eliya has 5 per cent.

79 Picking cardamoms which fruit close to the ground. Doteloya Estate in Kegalle District

Citronella, a perennial grass grown for its essential oil – now used in scented soap –, is restricted to western Hambantota and the adjacent part of Matara District, in the Wet Zone – Dry Zone transition (Fig. 5.15). From the grass, which is hand cut two or three times a year, the oil is distilled locally in small plants. Apart from weeding and maybe fertilising, the crop is undemanding, growing on slopes and often poor soils. Cuttings are row-planted and need replacing after six to eight years.

Coffee is grown throughout the Wet Zone and its transition to the Dry Zone. Sixty per cent of the area is in Kandy, Matale and Kegalle (Fig. 5.16). *Coffea arabica*, being tolerant of cooler conditions than *C. robusta*, does well over 600 m. For neither variety is shade essential, although each may be successfully grown as an undercrop to rubber or coconut. The bushes take three years to come into fruit and then have a useful life of 25 to 30 years. Picked when ripe, the berries are processed locally.

Pepper is a vine which must have tree trunks or poles on which to climb, protection from winds which might blow it down, and shade from excessive sunshine. Like cocoa, it needs high humidity, heat and abundant rainfall (1650–2500 mm). It is often seen growing as a cash crop using kapok, *areca* nut, or shade trees in tea or cocoa gardens as climbing support. Seventy per cent of the recorded pepper area is in the adjoining Districts of Kandy, Matale and Kegalle, but some is grown in every Wet Zone district (Fig. 5.16). The vines begin to fruit in two to three years, reaching a maximum

Table 5.10 Minor export crops, exports 1974–78
(tonnes, and value in Rs million)

Crop	1974	1975	1976	1977	1978	Value 1978
Pepper	335	97	10	630	1,204	35.1
Pepper oil	n.a.	n.a.	0.16	0.6	n.a.	0.24*
Cinnamon chips	2,631	462	508	533	406	2.5
Cinnamon quills	5,039	3,348	5,293	5,207	5,182	158.1
Cinnamon leaf oil	n.a.	n.a.	110	89	n.a.	4.6*
Cinnamon bark oil	n.a.	n.a.	n.a.	1	n.a.	n.a.
Cloves	574	158	478	1,224	472	32.3
Nutmeg and mace	122	1,544	325	152	396	9.4
Cardamoms	147	335	163	86	147	40.4
Cardamom oil	n.a.	n.a.	0.5	1.1	n.a.	2.5*
Cocoa beans	1,026	1,077	1,107	1,321	1,041	50.2
Coffee	n.a.	n.a.	1,709	986	n.a.	33.2*
Tobacco, unmanufactured	544	590	454	771	862	30.3
Papain	35	66	46	41	41	13.0
Citronella oil	135	102	227	132	n.a.	2.3*
Lemon grass oil	n.a.	n.a.	5.4	1.0	n.a.	0.14*
Nutmeg oil	n.a.	n.a.	8	3.5	n.a.	0.54*
Ginger oil	n.a.	n.a.	0.5	0.4	n.a.	0.2*

Source: as for Table 5.9.
* value 1977

at about eight years and declining after 15 years. The green berries are sun-dried on mats to produce black pepper.

Cloves are obtained from the unopened flower buds of the clove tree, grown generally in mixed gardens. The trees take eight years to come to fruiting, reaching peak production of 2500 from a tree (about one tonne per ha) in their twentieth year, and continuing to produce for up to 50 years. The trees grow up to 700 m in warm moist areas of the southwest Wet Zone.

The *nutmeg* tree grows in similar locations to cloves but may be found producing at higher levels. The nut kernel provides the nutmeg of trade, while mace is obtained from the outer skin.

Papaw (papaya) is a shortlived tree-like plant producing a fruit somewhat similar to melon. It is grown in every district but is of minimal importance in the east coast Dry Zone and at altitudes above about 500 m. Most is grown in the Wet Zone for fresh fruit, but on stabilized *chenas* on the margins of the Wet Zone in Matale and Kurunegala, and in the Uda Walawe area in Hambantota, the fruit is milked for papain which is exported for use in medicines and as a food tenderizer. The plant produces for five years, yielding best in its third year.

80 Girls grading cardamoms at Doteloya Estate, Kegalle District

Unlike most of the minor perennial crops which are suited only to the Wet Zone, *cashew* trees do best in some of the most extremely dry parts of the Dry Zone and will grow with as little rainfall as 500 mm. New plantations have been established on red sands in southern Mannar, and in Puttalam, Batticaloa and Hambantota Districts, often on lands otherwise useless. Smallholders and homestead gardeners can also grow the tree quite easily. Cashews are reported from every District, but of the total of 7037 ha in 1976, Mannar had 33 per cent, Batticaloa 21 per cent, Puttalam 12 per cent, Kurunegala 9 per cent and Colombo 8 per cent. The main threat to the Mannar plantation comes from marauding elephants from the neighbouring Wilpattu Wild Life Sanctuary. Apart from the edible kernel, the cashew nut shell yields a valuable

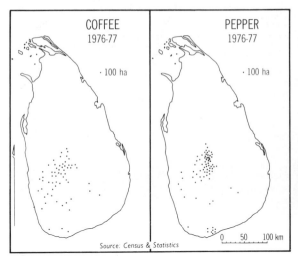

5.16 Coffee and pepper

oil used in heat-resistant brake linings and plastics. The fruits, or 'apples', are used to make wine, cordial syrup and jam. The tree bears in three to four years, reaching full production after nine to ten years when it will bear 1500–3000 fruit annually, but declining after 15 years. Processing involves separating the nuts from the apples, and roasting, shelling and peeling the nuts to obtain the kernel.

Mulberry has a somewhat uncertain future. Although the government has from time to time encouraged the development of a silk industry, orthodox Buddhists frown on the enterprise as one

81 Cutting cinnamon on an estate near Ambalangoda in Galle District

82 Peeling cinnamon bark off the stick is a skilled job. After scraping the stick and rubbing it with a brass rod, he eases the bark off with a knife. The 'pipes' of bark are packed one inside the other to make 'quills' about a metre long. Chips of bark are used to fill any gaps. Near Galle

83 Black pepper and cocoa beans (foreground) drying
    in the sun on the roadside near Teldeniya, Kandy
    District

requiring the worms to be put to death. The
government silk farm is still in operation near
Kandy, mulberry growing around it. It appears
that the area under mulberry is increasing and
there are plans to manufacture silk cloth.

One tree crop of importance in equatorial Southeast Asia and Africa but as yet only experimental
in Sri Lanka is the *oil palm*. An estate at Naka-
deniya in Galle District has 935 ha under oil palm.
Its tolerance of damp, acid soils would seem to
recommend it for the Wet Zone lowlands of
Kalutara, Galle and Matara where conditions are
somewhat similar to those in West Malaysia.

Overall, the economic survival of Sri Lanka's
plantation industries depends very largely on increasing their efficiency and thus their ability to
compete in world markets.

84 Cinnamon oil is distilled from the leaves and twigs,
    and sometimes the bark fragments in plants like this
    one near Ambalangoda in Galle District. The steam
    containing the oil is passed from the boiler on the
    right through the timber-cased still on the left and
    into the cement vat, extreme left, where it finally
    condenses to produce the valuable oil

85 Pepper vines climbing on grevillea shade trees on a
    tea estate at about 400 m in the Kelani Ganga Valley,
    Kandy District

Colonisation in the Wet Zone

Whereas in the Dry Zone there has been plenty of
opportunity for settling colonists on paddy lands,
such development in the Wet Zone has generally
been impossible due to the land shortage, and
colonisation has been on the basis of establishing
groups of cultivators to grow perennial plantation
crops. Thus, from 1956, colonies were begun to
grow tea on 0.9 ha blocks in Ratnapura, Galle and
Matara Districts, and rubber on 1.2 ha blocks in
Badulla, Ratnapura and Kalutara. Coconut colonists on blocks of 2 ha were set up in Kurunegala
and Badulla, as well as further into the Dry Zone
in Puttalam and Jaffna. Cocoa was the objective of
a colony in Matale District. The *Year Book* for 1959
reported that 3870 ha had been alienated to 2412
families in Highland Colonisation Schemes. Their
progress was supervised by a visiting official.

86 Coffee flowers and berries near Gampaha, Colombo District

87 Cocoa trees with glossy leaves growing beneath rubber (note the tapping scars on the trunk on the left). Picture taken near Matale in the dry season when rubber tends to shed its leaves

88 Afforestation with teak has been a widespread activity since Independence and makes more profitable use of the Dry Zone forest areas than does its natural vegetation. Here at a teak seed orchard in Polonnaruwa District, seedlings are prepared for planting

Tea was reported to be particularly successful. By 1968 there were 58 schemes, 21 in tea (supporting 3599 allottees), three in rubber, one in cinnamon, one in coffee, two in mixed crops, and 30 in coconuts (4633 colonists). Highland colonisation, in the sense of settling people from outside the area, seems now in abeyance, although after the 1972 Land Reform Law a scheme to provide small plots of land under tea and rubber for the landless rural population led to some subdivisions of estates to provide for this new category of smallholder.

Wet Zone 'highland' development, in this sense meaning non-paddy lands at any altitude, was included among the Youth Schemes established between 1961 and 1971. Five (involving 401 youths) were concerned with cinnamon and tea, three (580 youths) with passionfruit, two (246 youths) with tea and one (57 youths) with cardamoms.

Forestry

Very little, if anything, remains of the natural vegetation of Sri Lanka that has not been affected and altered by man who has cleared much of it for permanent agriculture, or has periodically burned the forest for *chena* and its fringing grasslands to promote palatable pasture. As suggested in Figure 5.17 (based on work by the French Institute in Pondicherry, India), the natural cover of the island is forest, ranging in type from open thorn forest in the dry northwest and southeast through grades

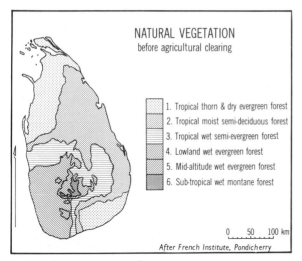

NATURAL VEGETATION
before agricultural clearing

1. Tropical thorn & dry evergreen forest
2. Tropical moist semi-deciduous forest
3. Tropical wet semi-evergreen forest
4. Lowland wet evergreen forest
5. Mid-altitude wet evergreen forest
6. Sub-tropical wet montane forest

0   50   100 km

After French Institute, Pondicherry

5.17 Natural vegetation

89 A ten-year teak plantation in Puttalam District. Teak is a deciduous tree losing its leaves during the dry season

90 Young teak interplanted with bananas in the early stages of establishing a teak plantation

of deciduous and semi-evergreen forest to evergreen forest in the Wet Zone.

The Forest Department takes a more empirical approach in mapping the actual forest types and its own plantations (Fig. 5.18). In the official statistics, 2.9 million ha of woodland constitutes 44 per cent of the total area of Sri Lanka, but much of this has been seriously degraded by *chena* cultivators. About 1.8 million ha is in reserves and State forests which include 118,000 ha of forest plantations made up in 1978 as follows:

teak	65,618 ha
mahogany	23,417 ha
eucalyptus	12,316 ha
pines/bamboo	12,403 ha
other	4,112 ha

Source: Department of Census and Statistics, *Statistical Pocket Book* 1979.

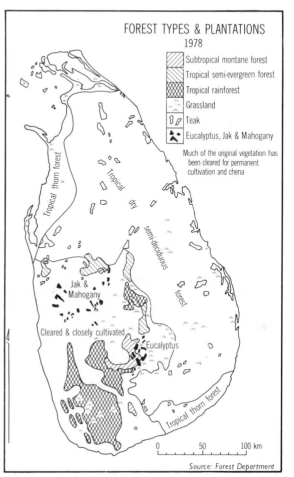

FOREST TYPES & PLANTATIONS
1978

Subtropical montane forest
Tropical semi-evergreen forest
Tropical rainforest
Grassland
Teak
Eucalyptus, Jak & Mahogany

Much of the original vegetation has been cleared for permanent cultivation and chena

Tropical thorn forest

Tropical dry semi-deciduous forest

Jak & Mahogany

Cleared & closely cultivated

Eucalyptus

Tropical thorn forest

0   50   100 km

Source: Forest Department

5.18 Forest types and plantations

91   Seedling teak has been planted here in an area of *illuk* (Imperata cylindrica), the coarse grass that often follows repeated chena cultivation and which is difficult to eradicate except by recreating a shaded environment

92   Five-month old teak (marked by a stick in the centre of the picture) is surrounded by cash crops of chillies, gourds and vegetables on this plantation. Chena cultivators are allowed to grow such crops for a year or two on forest land they have cleared for the Forestry Department. The teak plants are about three metres apart

Since Independence there has been a vigorous programme of forest planting with the object of upgrading the productivity of areas of medium and low yielding natural forest. Large areas of the Dry Zone have been established with stands of teak and eucalypts. In the Wet Zone lowlands, mahogany and jak (a fine hardwood as well as a fruit tree) have been planted, and in the hill country pines and eucalypts. Mahogany is also being planted in degraded rainforest to accelerate the restoration of its productivity.

For those areas of the Dry Zone beyond the reach of irrigation developments, forestry makes good sense, since the alternative is probably *chena*. Teak planting is a long term investment for fine-grade sawn timber for furniture and veneers; the thinned forest reaches maturity in 50 years, and the thinnings are also marketable. Extensive plantations have been made in the Dry Zone under a scheme which employs *chena* cultivators to clear the forest, and to inter-till their own crops with the young teak plants for three years. *Eucalyptus camaldulensis* has also been planted in the Dry Zone as a source of pulping timber for the paper making industry that currently has to import pulp to supplement local supplies of rice straw and waste paper. Eucalypts and pine are planted in the hill country where sub-tropical wet montane-forest would be the natural cover, but where much degradation resulting in grasslands known as *patanas* has taken place. Both trees become profitable for pulp or firewood in 10–20 years, whilst suitable species yield good constructional timber after 35 years.

The long-term annual production target of teak (by the year 2019) is 594,000 m³ compared with an expected annual output of 16,100 m³ in the period, 1980 to 1984. For eucalypts, yearly output is expected to increase from 11,860 m³ in the years 1979 to 1983 to 68,000 m³ by 2014.

Chapter 6

The Non-agricultural Resource Base and Manufacturing Industry

Introduction

The major resources are reviewed in the first part of this chapter, apart from those based on soil and climate which have been considered previously. Three of these, fisheries, sea-salt and hydro-electricity are renewable resources – fisheries, provided they are husbanded conservatively. Sri Lanka's mineral resources, in which the country is poorly endowed, are of course non-renewable. They include gemstones, graphite, ilmenite and rutile, all contributing in a small way to export earnings. Cruder materials like clay, kaolin, limestone and laterite are mainly of value in domestic manufacturing and constructional industries.

The range and scale of industrialisation is discussed in the second part, which also examines the division of manufacturing into public and private sectors, and the continuing existence of craft industries. The chapter concludes with a note on communications.

Fisheries

That fishing communities are among the poorest in society (and are generally the victims of economic exploitation) is probably true of all less developed countries, and indeed of many more developed ones. The fact that fisheries are more or less freely accessible to any who would try to harvest them leads inevitably to there being too many fishermen, a situation aggravated by limited availability of alternative livelihoods. An excessive number of fishermen in relation to the catch makes it harder for them to organise themselves to regulate sales so as to ensure a fair price, and easy for middlemen to exploit the situation. It is, however, difficult for governments to alter effectively the traditional systems that have evolved to suit existing social and economic conditions. In Sri Lanka, the fish trade is traditionally structured around the *mudalalis*. These are the middlemen with access to the main markets who organise the transport of the catch, the seasonal movement of the fishermen and

93   A fisherman throws his net in Batticaloa Lagoon

94   The beach at Hambantota (Fig. 7.7) is sheltered from the west, south and north. In the morning the outrigger fishing boats sail home with their catch some of which is offered for sale on the beach

the capitalisation of their boats through loans against the expectation of the catch.

Modernisation and expansion of the fishing industry, while perhaps theoretically desirable, comes up against many practical and economic problems. There is considerable domestic demand and a dietary need for low cost fish, as is indicated by the scale of imports. For many, fish is the chief source of protein. So far, deep sea fishery resources have been exploited only slightly, their full potential awaiting the provision of boats and harbour facilities. Technological development has taken place in the lucrative and growing export trade in frozen prawns and lobsters, where international competition in a hygiene-conscious market sets high standards. For the domestic market, high technology can be over-expensive. In the hot climate deterioration is rapid and the fresh catch is usually marketed and consumed close to the point of landing, or transported quickly to the towns packed in ice. Longer-term preservation is achieved traditionally by salting and sun-drying. At Pesalai, near Mannar, a factory has been built to can fish and to make fish meal.

The scale of the fishing industry and some of its characteristics may be gauged from Tables 6.1 and 6.2 and the four maps in Figure 6.1 (a-d). Production is clearly heaviest from the west coast fisheries where the continental shelf extends across Palk Strait and the head of the Gulf of Mannar into Indian waters. The proximity of the Colombo market is an additional incentive (a). There is some variation in production according to season (b), but this is probably becoming less marked than

96   At Talaimannar on Mannar Island, fish of various sizes are laid out on mats on the beach to dry in the sun. The fishing families live in the huts behind. These and the fences are built largely from the wood and leaves of the palmyra palms seen in the background

formerly due to increasing mechanisation of the fishing fleet which is now better able to fish independently of the wind direction, and to go further out to sea in the time available.

The less developed fishing communities on the southwest coast show a rise in production during the calms late in the year, whilst on the east coast there is generally a reduction in the catch during the northeast monsoon. In Figure 6.1 (c), showing the variation in the number of days per month suitable for fishing at seven ports, the effect of the southwest monsoon along the southwest coast and of the northeast monsoon on the east coast is demonstrated.

To take advantage of these seasonal variations a certain amount of migration takes place. During the southwest monsoon fishermen move from Galle and Kalutara Districts to Batticaloa District, and from the Negombo area to Batticaloa, Trincomalee, Jaffna and the sheltered waters north of Mannar.

95   A fisherman mending his nets beside his boat, drawn up on the beach at Yala, on the south coast east of Hambantota

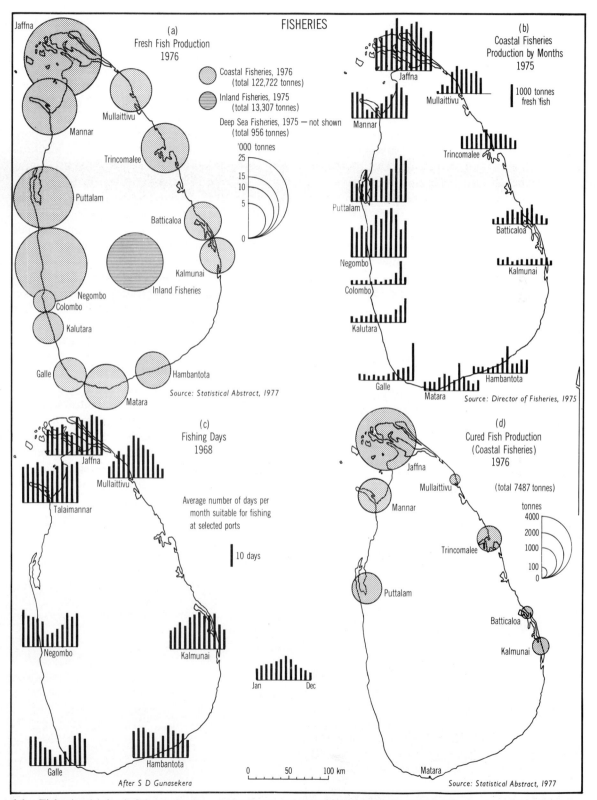

6.1 Fisheries (a) fresh fish production, 1976 (b) coastal fisheries production, 1976 (c) days per month suitable for fishing, 1968 (d) cured fish production, 1976

All major communities are involved in fishing. From Negombo south to Galle and Hambantota, Sinhalese dominate. Mannar, Jaffna, Trincomalee and Batticaloa have a majority of Tamils, with sizeable numbers of Moors in the two east coast districts.*

Fishing techniques in Sri Lanka extend through a wide range from primitive to advanced. Throughout the island 'one-man' nets are thrown into lagoons, tanks and rivers. In the southwest, *madel* or beach seine nets are used, sometimes involving considerable co-operation from villagers on shore, who help to drag in the 500 m of rope and the attached net which is capable of holding two tonnes of fish. Also along the southwest coast, fishermen perched on stilt-like poles may be seen casting with rod and line in reef-sheltered waters. The most common traditional fishing boat is an out-rigger sailing canoe carrying a crew of three or four. Simpler craft, little better than rafts, are made by lashing together crudely shaped trunks, which have to be dried out periodically. Even vessels such as these may now be propelled by outboard

*Gunasekera, S. D. *A Study of the Social and Economic Geography of the Coastal Fishing Industry of Ceylon,* unpublished Ph.D. thesis University College, Swansea, 1970.

97   Fishing boats on the north coast of Jaffna. A coral breakwater provides some shelter. In the foreground is a simple log boat driven by an outboard motor. The other craft are more conventional

motors! The most modern fishermen use fibreglass motor boats, and larger trawlers of reinforced cement are being built in Jaffna for deep-sea fishing. Of the total production of 129,139 tonnes in 1975, almost 86 per cent was marketed fresh, and 13 per cent was cured by drying and salting. Over half the dried fish production is from Jaffna, with Mannar, Trincomalee and Puttalam also important (Fig. 6.1d). All these are Dry Zone locations with climates suited to sun-drying the fish on the beach. Private firms are engaged in freezing for the export trade, while the Pesalai factory of the Ceylon Fisheries Corporation has begun, somewhat fitfully, to can what catch it is able to persuade fishermen to part with. Fish meal is made from unmarketable material both at Pesalai and at Mutwal, near the Colombo fisheries harbour. The strength of the fish *mudalis*' organisation, however, makes it difficult for the Corporation's activities to reach the economic scale anticipated.

By 1978 fish production had reached 156,569 tonnes, almost four times the size of the catch twenty years previously.

Fresh water fisheries represent a relatively underdeveloped resource in a country so generously supplied with controlled water bodies in the form of tanks. The market's conservative preference for sea fish, and its dislike of fresh water fish (regarded as mud-flavoured) has yet to be overcome, but considerable efforts are being made to stock tanks with tilapia and carp. Freshwater

fish now account for about 12 per cent of domestic production, and might eventually displace a large part of the imports. 1975 details are shown in Table 6.1.

Table 6.2 lists the fish imports and exports by value and quantity in 1975, the latest year for which such detailed data are available. Imports came mainly from Pakistan (54 per cent by value), the

98   Boiling *bêche-de-mer* in brine near Mannar. This sea food is a valuable export but is collected only seasonally

Maldives (23 per cent), Ethiopia, Malaysia, India and Aden.

In 1976 imports were down to Rs 25 million, far below the 1959 total of Rs 92 million – the more so when inflation is taken into account. Exports have been increasing over the years, from Rs 560,000 in 1959, to RS 52 million in 1973, and to Rs 233 million in 1978, when 90 per cent consisted of prawns and lobsters, mainly destined for Japan and the USA.

99   Quarrying coral limestone on the coast north of Galle. Coral is also brought in from the sea to be used to make lime

Table 6.1   Total landings of fresh fish, 1975

	Tonnes	Per cent
Deep sea fisheries		
i.e. by trawlers, 11-tonne boats and tuna boats	970	0.8
Coastal fisheries		
by mechanised 3.5-tonne boats	43,024	33.3
by smaller mechanised and non-mechanised craft, and by other methods	71,839	55.6
Inland fresh water fisheries	13,306	10.3
Total	129,139	100

Source: Administration Report of the Director of Fisheries for 1975, Ministry of Fisheries, Colombo, 1977.

Table 6.2   Fish imports and exports, 1975

Imports	Value (Rs thousand)	Tonnes
Maldive fish*	10,173	1,637
Sprats	1,689	678
Dried fish	31,828	12,870
Prawns	1	–
Preserved fish	32	2
Cod-liver oil	248	7
Fresh fish (chilled or frozen)	28	–
Total	43,999	15,194

*A highly flavoured fish preparation imported only from the Maldives.

Exports		
Prawns	11,061	532
Lobsters	2,919	77
Other fish	3,460	218
Shark fins etc.	3,321	55
Bêche-de-mer	3,208	122
Shells	84	21
Other	132	–
Total	22,185	1,025

Source: as for Table 6.1.
Note: the total value of exports (22,185) is as shown in the Report; the column in fact totals 24,185.

Salt

The combination of long, sunny, dry periods with a
lagoonal micro-relief provides excellent sites in
northwestern and southeastern Sri Lanka for the
solar evaporation of sea water. There are some 16
salterns, 86 per cent of capacity being owned by the
National Salt Corporation which controls the
whole industry (Fig. 6.2). The bulk of production
is accounted for by five salterns, two of them at
Elephant Pass, close to the causeway joining
Jaffna Peninsula to the mainland, one near
Hambantota on the south coast, and two beside
Puttalam Lagoon on the west coast.

Production fluctuates according to season,
untimely heavy rainfall being the greatest hazard
since it dilutes the evaporating brine in salterns
and sets the whole process back. In 1976 a peak
of 140,497 tonnes was achieved but the next
year saw a slump to 47, 853 tonnes, followed by
a recovery to a new record of 152,779 tonnes
in 1978. An even more dramatic decline followed
the floods of December 1957, resulting in an output of only 18,163 tonnes in 1958 compared with
108,270 and 81,475 in the two preceding years.

The process at Hambantota is shown in Figure
6.2. Sea water enters the eastern lagoon, Koholan-
kala Lewaya, at a height of 0.4m above mean sea
level. It circulates slowly, evaporating the while, to
be fed at 0.3 m above sea level into the western

100   Lime kiln near Matale. Blocks of limestone (right)
are hand broken to size (centre) and burned to
make lime using as fuel logs of rubber trees (left)

101   In the Wet Zone soft laterite is found close to the
surface and may be cut into blocks to make a
strong building material when dry

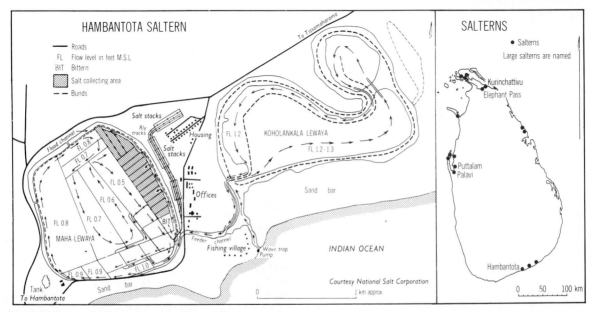

6.2   Salterns: Sri Lanka and Hambantota

102 Brickmakers at work near Gampaha, Colombo District. The man on the right shapes the bricks in a wooden mould while the other takes them to stack (in rear) for a period of air-drying before being finally fired in a kiln nearby

lagoon, Maha Lewaya, which has been partitioned by bunds into a number of pans through which the brine moves eventually to start crystallising in the smaller pans. Labourers rake the crystallised salt into heaps from which it is shovelled into baskets and carried by head load to trucks on a light railway leading to the storage stacks. Here, the trucks are lifted mechanically and the salt tipped into huge heaps that are then thatched with cadjans as a protection against the occasional rainstorm in this dry climate.

Sri Lanka has the potential to become a regular exporter of sea salt but is handicapped by problems of handling since none of the salterns is conveniently located close to a port or roadstead. Exports to Bangladesh from the roadstead at Kankesanturai have to be manhandled at several stages: while being put into sacks at Elephant Pass; loaded onto trucks; unloaded at Kankesanturai; and transferred to lighters from which the sacks are transhipped for stowage aboard a freighter. Small non-domestic users of salt are the fish-drying industry and the Paranthan Chemical Corporation at Elephant Pass which makes caustic soda, chlorine, hydrochloric acid and table salt.

Hydro-electric Power

Since Sri Lanka has neither coal, nor oil, nor natural gas, it is fortunate in possessing good water power resources. The need for electricity is increasing not only because of the escalating cost of imported fuels, but also on account of the demands made by expanding industries and improved living standards. There is considerable potential for electrification of railways and of the rural sector, including tea and rubber factories and irrigation pumps.

Potential hydro-electric power is estimated at 1540 MW from about 30 specific sites.* Some 21 per cent of this potential has been harnessed with an installed capacity of 331 MW, or 82 per cent of the country's present total of 405 MW from all sources.

The Wet Zone hill country provides Sri Lanka with several good sites for hydro-electric power development on the rivers that cascade down steep slopes, and can be impounded relatively inexpensively in confined valleys. The power stations and their connecting 132 kV grid are shown in Figure

*UN World Water Conference, *Country report from Sri Lanka to the ESCAP Regional Preparatory Meeting, Bangkok, Thailand*, Colombo, 1976.

103 In the driest parts of Sri Lanka sea salt can be evaporated in the sun as here near Hambantota. (Fig. 6.2) A small diesel operated railway in the background takes the salt to be stacked nearby under a cadjan thatch until it is sent to market by road

6.3. Thermal stations are at Colombo (56 MW) and Chunnakam, Jaffna (14 MW). The hydro-stations are at Laxapana (150 MW), Polpitiya (75 MW) and Canyon (30 MW) on the Maskeliya Oya, Norton (50 MW) on the Kehelgomu Ganga, Ukuwela (40 MW) in the Mahaweli Ganga Scheme, Inginiyagala (10 MW) at the Senanayake Samudra on the Gal Oya, and Uda Walawe Reservoir (6 MW) on the Walawe Ganga. Stations are being developed at Bowatenna (40 MW), at Kotmale (150 MW) and at Victoria (210 MW to be increased to 360 MW) in the Mahaweli Ganga Scheme (Fig. 4.17). Another is planned at Samanalawewa (120 MW) on the Walawe Ganga.

Total electrical energy production amounted to 1380 million KWh in 1978. Power use is not widely distributed through the community judging by the statistics of consumer numbers: 96,000 domestic (presumably householders), 24,311 commercial, and 3296 industrial. Almost half the sales is to industry and only 10 per cent is to domestic consumers.

Mineral Resources

Although Sri Lanka was a fragment of the vast Gondwanaland Continent to which also belonged the Indian Peninsula, Western Australia and South Africa, it contains little of the mineral wealth that characterises parts of these areas. As Figure 6.4 shows, Pre-Cambrian granite, gneiss and metasediments are exposed over much of the island, being overlaid by Jurassic, Miocene and Pleistocene sedimentary formations in a restricted coastal zone extending northwards from Colombo.

Lacking coal or substantial deposits of iron ore, Sri Lanka cannot look to an economic future in heavy industry. At best, the scattered pockets of

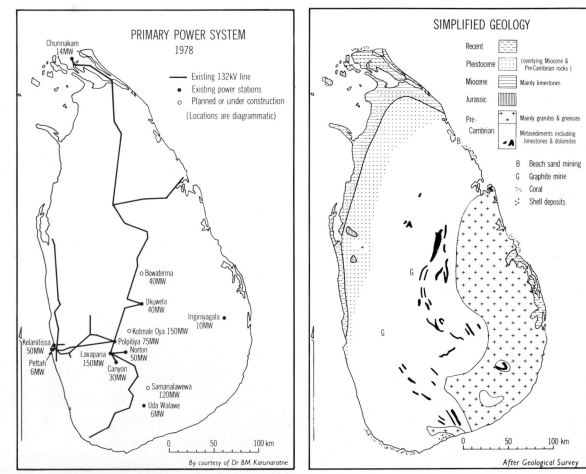

6.3   Primary power system

6.4   Simplified geology and minerals

limonitic iron ores in the southwestern hill country could help support a small scale iron industry. The mineral wealth that exists supports a modest export trade in graphite, gemstones and mineral sands, i.e. ilmenite and rutile.

Graphite

Graphite – a form of carbon used as a lubricant in carbon rods and electrodes, and in the metallurgical and nuclear industries – has long been mined from vein deposits. Three deep mines are in production, the largest in Kegalle District, and two, connected underground, in Kurunegala District. Graphite is also recorded from a number of sites mainly in the southwest. The industry is now nationalised. Production fluctuates in relation to overseas demand which reached peaks in the two World Wars. Since Independence, exports have ranged between 5,722 and 14,220 tonnes. Output in 1978 totalled 10,697 tonnes and exports were valued at Rs 59.3 million. Practically the whole production is exported, mainly to Japan, the USA and the UK. The value of exports has increased relative to quantity as grading has improved.

For centuries Sri Lanka has been famous for its *gemstones* – precious stones like sapphires and rubies and semi-precious gems such as topaz, garnets and moonstones. The last named are found in the weathered pegmatite rock near Ambalangoda. The other gems are mined from alluvial deposits, Ratnapura District being the principal source, where the shallow pits may be seen in the middle of the paddyfields. Mining methods are essentially crude, although power pumps are now often employed to control water. Production units are small, and close government supervision of exports by the State Gem Corporation seeks to protect small producers and consumers against the once all-powerful dealers. In 1978 gems valued at Rs 531 million made up 4 per cent of the total value of exports. Hong Kong, Japan and Switzerland took 83 per cent of the total.

Mineral Sands

Mineral sands are mined to obtain ilmenite and rutile, the sources of titanium used in paints and metallurgy. The Pulmoddai deposit north of Trincomalee yielded 37,260 tonnes of ilmenite in 1978 and exports worth Rs 23.8 million. In the same year rutile production was 11,497 tonnes.

104 An elephant working in a timber yard near Negombo in the 'coconut triangle'

105 A sawpit at Potuhara, Kurunegala District operated by two men, is indicative of the persistence of manual labour in Sri Lanka even in activities where mechanisation exists in competition

106 A gem mine near Avissawella has been dug into the alluvial valley floor among the paddy fields. A motor pump is used to drain the mine which is about four metres deep. In the background, a rubber plantation and a homestead with coconuts and bananas

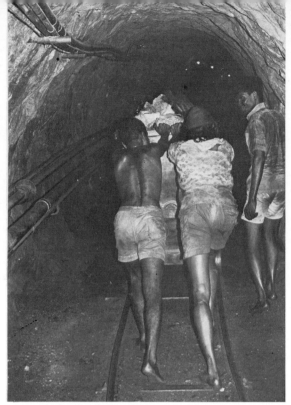

107 Working in a gem pit near Avissawella, the gravel is extracted in baskets to be sorted on the surface for gemstones

108 Down a graphite mine in Kurunegala District. The graphite gives a gloss to the workmen's skin

Other Minerals

While other minerals extracted for export do not make a very impressive show economically speaking, there are considerable local industries based upon other more humble materials from the ground.

Limestones are found in the sedimentary Miocene deposits that stretch from south of Puttalam into the Jaffna Peninsula, and provide the basis for the cement industries at Kankesanturai in the Jaffna Peninsula and near Puttalam; 647,142 tonnes were quarried in 1976, when cement production was 367,225 tonnes. In 1978, 575,061 tonnes were made. Small lime works supplying local needs utilise the Pre-Cambrian limestones and dolomites, and coral and shell limestone which are found on the coast in several areas (Fig. 6.4).

China clay, for fine ceramics, is worked near Colombo and ball clay, for china and earthenware, is found in the alluvial deposits of several rivers of the southwest. Clay suitable for brick and tile making is more widespread in both Wet and Dry Zones and is the basis for both large and craft-scale industry. In the Wet Zone a traditional building material, *laterite*, is available. A metre or so below the surface may be found easily workable beds of laterite, the product of tropical soil forming processes. Blocks are cut by hand while the material is still relatively soft, but on exposure to the air they harden into a construction material of considerable engineering strength.

Manufacturing Industry

It was seen in Table 2.2 that the contribution of manufacturing industry to GNP showed an upward though somewhat erratic trend from 4.7 per cent in 1953 to 20.7 per cent in 1978. Like many less developed countries, Sri Lanka has been trying since Independence not only to encourage industries manufacturing substitutes for imported articles, but also to promote the export of such goods. By 1978, 14 per cent of all exports consisted of manufactures.

In attempting to develop an economically sound range of manufacturing industries, successive governments have had to contend with many difficulties, including some slow changing constraints such as the limited size and purchasing power of the domestic market, the lack of raw materials, and a shortage of skilled manpower and capital. In addition the export-based economy, subject to fluctuating world markets, has from time to time run into crises, forcing the reduction of imports of capital and intermediate (semi-finished) goods. On top of all these handicaps, political ideology at home has at times made manufacturing industry a 'political football'. Left-wing governments have sought to take over industry to develop it as an instrument of social policy, while more right-wing governments have encouraged private (including foreign) enterprise.* The UNP government coming to power in 1977 appears to be promoting private investment while leaving intact the many State Industrial Corporations set up by its predecessors, although the problem remains of getting them to run efficiently. Under-utilisation of capacity and overemployment are common failings contributing to inefficiency.

Industrial statistics in a developing country like Sri Lanka present an incomplete picture since most craft industries and many small-scale enterprises

*For a study of industrial policy and development since Independence, see N. Balakrishnan's Chapter 8 in de Silva, K. M. (ed) *Sri Lanka: a Survey*, London, 1977, pp. 192–212.

109 A woman breaking road metal in a quarry near Ella Badulla District. She holds a metal ring in her left hand to prevent the fragments flying as she strikes with her hammer

110 Near Kandy specialised brass work is carried on in a number of villages. Here a tray is being hammered into a traditional design

probably go unrecorded. In Table 6.3 the relative importance of State Corporations and those private industrial establishments that are registered with the Ministry of Industries and Scientific Affairs, is shown by employment and value of production in nine main categories of industry. Because published official data for State owned and private industries separately do not exactly correspond with other data for national totals, Table 6.3 contains two versions of the totals which, while being very similar in terms of value of production, diverge considerably on employment.

Group 5 including petroleum refining, chemicals, rubber and plastics dominates the total value of production with 38 per cent, followed by Groups 1 (food, drink and tobacco), 2 (textiles etc.) and 8 (metal fabrication etc.). The same four groups head the list for employment but in different order, Group 2 (textiles) leading well ahead of Groups 8, 1 and 5.

Employment in private industry is almost two-thirds of the total compared with its 40 per cent

111   At Kundasale near Kandy, many villagers are brass workers. In this small foundry brass is being heated in a fire stimulated by a hand bellows

Table 6.3   Industry, value of production and employment, 1976
(Rs million; and percentages of totals)

Industrial Groups	Total 1 af		Value Total 2 bf		State owned 3 cg		Private 4 dg		Total 5 af		Employment Total 6 ef		State owned 7 cg		Private 8 dg	
Food, drink, tobacco	1,715	28	1,711	28	718	42	993	58	23,667	21	20,207	15	9,472	47	10,735	53
Textiles, clothing, leather	680	11	711	11	194	27	517	73	30,477	27	38,471	29	11,679	30	26,792	70
Wood and wood products	129	2	124	2	120	98	3	2	6,510	6	6,074	5	5,959	98	115	2
Paper and paper products, printing	203	3	163	3	96	59	67	41	6,416	6	6,035	5	3,605	60	2,430	40
Chemicals, petroleum, rubber, plastic products	2,336	39	2,366	38	2,091	88	275	12	14,592	13	16,965	13	4,254	25	12,711	75
Non-metallic minerals	360	6	226	4	167	74	59	26	12,483	11	10,541	8	4,773	45	5,768	55
Basic metal products	138	2	179	3	138	77	41	23	1,429	1	3,182	2	1,429	45	1,753	55
Fabricated metal, machinery	474	8	476	8	20	4	456	96	16,545	15	24,279	18	1,595	7	22,684	93
Other industries	26	0.4	245	4	157	64	88	36	1,344	1	5,524	4	4,027	73	1,497	27
Total	6,061	100	6,201	100	3,701	60	2,497	40	113,463	100	131,278	100	46,793	36	84,485	64

Source and Notes:
a. Central Bank of Ceylon, *Review of the Economy*, Colombo, 1976, Table 11(c)1.
b. Sum of columns 3 + 4.
c. Central Bank of Ceylon, *op. cit.*, Table 11(D)2 apportioning each State Corporation to an appropriate group.
d. Department of Census and Statistics, *Statistical Pocket Book*, Colombo 1977, Table 55(h). Totals may not tally due to rounding off of individual items.
e. Sum of columns 7 + 8.
f. Percentages in columns 1, 2, 5 and 6 are of the totals in those columns.
g. Percentages in columns 3 and 4 are of their summed totals by groups in column 2; those in columns 7 and 8 of their summed totals by groups in column 6.

share in the value of production. The disparity is largely due to the high value of refined petroleum products in Group 5. If this group is omitted from both employment and value totals, private industry's share of these becomes 63 and 58 per cent respectively. As the table stands, private industry has 75 per cent of the work force in Group 5 but accounts for only 12 per cent of production. The lesser discrepancy which may be noted in the case of Group 6 (non-metallic minerals) is attributable to the State's hold on the more valuable mineral sands and graphite industries, and that in Group 7 (basic metal products) to the scale and advanced technological level of the Ceylon Steel and State Hardware Corporations.

Table 6.4 lists 19 of the State Corporations with their employment in 1976, and production data for 1976–78. Details of production in private industry are not available beyond the data presented in Table 6.3.

Table 6.4 State Industrial Corporations, production and employment

Corporation	Employment 1976	Unit of output	Production 1976	1977	1978
Ceylon Cement	2,625	tonnes	335,652	361,442	575,064
Ceylon Ceramics	3,649				
ceramics and sanitary ware		tonnes	2,964	3,600	4,428
kaolin		tonnes	4,353	5,182	5,724
Ceylon Leather Products	938	thousand pairs shoes	167	177	179
Ceylon Mineral Sands	422				
ilmenite		tonnes	55,810	20,137	37,260
rutile		tonnes	1,039	1,070	11,496
Ceylon Oils & Fats	899				
animal food		tonnes	46,741	42,017	41,736
Ceylon Plywoods	4,353	thousand m²	4,282	3,564	3,096
Ceylon Steel	1,429				
rolled products		tonnes	28,295	24,558	33,108
wire products		tonnes	9,028	7,604	14,148
National Milk Board	2,280				
processed milk liquid		thousand litres	11,848	16,862	17,292
condensed milk		thousand cans	16,767	14,834	12,792
powdered milk		tonnes	970	938	1,190
National Paper	3,605	tonnes	17,257	19,740	25,500
National Salt	678	tonnes	140,497	47,101	152,784
National Textile	9,894				
yarn		thousand Kg	7,374	5,030	5,736
cloth		thousand m²	10,886	14,918	18,276
Paranthan Chemicals	399				
caustic soda		tonnes	1,571	1,515	1,860
Sri Lanka Petroleum	627				
petrol		tonnes	99,371	103,348	120,624
kerosene		tonnes	188,331	185,447	211,932
naphtha		tonnes	103,484	102,197	n.a.
diesel		tonnes	320,394	368,428	359,436
aviation turbine-fuel		tonnes	76,884	71,592	35,088
furnace oil		tonnes	513,678	545,349	548,136
Sri Lanka Sugar	3,068	tonnes	23,275	23,053	24,780
Sri Lanka State Flour	521	tonnes	93,639	72,740	61,788
Sri Lanka Tyre	2,082	numbers	181,416	156,496	256,968
State Graphite	1,726	tonnes	8,135	8,724	10,697
State Hardware	1,595				
castings		numbers	2,053	2,055	n.a.
mamotties		numbers	199,476	384,720	361,368

Source: Department of Census and Statistics, *Statistical Pocket Book*, Colombo, 1978; and Central Bank of Ceylon, *Bulletin*, Colombo, Feb. 1979.

112 Molten brass is being poured into a sand mould to make a casting. At Kundasale, near Kandy

113 Finishing pots beside a village kiln near Trincomalee

Craft Industries

Craft industries both at the level of the family household or in small organised units are a feature of Sri Lanka life. Under the Industrial Development Board (National Industries Corporation), assistance and guidance is being given to small-scale industry both to preserve traditional crafts from extinction and to promote their products at home and abroad. Among specialisations being assisted are pottery, coir fibre industries, carpentry, hand-loom weaving, and working in brass, silver and gold. Some of these crafts are highly localised, such as brass working in villages near Kandy. Here, attempts are being made to introduce the making of modern brass products such as taps to help sustain the fine traditional crafts making beaten brass trays, etc. The Board is also assisting new medium-scale industries in the private sector in order to create employment opportunities. Traditional goldsmiths can be seen at work in the Pettah in Colombo and in Jaffna where extremely fine chain work is done. In the 'tourist' zone between Colombo and Negombo and along the Kandy Road, batik workshops and showrooms are proliferating.

Industrial Estates

Industrial estates providing the basic material infrastructure for small factories have been set up at Ekala near Ja-ela, between Colombo and Negombo, near Kandy at Pallekelle, and at Achchuveli near Jaffna. Ekala has plants making leather goods, canned foods, paints, packaging materials, agricultural machinery, fans, radios, etc. Pallekelle has a textile mill and plants processing oils and fats, peanut butter, cocoa, milk, and local silk; Achchuveli includes fruit canning, textile finishing, and the manufacture of soap, match boxes and writing chalk among the products of several small factories.

Free Trade Zone

A recent government initiative in 1978 aims to attract manufacturing industry by the setting up of a 'Free Trade Zone' close to Colombo's International Airport, 29 km north of the city. The idea is to allow foreign entrepreneurs and mixed foreign and Sri Lanka enterprises to import materials not available in Sri Lanka free of duty and harbour dues, provided they are to be made up into goods mainly for export, when again they will escape customs duty. It is hoped thereby to increase export earnings and employment opportunities.

Firms operating in the Zone enjoy a 7–10 year tax 'holiday' and low rates of tax for a further 15 years, as well as a reduced tax of 75 per cent of the prevailing import duty on goods sold in Sri Lanka for 20 years.* The Zone is under the control of the Greater Colombo Economic Commission. By February 1980, 92 enterprises had been approved and 45 were in operation or under construction; 13 were Hong Kong firms, many of them in the clothing trade, and one in cashew oil; six were from the USA (one, part-Indian), engaged in clothing manufacture, gem-cutting and making hair-dryers; two Thai companies were in gems and clothing. Japan provided two firms and 12 other countries one project each. The total labour force involved is 6–7,000.

Location of Industries

A precise picture of the overall distribution of industry is impossible to obtain in the absence of data for employment and location of individual plants both in State Corporations and in the private sector. The *Preliminary Report on the Field Survey of Manufacturing Industry 1975/76*† does, however, detail employment in private industries by districts. Of the total of 75,184 employees recorded in that survey, 81.7 per cent were in Colombo District and a further 4 per cent in the adjoining district of Kalutara. Only four other districts exceeded a 1 per cent share: Galle 1.8 per cent, Matara 2.5 per cent, Kandy 2.8 per cent and Jaffna 2.2 per cent. The dominance of Colombo District is even more marked in its 90 per cent share of the value of private industrial output, followed by Kalutara with 3.4 per cent. Matara 1.1 per cent, Kandy 1.8 per cent, and Jaffna 1.0 per cent are the only others with 1 per cent or more.

Away from this focus, industries are specifically located either because of some available resource,

114 The village of Puwakdandawa in western Hambantota District specialises in pottery in which women play an important part. Here a large pot takes shape on a hand turned wheel

115 Weaving cloth on a hand loom near Beliatta, western Hambantota District. The girl uses her feet as well as her hands

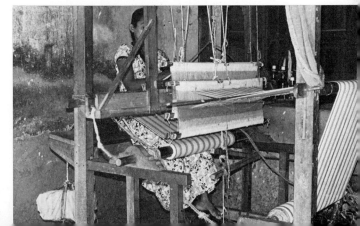

* Central Bank of Ceylon, *Bulletin*, Colombo, November, 1978, p.951.
† Published by the Ministry of Industries and Scientific Affairs, Colombo, 1977.

or because they represent survivals of traditional crafts earlier located there. It is true that there have been efforts to establish small factories such as textile mills in some district towns, but certainly in the private sector, in none of the manufacturing categories listed in Table 6.3 does Colombo District account for less than 73 per cent of total employment, and in five of the nine the figure is over 85 per cent.

Clearly, the primacy of Colombo (with the closely associated urban settlements in its immediate hinterland) has proved an irresistible magnet for industry. Because of the relatively recent development of modern manufacturing, the Colombo factories tend to be on the fringes of the built-up area, particularly along the main approach roads from Negombo and Galle.

A brief survey of the major State Corporation plants will serve to underline the fact that most of those outside Colombo District are materials-oriented. (See Fig. 6.5 for locations.)

Ceylon Cement has three plants: at Kankesanturai, at Palavi near Puttalam (both sited near limestone deposits), and at Galle. At the latter – for no obvious economic reason – clinker brought by rail from Kankesanturai is crushed. The argument for setting up the Galle plant was that a harbour was to be built at Kankesanturai and surplus clinker could be shipped economically by sea to Galle. In the event, however, no harbour materialised.

The Sugar Corporation has mills at Kantalai near Trincomalee, and at Hingurana in the Gal

6.5   Location of industries

116   Silk screen printing of cotton fabric at a cooperative powerloom factory near Jaffna

117   A Jaffna Tamil goldsmith at work on a fine chain necklace, with his forge in the foreground

118 Applying wax to a batik design at a factory at Marawila, north of Negombo. After waxing, the cloth will be dipped in dye which will colour all but the waxed area

19 Rolls of finished paper at the Eastern Paper Mill at Valaichchenai, Batticaloa District

20 A tractor pulling a load of rice straw for the paper mill at Embilipitiya in Hambantota District. Tractors are commonly seen on the roads pulling trailer loads of people or commodities or both

Oya Scheme, producing refined sugar and distillery products from cane grown in their own large, monocultural sugar estates sited there. *Jaggery* manufacture in small scale operations is very widespread in the moister parts of the island, expanding and contracting in relation to the price of refined sugar as fixed by the government, and the latter's import policy.

The National Paper Corporation has two plants. That at Valaichchenai (north of Batticaloa) was sited in the expectation that *illuk* grass *(Imperata cylindrica)* could be grown nearby on a commercial scale to supplement local paddy straw. These together would constitute 70 per cent of the raw materials, the remainder being imported pulp. When this proved not to be the case, the mill had to rely on rice straw and waste paper, and has continued to fortify the feed stock with high-grade imported pulp. The second mill is at Embilipitiya in the Walawe Ganga basin. A reliable water supply is essential in papermaking and has been a problem at Valaichchenai where, in very dry seasons, the tank supply is inadequate and the mill has to shut down.

With the tea industry taking most of its production (mainly of tea chests), the Ceylon Plywoods Corporation runs plants at Gintota and Kosgama, both near forests in the wet southwest.

The Ceylon Ceramics Corporation has been one of the few really profitable State undertakings. Its major plants at Negombo and Piliyandala use kaolin from deposits at Boratesgamuwa. Crockery, decorated tiles and sanitary ware are supplied to both domestic and export markets. A sheet glass factory is being built at Dankotuwa, north of Negombo, to exploit glass-sand deposits nearby. In several parts of the island in the Wet Zone, particularly in the southwest, clays suitable for brick and roof-tile manufacture are quarried, but in only a few localities is high-grade ball clay found for making refractory bricks.

The Leather Products Corporation tans leather and makes footwear and other goods, some of which are now being exported. The tanning factory is on the northern outskirts of Colombo, while leather goods are made at the Ekala Industrial Estate at Ja-ela.

The National Textile Corporation is the largest employer of labour, operating spinning and weaving mills at Veyangoda, Tulhiriya and Pugoda.

Additional plants are being set up at Mattegama and Minneriya. Labour supply and the Colombo market are the major locational factors in the textile industry. That there is still unsatisfied demand for cloth is revealed every New Year when better grades and designs of sari are imported from India. As Table 6.3 indicates, there is a large private sector in textiles and clothing manufacture.

Ceylon Petroleum has a refinery at Sapugaskanda, northeast of Colombo, where imported crude is processed. A plant at Kolonnawa, on the eastern side of Colombo, makes candles and blends lubricants. The export of bunker oil and naphtha have become a valuable source of foreign exchange.

At the Ceylon State Hardware Corporation's plant a wide range of hand tools, implements and castings are made from iron and non-ferrous metals. *Mamotties*, the large hoes widely used in cultivating paddies, are the major product. Heavier iron and steel goods are made by the Ceylon Steel Corporation at Oruwala, east of Colombo, which runs a rolling mill and a wire mill. Imported mild steel billets are heated in an oil furnace and rolled to make rods and angles. A start has been made on building machine tools such as grinders, drills and presses.

At Kelaniya, northeast of Colombo, the Sri Lanka Tyre Corporation makes rubber tyres and tubes. Although locally produced rubber is used, imported materials (included synthetic rubber and petro-chemicals) make up 83 per cent of the cost of raw materials.

The National Milk Board has plants processing fresh milk and reconstituting powdered milk on the outskirts of Colombo. A new plant making powdered milk is at Ambawela in the hill country, while a condensed milk factory at Polonnaruwa uses imported milk powder and local fresh milk.

At Seeduwa, near Negombo, the Ceylon Oils and Fats Corporation makes animal feedstuffs from copra residue. Nearby is the Distilleries Corporation's arrack factory.

Some Corporations handle imported materials without much processing. Thus the Ceylon Fertiliser Corporation mixes and packs fertiliser, the Jute Industries Corporation reconditions second-hand gunny bags, and the State Flour Mill operates at Mutwal on Colombo Harbour.

In conclusion, it must be reiterated that a great deal of manufacturing goes on in small workshops using simple equipment, some to process primary products on site throughout the country, others engaged in craft manufacture or in making more modern artifacts on a small scale or in building local bodies on imported vehicle chassis, etc. In the private sector, 78 per cent of the establishments that report to the Ministry have less than Rs 100,000 capital and account for 48 per cent of employment and 28 per cent of the value of output. Only 8 per cent of reporting plants exceed Rs 1 million capital, but these produced 56 per cent of the value and used 34 per cent of the labour force covered by the returns.

Communications

Good communications are an essential prerequisite for economic and social development. By South Asian standards, Sri Lanka is well provided with bitumen roads on which State managed bus services provide a remarkably extensive and well-patronised service throughout the island. The Transport Board buses totalled 19,361 million passenger-kilometres in 1978 compared with 3,708 million by the Government Railway.

The railways all radiate from Colombo (Fig. 6.6). In clockwise order the lines are as follows:

to Puttalam, with a mineral line extending 29 km beyond; to Talaimannar, the ferry terminal for India; to Jaffna and Kankesanturai, the Northern Line; to Trincomalee; to Batticaloa; to Kandy and Matale; to Badulla and the hill country, the Main Line; to Galle and Matara, the Coast Line.

These tracks are of standard guage. A narrow guage (2 ft. 6 in.) line, the Kelani Valley Line, formerly reached beyond Ratnapura, but now terminates at Padukka. Colombo's rail-commuter catchment, measured by sections carrying more than 1,000 passengers daily to the Colombo area, extends as far as Puttalam, Polgahawela, Padukka and Galle.

Air Lanka operates international flights to Madras, Bombay, Singapore, Bangkok, Paris and London. Many foreign airlines and charter companies serve the island. The former domestic services from Colombo to Jaffna and Trincomalee have been discontinued.

121 The Cement Factory at Puttalam. Limestone and clay quarried in the district are brought in by rail

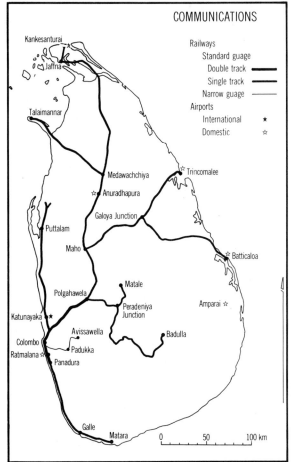

COMMUNICATIONS

Railways
  Standard guage
  Double track
  Single track
  Narrow guage
Airports
  International ★
  Domestic ☆

Kankesanturai
Jaffna
Talaimannar
Medawachchiya
Anuradhapura
Trincomalee
Galoya Junction
Puttalam
Maho
Batticaloa
Matale
Polgahawela
Peradeniya Junction
Amparai ☆
Katunayaka ★
Avissawella
Badulla
Colombo
Ratmalana ☆
Padukka
Panadura
Galle
Matara

0   50   100 km

Foreign shipping is also dominated by Colombo which handled 7 million tonnes of shipping in 1970 compared with its nearest rival, Trincomalee, with 294,000 tonnes. Cargo handled in 1976 amounted to 2.3 million tonnes at Colombo (92 per cent of the total), 130,000 tonnes at Trincomalee (mainly tea exports) and 54,000 tonnes at Galle. Exports totalled 1.1 million tonnes in 1976 compared with 0.56 million tonnes in 1959; for imports the totals were 1.38 million tonnes and 2.07 million tonnes respectively.

6.6 Communications

Chapter 7

Population Distribution and Urbanisation

Population Density

Population density at the 1971 Census is mapped in Figure 7.1 by the 145 electoral districts. These provide a much finer mesh for the purpose of density mapping than do the 22 administrative districts, but the latter are used for considering changes over time because of changes in the electoral districts.

The density map (Fig. 7.1), and that of urban centres in 1971 (Fig. 7.2), have been placed side by side to indicate those areas of high density which are attributable largely to the presence of towns.

The average density of population per km^2 in 1971 was 195. Taking the value 200 in Figure 7.1 as approximately this average, it is apparent that if exceptions are made for rugged ridge-and-valley

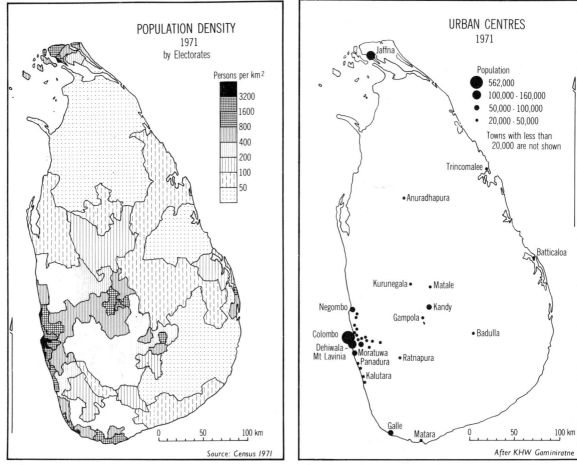

7.1 Population density

7.2 Urban centres

122 Colombo Harbour and the channel linking it to Beira Lake in the foreground. In the right distance is the silo of the flour mill, and on the left the eastern edge of the city centre of Fort. Warehouses occupy much of the land to the right of the channel which has lock gates to control the level of Beira Lake (Fig. 7.12)

123 Temple of the Sacred Tooth of the Buddha in Kandy, from which every year with great pageantry the relic is paraded through the town. (Fig. 7.10)

124 A terrace of shops with balconied homes above Colombo, now partly occupied by the Hotel Nippon, 1 km southeast of Fort

country in Ratnapura District, this isoline follows very closely the Wet Zone-Dry Zone boundary (cf. Fig. 1.6). The Wet Zone electorates contain 65 per cent of the total population on 23 per cent of the total land area.

Within the Dry Zone only two areas exceed densities of 200 persons per km². Outstanding is the western two-thirds of the Jaffna Peninsula with its intensive cultivation supported in part by well irrigation. A smaller area lying south of Batticaloa consists of two electorates in which the population is topographically confined by the inland lagoons to a narrow coastal strip.

A striking feature revealed by the map is that such large areas of the Dry Zone support quite sparse populations. Thus 'mainland' Jaffna, Mannar, Vavuniya and the northern two-thirds of Anuradhapura Districts and a large part of the Districts of Polonnaruwa, Batticaloa, Monaragala and Amparai, have less than 50 per km². With 23 persons per km², Monaragala electorate has the lowest density in the island, followed by Vavuniya (26 per km²) and Mannar (31 per km²). Those areas with between 50 and 200 per km² contain the major colonisation schemes based on tank renovation and irrigation development.

Within the Wet Zone, those areas with over 400 per km² stand out. From north of Negombo southwards to just east of Matara, the coastal belt with its several towns forms a zone of high density (broken only by the 'accident' of one basically inland electorate projecting its medium overall density to the coast). Colombo spreads its urban influence inland in a cluster of semi-suburban towns leading into what may be described as the Colombo – Kegalle – Kandy axis of high population density. North and south of Kandy the axis widens to include the Matale and Gampola electorates respectively. The third area comprises Badulla, Bandarawela and Uva-Paranagama, small electorates with intensive traditional agriculture in the valleys.

Figure 7.3a shows by the 1946 districts (i.e. prior to the subdivison of Anuradhapura, Batticaloa and Badulla) the actual increase in population in the 30 years 1946–76. The impressive percentage increases in the belt of Dry Zone districts from Mannar to Batticaloa–Amparai, particularly in Vavuniya (338 per cent) and Anuradhapura-Polonnaruwa (327 per cent), are mainly accounted

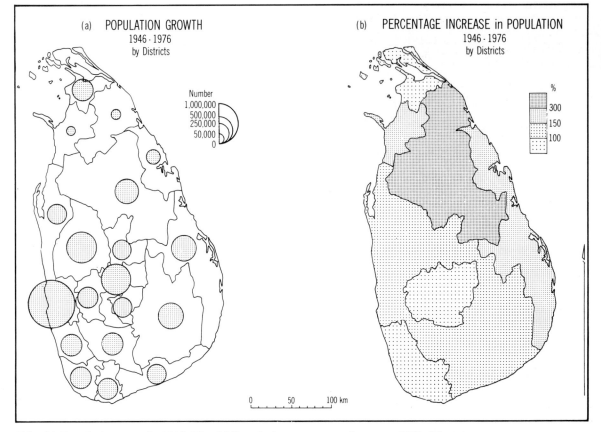

(a) POPULATION GROWTH
1946 - 1976
by Districts

Number
1,000,000
500,000
250,000
50,000
0

(b) PERCENTAGE INCREASE in POPULATION
1946 - 1976
by Districts

%
300
150
100

0   50   100 km

7.3   (a) Population growth, 1946–76   (b) Population percentage increase, 1946–76

125   Next door to the Hotel Nippon empty lots are occupied by squatters' huts. Old tyres on the roof keep the corrugated iron from blowing away in a storm. Bamboo curtains in the doorway provide privacy and shade. In the right foreground is the communal tap

for by colonisation schemes, but relate to small initial populations (Fig. 7.3b). In the period in question, Sri Lanka's population rose by 106 per cent. Colombo District (104 per cent) lies close to the average, separated by an appreciable gap from the group of districts with lower values (Table 7.1). These include the hill country and its western margins, i.e. Nuwara Eliya, Kandy and Kegalle, and the southwest coastal Wet Zone: Kalutara, Galle and Matara. Emigration of Indian Tamils returning to India has been substantial from the tea growing areas. The move of Sinhalese from the crowded Wet Zone into the Dry Zone colonies has been largely responsible for the pattern of differential increase. The map of net migration between 1946 and 1971 (Fig. 7.4a) must be seen as highly tentative, based as it is on the summation of intercensal estimates using vital statistics as an indirect indication. There is a total excess of losses over gains of 231,000 which must be assumed to be the result of net emigration overseas. At face

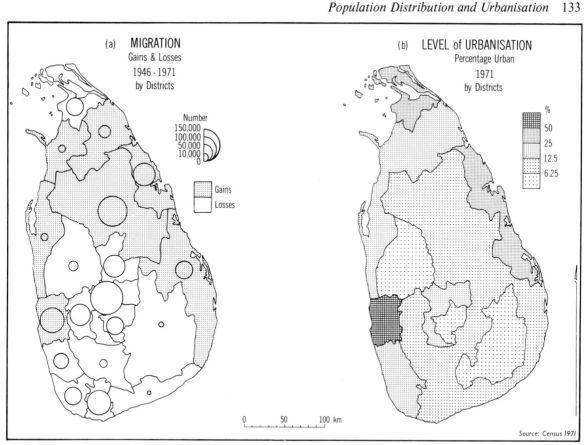

(a) MIGRATION
Gains & Losses
1946 - 1971
by Districts

Number
150,000
100,000
50,000
10,000
0

Gains
Losses

0   50   100 km

(b) LEVEL of URBANISATION
Percentage Urban
1971
by Districts

%
50
25
12.5
6.25

Source: Census 1971

Table 7.1 Percentage increase of population by District 1946–76

District	Increase
Vavuniya	338
Anuradhapura-Polonnaruwa	327
Batticaloa-Amparai	182
Trincomalee	168
Mannar	163
Hambantota	145
Badulla-Monaragala	135
Kurunegala	129
Puttalam-Chilaw	121
Matale	119
Ratnapura	108
Colombo	104
Nuwara Eliya	82
Kandy	81
Matara	80
Jaffna	79
Kegalle	76
Galle	73
Kalutara	71
Sri Lanka	**106**

Source: Department of Census and Statistics, *Statistical Pocket Book,* Colombo, 1978 and *Statistical Abstract of Sri Lanka 1973*, Colombo, 1975.

7.4 (a) Migration gains and losses
(b) Level of Urbanisation

126 New flats near Maradana in inner Colombo help the resettlement of squatters

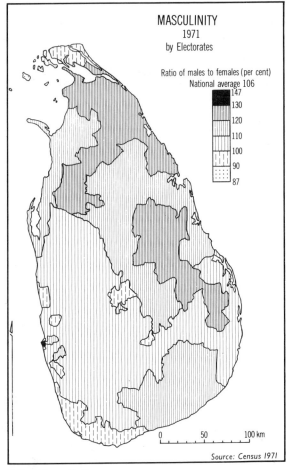

7.5 Masculinity

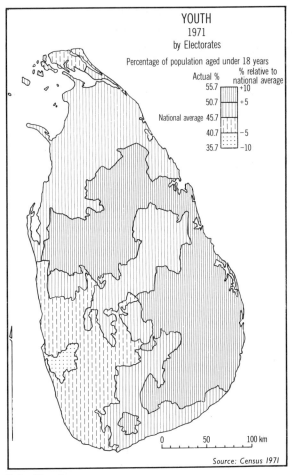

7.6 Youth

value, the map indicates the attraction of urban Colombo and of the Dry Zone districts with colonisation schemes, and the heavy outflow from the most crowded Wet Zone districts in the southwest and centre.

The levels of masculinity in the population (Fig. 7.5), i.e. the ratio of males to females, and its youthfulness (Fig. 7.6) are indirect indices of migration. Apart from central Colombo city, the highest masculinity is found generally where agricultural colonisation has attracted single male workers in the period immediately prior to the census. The lowest masculinity is seen in Jaffna and its islands from which able bodied males migrate in search of work, and in Galle and Matara, Negombo and Kandy, where a higher proportion of the population than the average is retired, and womenfolk are outliving their husbands. The least youthful areas, in the Wet Zone generally,

suggest the effect of emigration of young couples to the colonisation schemes.

Youthfulness is more pronounced where the colonies have become established. It is lowest in Colombo to which there is significant adult male migration in search of work, and where also the practice of family limitation is more widespread.

Urbanisation

Although 22 per cent of the population was recorded as 'urban' in the 1971 Census, the proportion is only a modest 16 per cent if one restricts the term to towns with over 20,000 inhabitants. The increase since 1946 has been relatively slight; from 21 to 22 per cent of the total urban population according to the Census and from 11.4 to 16 per cent if only towns exceeding 20,000 are considered.

An ESCAP* study concludes that urbanisation in Sri Lanka has not been associated with industrialisation, but rather with commercial activity generally, and the trading functions of Colombo in particular. The colonisation schemes and other government investment in rural areas have taken up some of the pressures of population growth, while the compactness of the island and its easy communications perhaps reduce the urge to settle permanently in the city while the social contacts with the rural ancestral home can be maintained. The Colombo conurbation, Jaffna and Kandy (all over 100,000 people) are the only cities that emanate a truly individual and independent atmosphere, and it is probably no accident that they represent the three main strands in the fabric of Sri Lanka. These are respectively the commercial, cosmopolitan, former colonial capital; the cultural capital of the Sri Lanka Tamils; and that of the traditional Kandyan Sinhalese. The smaller centres are generally no more than district headquarter towns, graced perhaps with some reminders of a colonial past, as in Galle, Trincomalee, Matara, and Batticaloa, or with relics of Sinhalese history as in Anuradhapura and Polonnaruwa.

In the 1971 Census, the urban population is defined as that living in Municipal, Urban and Town Council Areas, irrespective of their size. The level of urbanisation by districts, i.e. the urban population as a percentage of the total, is shown in Figure 7.4b. Colombo District with 55 per cent urban stands on its own. Jaffna and Trincomalee both have upwards of one-third of their population in towns, followed by Batticaloa with almost 28 per cent. With between 12.5 and 25 per cent are the west coastal Districts from Galle to Mannar, Vavuniya in the north and Kandy inland. Apart from the latter, the level of urbanisation has relied in good measure on the existence of coastal towns. The low levels general elsewhere reflect the dispersed nature of the population whether in paddy growing districts where a measure of subsistence persists, or in areas dominated by estates where labourers live close to their work. Closely nucleated settlement is the exception, and even in towns the preference for a home surrounded by its garden tends towards dispersion.

* ESCAP, *Population of Sri Lanka*, Country Monograph Series No. 4, Bangkok, 1976.

127   The jewellers' quarter of the Pettah, Colombo at opening time in the morning. Note the handcart load of fresh coconuts and the boards securing the shop fronts

128   Old colonial style upper class residence in Cinnamon Gardens, Colombo. Many such houses are now used as offices for government departments, foreign legations, etc.

129   Modern upper class residence in Cinnamon Gardens, built two or more to the plot formerly occupied by a more gracious mansion

Figure 7.2 shows that 18 of the 32 centres with more than 20,000 are in Colombo District. These account for 52 per cent of the urban population. Colombo and the suburbs of Dehiwala–Mt Lavinia to the south together have 25 per cent of the total urban population of the island. However Colombo is defined, it is clearly a 'primate' city. Colombo Municipal Council Area had a population of 616,000 in 1977, and Dehiwala – Mt Lavinia 169,000. The next largest town was Jaffna with 118,000 followed by two more of Colombo's close satellites, Moratuwa (104,000) and Kotte (102,000), and Kandy had 103,000. Of the total population in the towns of over 20,000, 82 per cent were in the Wet Zone.

The Sri Lanka Town

As a rule, towns in Sri Lanka are an agglomeration of one or two-storey buildings, the most important of which are the local offices of Government departments. A street or two of open-fronted shops along with the market place, provide the commercial needs of the neighbourhood. Day to day requirements of fresh foods are obtained in the market where producers and small entrepreneurs offer their wares for sale, or provide minor services as shoemenders and repairers of umbrellas. A bus station generally occupies a central location near the market. Immediately adjacent to such a centre residential density is fairly high, although seldom do houses rise above a single storey. The services to these homes may be very limited, some

residents having to use public stand pipes for their water supply, and maybe public latrines. The quality of houses may vary greatly within a single block. At a distance of a block or two from the centre, the tight nucleation gives way to homes standing in gardens more or less intensively planted with subsistence fruits and vegetables depending on the climate.

Thumbnail sketches of two small towns, Hambantota and Mannar, will serve to illustrate how modest in scale and unpretentious such district towns are. They are followed by closer studies of Kandy, Jaffna and Colombo.

Hambantota

Without its district headquarter functions, Hambantota (with an estimated population of 8,000 in 1977) would be diminished practically to the level of a fishing village (Fig. 7.7). It is poorly located to serve the developing agricultural colonies in its district, and was clearly established with its maritime possibilities in mind. It is the most easterly haven of any size along the south coast of Sri Lanka, giving shelter from the southwest monsoon. A headland standing maybe 30 m above sea level protects a kilometre of east-facing sandy beach up which today's fishermen drag their sailing craft. On the headland is a cluster of substantial administrative buildings: the Dutch-built *Kachcheri* (District Headquarters), the Government Agent's Residency, the Court House, Land Registry, Public Works Department Office, the Rest House and the old lighthouse. Immediately back from

7.7   Hambantota

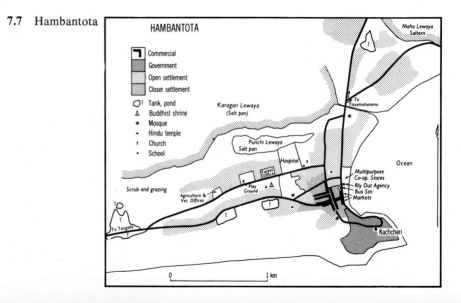

the beach are the fish market, the Railway Out Agency where goods may be forwarded by road to the railhead at Matara, 80 km to the west, and a multi-purpose Co-operative.

Across the road the daily fresh food market is held in an open space, and there are a few shops, with the bus station just behind. The cross streets immediately adjacent are lined with shops, and 150 m further on the closely built-up town centre gives way to open development of houses in big gardens. Here, too, are the main mosque and Muslim burial ground, the Buddhist temple and Hindu *kovil*. More recent administrative growth, including the Agricultural Department and Veterinary Offices, lies to the northwest, past the Christian church and school, the hospital and the Forest Offices. Three mosques in so small a town underline the strong concentration of Muslims in the small fishing ports of Sri Lanka. Like many of these, Hambantota occupies in part a beach ridge backed by lagoons, those to the northeast providing salterns for one of the country's major salt evaporating works (see Fig. 6.3).

Mannar

The little town of Mannar, with 13,000 inhabitants in 1977, is approached from mainland Sri Lanka by a causeway three kilometres long across the shallows that separate it from the bulk of the district it serves (Fig. 7.8). The Fort commanding the link to the mainland bears the date 1686 over the gateway, indicating Dutch construction, although the Dutch were probably not the first to recognise the strategic potential of Mannar. It was hardly the traffic from the arid little island

130 Colombo harbour and the Central Business District of Fort on the rocky promontory on the right and to the left the retailing district of Pettah, with Beira Lake beyond. The beach stretches to Mount Lavinia in the distance (Fig. 7.12)

that accounted for Mannar's importance, but rather its position along the shortest route from India now serving the rail-ferry link between Dhanushkodi and Talaimannar. Further, the shallow strait between Mannar Island and the mainland was a convenient route for small craft plying between Jaffna and Colombo, and a safe passage for fishing boats moving seasonally from the threat of the southwest monsoon on the south side of the Island to sheltered waters on the north.

Like that of Hambantota, the central business district of Mannar is very circumscribed. Boats serving the local market moor beside the bridge, close to the shopping centre between the Fort and the Kachcheri. The residential town extends northwest, seemingly segregated into Muslim and Tamil quarters. There are Hindu *kovils* and Muslim mosques, and three large churches bear witness to the strong Christian missionary activity under the Portuguese. Evidence of Buddhist Sinhalese

7.8 Mannar

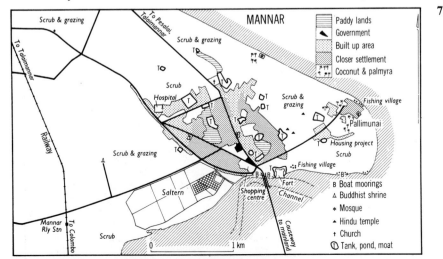

131 Downtown Kurunegala, a private passenger bullock
cart in the foreground. Note the street vendor to
the right, and the open fronted shops with neatly
stacked boards for shutting up shop at night. Sign
boards in Sinhala and English

culture is hard to find in the heart of this firmly
Tamil town with its substantial Muslim minority
stronghold. Fishing and salt evaporating are the
most evident primary economic occupations. On
the beaches east of Mannar, *bêche-de-mer* are
boiled in brine for export. Several small temporary
fishing villages are sited on the beaches, as at
Pallimunai.

Jaffna

In some respects Mannar may be seen as a micro-
cosm of Jaffna, the capital of the Sri Lanka Tamils
and the country's second urban agglomeration
numbering about 118,000 inhabitants in 1977.
Jaffna's Fort, used in turn by Portuguese, Dutch
and British, stands on the shore of the wide lagoon
that separates Jaffna Peninsula from the mainland
portion of Jaffna District (Fig. 7.9). While the

7.9 Jaffna

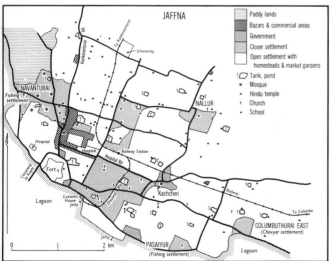

Town Hall, Police Station and Courts face the
Fort across the open Esplanade, and mark the
western edge of one nucleus of the city, the
other emblems of government – *Kachcheri*, Residency, Fiscal's Office, Forest and Agricultural
Offices – are grouped almost two kilometres away
to the east. The third and major nucleus is the
commercial area identified in the bazaars and
goldsmiths' shops lying north of the Fort in the
Kankesanturai Road – Hospital Road angle,
and extending almost one kilometre along the
former.

The general impression one gains of Jaffna is
of dispersion along lanes of homesteads hidden
in their gardens by fences of palmyra leaves or by
eye-level screens of these leaves, or of coconut
cadjans or strips of corrugated iron. There are
a few more tightly grouped clusters of residential settlement. Thus the middle-class area
just east of the Fort occupies a one kilometre
square area in the angle of the old railway track
to the Customs House and jetty. Another cluster,
the mainly Muslim quarter with several mosques,
lies to the northwest, and a third, occupied by a
fishing community, at Pasaiyur on the shore of
the lagoon three kilometres to the east of the Fort.
Further east again is a cluster where the Chevyar
community lives, the former palanquin carriers
in the Tamil Hindu caste system. Some goldsmiths
and other artisans are grouped near Nallur, more
than three kilometres northeast of the Fort. Jaffna
has grown to absorb these caste-defined nuclei,
linking them in a matrix of semi-urban, semi-rural
settlement, liberally dotted with *kovils* and schools.
The closer the settlement the lower the class or
caste, is the characteristic pattern. On the northern
edge of the loosely built up area is the University.

132 Coir ropes, baskets and brooms in a shop in
Mannar. The Muslim man can be recognised as
such by his fez

Kandy

The sprawling city of Kandy, with a population of c. 103,000 in 1977 (Fig. 7.10), holds a unique place in the Sinhalese Buddhist national consciousness as the former seat of the Kandyan kings and also as the place where the Sacred Tooth of the Lord Buddha is preserved, making it a most revered location. Kandy celebrates the veneration of the Sacred Tooth every year in the Buddhist month of *Esala*, usually in August. Ten days of colourful festival, the *Esala Perahera*, draw pilgrims and tourists from far and wide, and incidentally help keep alive the many craft industries of the region.

Because of its historic and religious associations and no doubt partly on account of its relatively healthy semi-hill station climate, Kandy has developed into a major educational centre. British missions and later Sinhalese institutions established boarding schools here on British models to serve upper-class Lankans, and the country's major university campus established at Peradeniya after Independence reinforced this educational function.

The site of Kandy has in a broad sense defensive advantages, situated as it is within a tight bend of the Mahaweli Ganga, although the town itself lies in a basin around Kandy Lake and the valley to the southwest. It is thus separated by hills from the Mahaweli. From the floor of the basin lying at about 500 m, hills rise to over 900 m within the municipal limits and to 1338 m at a distance of seven kilometres to the south.

In form, Kandy is much influenced by its religious and administrative functions within the physical constraints of its hilly site. The Temple of the Tooth stands above the artificial Kandy Lake. Close by are the High, District and Magistrate's Courts, the Residence of the Government Agent, and the Kandy Presidency. This latter is in itself an indication of the psychological importance that Kandy holds for the Sinhalese, as it occupies the site of the former King's Palace, now the residence of the President when he visits the town. Close by is the commercial centre, consisting of 14 or so small blocks delineated by half a dozen rectilinear streets. The main street, Dalada Vidiya,

7.10 Kandy

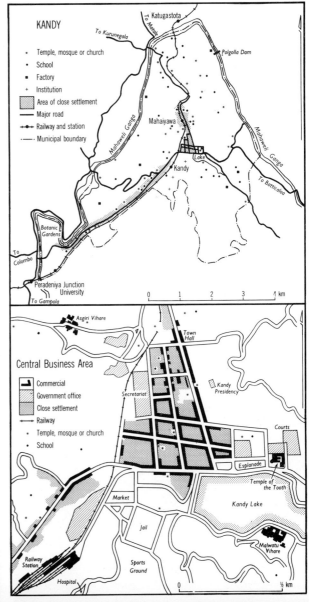

133 The morning vegetable market in Hambantota. Green coconuts previously opened for their milk are being investigated by the goats

fronts onto Kandy Lake and extends west and southwest as the main road paralleling the railway in the valley to Peradeniya where it crosses the Mahaweli Ganga and continues towards Colombo. Eastwards, this road extends to cross the Mahaweli, on its way to Teldeniya and Batticaloa, while at right angles to it the D. S. Senanayake Vidaya leads north across the river to Matale, to Kurunegala, and the north.

From the grid of the town centre, where the major and oldest development is situated, minor roads wind up the slopes to serve the numerous better-class residences, many of them the homes of the retired. Some of these lead further up to reach the tea estates above the town, others to the small agricultural valleys with their narrow strip of paddy fields.

While Kandy itself can claim a wide range of small consumer industries from batiks to woodworking, the traditional crafts of brass, copper and silver beating and engraving, brass casting, mat weaving, wood carving and lacquering, tend to be located in agricultural villages particularly to the northeast.

Colombo*

As is so often the case, the problem of defining realistically the functional boundary of Colombo

*With acknowledgements to Panditharatna, B. L. *Colombo*, University of London Ph. D. Thesis, 1973; and de Silva, S. K. *Socio-spatial Patterns of the City of Colombo; a Factorial Ecology*, University College, Swansea M. A. Thesis, 1973.

134   Typical traditional single storeyed houses and shops in Kandy. The curved clay tiles are typical of older buildings whose front doors open onto the street. The street tap on the pavement outside 'City Dental Work' supplies water to the residents

is difficult. The Colombo *Municipal Council Area* (Fig. 7.11) had 562,000 people in 1971, but effectively the city is much more extensive, continuing southwards without a break, into Dehiwala-Mt Lavinia (154,000), and inland into a number of quite populous suburbs. Northwards, it is contained by the Kelani Ganga, crossed by a rail and two road bridges. The Colombo *Urban Area*, however, had 1.346 million inhabitants in 1971 and this is likely to have reached 1.5 million by 1979. In the Draft Colombo Master Plan Project (1978), the Colombo *Metropolitan Region* was estimated

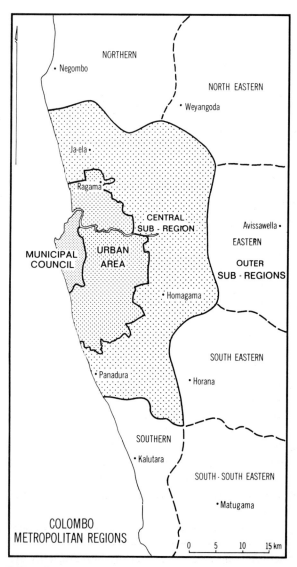

7.11   Colombo

to have had 3 million in 1971, of which 1.6 million were urban dwellers. The Project identifies an inner Central and six outer Sub-Regions, partially shown in Figure 7.11.

Colombo's Fort was first built by the Portuguese in the sixteenth century to defend their commercial interests in the area of the city now occupied by the CBD immediately adjacent to the harbour. Under the Dutch in the seventeenth and eighteenth centuries, and the British from the nineteenth century, Colombo expanded to dominate the commerce and administration of the Colony. It now stands unchallenged in its primacy.

The three maps in Figure 7.12 show some of the main features of Colombo: physical, demographic and functional. The rocky outcrop where the 'mantled plain' reaches the sea to form the promontory on which stood the Fort, an area still so named, gave some shelter from the southwest monsoon on an otherwise exposed coastline. Here, Muslim traders had established a settlement before the arrival of the Portuguese. The immediate coastal belt consists largely of sand barriers behind which the coastal streams have been impounded to form a discontinuous line of lagoons, still apparent in Beira Lake and again north of the Kelani Ganga. A canal linking the Beira Lake to the harbour continues to provide access by barges to warehouses around the lake. Another canal northwards from the Kelani Ganga formed a protected waterway as far north as Puttalam Lagoon.

Low-lying ground in the flood plain of the Kelani Ganga and its tributaries, and around the coastal lagoons, has effectively limited the direction of urban growth encouraging it to spread north, and more particularly to the south along the coastal sand plain, and on the patches of mantled plain that stand above it. The latter are remnants of a much dissected surface (increasingly extensive inland), deeply weathered and carrying a generally lateritic soil cover. The low ground, ill-drained and very prone to flooding, provided some protection for the early foreign mercantile settlement of the Fort and nearby Pettah, and the extension northeast from this towards the mouth of the Kelani Ganga.

Portuguese and Dutch interests lay in the coastal lowlands where spices could be obtained, but the British penetrated the interior, building railways to Kandy and into the hill country beyond as they

135 A vendor in Colombo Fort occupies a square metre of pavement in a busy street

136 On the steps of the Chartered Bank in Fort, Colombo, this woman sells cashew nuts, one of which she is splitting

COLOMBO LANDFORMS

COLOMBO POPULATION DENSITY: 1971

7.12 Colombo, Landforms, Population density, Land Use

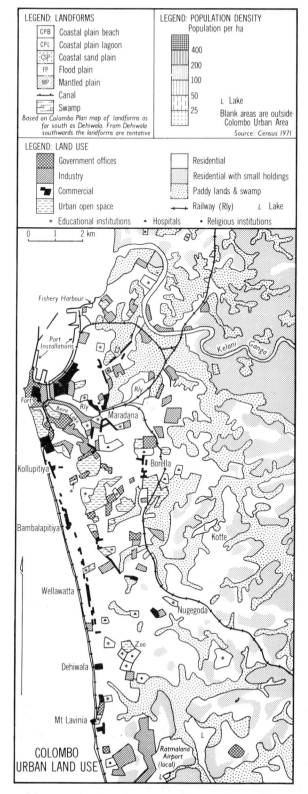

LEGEND: LANDFORMS

CPB	Coastal plain beach
CPL	Coastal plain lagoon
CSP	Coastal sand plain
FP	Flood plain
MP	Mantled plain
	Canal
	Swamp

Based on Colombo Plan map of landforms as far south as Dehiwala. From Dehiwala southwards the landforms are tentative

LEGEND: POPULATION DENSITY

Population per ha

400
200
100
50
25

L Lake

Blank areas are outside Colombo Urban Area

Source: Census 1971

LEGEND: LAND USE

	Government offices
	Industry
	Commercial
	Urban open space
	Residential
	Residential with small holdings
	Paddy lands & swamp
	Railway (Rly)	*L* Lake

* Educational institutions   ▲ Hospitals   • Religious institutions

0   1   2 km

Fishery Harbour

Port Installations

Kelani Ganga

Rly

Fort   Rly

Beira Lake   Maradana

Kollupitiya

Borella

Bambalapitiya

Kotte

Wellawatta

Nugegoda

Zoo

Dehiwala

Mt Lavinia

Ratmalana Airport (local)

COLOMBO URBAN LAND USE

developed plantations of coffee and later, tea. Colombo expanded greatly under the impetus of trade, and as a key coaling station in the British sea-based strategic and commercial system, conveniently situated between the Suez Canal and Singapore. After the opening of Suez the harbour was protected from the southwest monsoon by moles.

The map of present day functional regions reflect the historical factors in Colombo's growth. Government and financial institutions are concentrated in Fort and close by, although with their expansion since Independence many Government offices have had to be housed in former large residences, and commercial developments scattered through the high-class Cinnamon Gardens area and adjacent suburbs.

Commerce, wholesale handling of export commodities, and some related industries cluster around Beira Lake, goods being transported by barges through the canal to the harbour, (although with improved wharf facilities much cargo is moved to the dockside by road). Some industries like flour milling, tobacco and tea packing are located close to the harbour, but many of the modern factories have found sites on low lands unattractive to housing, on the fringes of residential development particularly to the east. The cluster of industrial sites alongside Ratmalana Airport near Mt Lavinia owes its origin to military installations established by the British during World War II.

Retailing is most concentrated in Pettah, the traditional focus of Muslim traders and Tamil craftsmen. The shops here are open-fronted but are boarded up at night, giving the streets a deserted look. On the southern edge of Pettah is the fresh food market, close to Colombo Fort railway station. Modern shops in the style of departmental stores were established in Fort to serve the British plantation and administrative population. Now they linger on as somewhat pathetic relics. Here, and in the suburban retail centres strung along Galle Road and at a few road junctions, shops resemble those in Western cities. Beira Lake is today much reduced in size. Reclamation, particularly of its northern extension has enabled the railway yards and the Fort station to be built west of the original terminus at Maradana. From the latter, a branch line serves Colombo harbour and the Coast Line continues south through the suburbs to Galle and Matara. East of Maradana are the sidings of the railway workshops beside the Main Line to Kandy and the north. The narrow gauge line serving the southeastern suburbs runs out to Padukka.

The map of gross population density shows the highest concentration to be in Kochchikade just east of Pettah, rather than in Fort which is dominated by office blocks or in Pettah itself. East of Pettah, the low-status Tamil and Muslim areas are densely settled, with diminished density northwards into lower middle-class Tamil areas, and beyond these again, in the bend of the Kelani Ganga, low-status housing mixed with industry and market gardening. Gross densities south of Fort and Pettah are reduced by the considerable areas of open space in the Galle Face and Beira Lake, but net residential densities in tenements exceed 500 persons per ha in Kollupitiya. Cinnamon Gardens with only 47 per ha (gross density) is Colombo's highest-class residential area, but is under invasion from institutional functions which are taking over some of the mansions and former open space. Thus the University, Meteorological Office and other Government departments, and various embassies are found among the homes of the wealthy. High status residential areas of moderate density, between 50 and 100 persons per ha, extend southwards over the coastal sand plain. Lower overall densities occur inland as more of the land is low-lying and unsuited to housing. The urban area gives way ultimately to a 'rurban' fringe, where houses set in homestead gardens become more common than strictly urban residences, and the population tends to be Sinhalese speaking, Buddhist and middle-class.

A high proportion of Colombo's population (67 per cent) live in 'sub-standard' housing, and some 157,000 in shanties as squatters on generally low-lying marshy areas, on patches of government land, and often strung along canal, road and railway reservations. The map of shanties* (Fig. 7.13), although dating from the late 1960s, shows them more common on the northern half of Colombo, particularly towards the fringe where the built-up area gives way to lower ground, as in Borella and in the neighbourhood of the Kelani Ganga bridges.

*Based on de Silva, S. K. *op. cit.*, Map. 5.6.

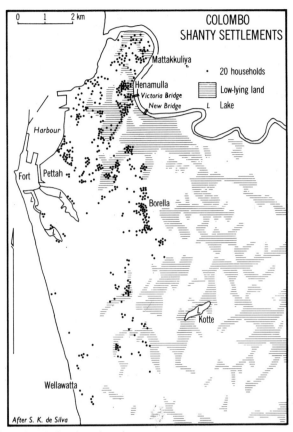

7.13 Colombo, shanties

137 This tailor works in the open front of his shop in Hambantota using a treadle machine

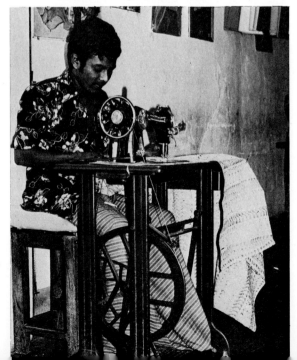

Squatter settlements such as these are a feature of many growing cities in the Third World, and tend to persist however fast the authorities build more permanent homes for their occupants, since there are generally new arrivals to the city ready to take over the shanties of those re-housed. The advance guard in rural-urban migration shows a high degree of masculinity, the men finding work and space in which to live before bringing their families to join them or perhaps leaving them behind. The age-sex pyramid for Colombo (Fig. 7.14) demonstrates the imbalance in the sexes in the working age groups from 15 to 55.

138   In a street in Pettah, Colombo, the itinerant knife-grinder sets up his simple workshop

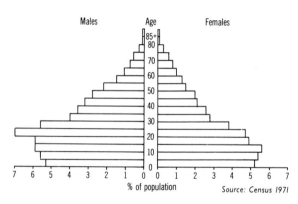

AGE - SEX PYRAMID
Colombo &
Dehiwala-Mt Lavinia Municipalities : 1971

Source: Census 1971

7.14   Colombo, age-sex pyramid

The Colombo Urban Area extends as a coastal linear city from the Kelani Ganga in the north, to Moratuwa 19 km to the south of Colombo Fort, a distance of almost 25 km. The lateral development of the city is severely constrained by the sea on one side and by low-lying flood-prone areas inland, and is seldom as much as 5 km wide. In a city whose inhabitants are mainly dependent for mobility on public transport, the road system and its bus services are all important. The future functioning of the urban region will depend in large measure on ensuring the smooth flow of traffic not only within this core but also between this core and sub-regional centres developing on the periphery – inland beyond the zone of swamps and paddy lands, and along the coastal sand plain, north towards Negombo and south to Kalutara and beyond.

A new parliamentary and administrative capital, Sri Jayawardhana Pura, is being built on 104 km² at Kotte about 9 kilometres southeast of Fort. The site is ill-drained but is to be planned to create an island in a lake. To serve the capital a rail loop is to be constructed from the Coast Line at Ratmalana, through Sri Jayawardhana Pura to Colombo.

Select Bibliography

The sources listed below are not exhaustive of the material available or used by the authors but rather are selected to guide the interested reader to what they regard as the most useful material.

1 Government Publications

Census of Population, 1971, Department of Census and Statistics, Colombo.

Ceylon Customs Returns Ministry of Finance, Customs Department, Colombo, (monthly).

Population of Sri Lanka, Department of Census & Statistics, Colombo, 1974.

Preliminary Report on the Field Survey of Manufacturing Industry in Sri Lanka, 1975–76, Ministry of Industries and Scientific Affairs, Colombo, 1977.

Socio-Economic Survey of Sri Lanka 1969–70: Special Report on Food and Nutritional Levels in Sri Lanka, Department of Census and Statistics, Colombo, 1972.

Sri Lanka Year Book, Department of Census and Statistics, Colombo, 1977 and earlier years.

Statistical Abstract of the Democratic Socialist Republic of Sri Lanka 1977, Department of Census and Statistics, Colombo, 1979.

Statistical Pocket Book of Sri Lanka (Ceylon), Department of Census and Statistics Colombo, 1978.

2 Periodicals

Review of the Economy, Central Bank of Ceylon, Colombo, 1976.

Annual Report, Central Bank of Ceylon, Colombo, 1977, 1978.

Bulletin, Central Bank of Ceylon, Colombo (monthly).

Economic and Social Statistics of Sri Lanka, Central Bank of Ceylon, Colombo.

Staff Studies, Central Bank of Ceylon, Colombo (periodically).

Report on the Sample Survey of Economic Conditions in the Mahaweli Development Area 1974, Central Bank of Ceylon, Colombo, 1975.

Ceylon Geographer, Bulletin of Ceylon Geographical Society, Colombo (irregular).

Ferguson's Ceylon Directory, Associated Newspapers, Colombo, 1978 and earlier years.

Marga, periodical published by the Marga Institute, Colombo, 1971.

Modern Ceylon Studies, University of Sri Lanka, Peradeniya, 1970.

Economic Review, Peoples' Bank, Colombo (monthly).

Quarterly Economic Survey of Sri Lanka, Economist Intelligence Unit London.

3 Other Publications

Agrarian Research and Training Institute (ARTI). Numerous Research Reports and Occasional Publications, e.g. *The Agrarian Situation Relating to Paddy Cultivation in Five Selected Districts of Sri Lanka*, 1974–75; *New Settlement Schemes in Sri Lanka*, 1974; *Kurundankulama Dry Farming Settlement*, 1977.

Arumugam, S. *Water Resources of Ceylon*, Water Resources Board, Colombo, 1969.

Coelho, V. H. *Across the Palk Straits*, Palit and Palit, Dehra Dun, 1976.

Cook, E. K. (revised Kularatnam, K.) *Ceylon*, Macmillan, London, 1951.

Child, R. *Coconuts*, Longmans, London, 1974.

de Alwis, K. A. and Panabokke C. R., *Handbook of the Soils of Sri Lanka*, Soil Science Society of Ceylon, Colombo, 1972.

de Silva, K. M. (ed.), *Sri Lanka: a Survey*, Hurst, London, 1977.

Domros, M. *Sri Lanka: die Tropeninsel Ceylon*, Wissenschaftliche Buchgesellschaft, Darmstadt, 1976.

Domros, M. *The Agroclimate of Ceylon,* Steiner, Wiesbaden, 1974.

Economic and Social Commission for Asia and the Pacific (ESCAP), *Comparative Study of Population Growth and Agricultural Change: Case Study of Sri Lanka*, Bangkok, 1975.

ESCAP, *Population of Sri Lanka*, Country Monograph Series No. 4. Bangkok, 1976.

Farmer, B. H. *Pioneer Peasant Colonisation in Ceylon,* Oxford University Press, London, 1959.

Farmer, B. H. *Ceylon, a Divided Nation*, Oxford University Press, London, 1963.

Farmer, B. H. (ed.), *Green Revolution? Technology and Change in Tamil Nadu and Sri Lanka*, Cambridge University Press, London.

Herath, J. W. *Mineral Resources of Sri Lanka,* Geological Survey Department, Colombo, 1975.

International Bank for Reconstruction & Development Mission to Ceylon, *The Economic Development of Ceylon*, Ceylon Government Press, Colombo, 1953.

Jones, G. W. and Selvaratnam, S. *Population Growth and Economic Development in Ceylon*, Hansa Publications, Colombo, 1972.

Karunatilake, H. N. S. *Economic Development in Ceylon*, Praeger, New York, 1971.

Ludowyk, E. F. C. *The Story of Ceylon*, Faber and Faber, London, 1962.

Ludowyk, E. F. C. *The Modern History of Ceylon*, Weidenfeld & Nicolson, London, 1966.

Marby, H. *Tea in Ceylon*, Franz Steiner Verlag GMBH, Wiesbaden, 1972.

Mendis, G. C. *Ceylon: Today and Yesterday*, Associated Newspapers of Ceylon, Colombo, 1963.

Pakeman, S. A. *Ceylon*, Bern, London, 1964.

Sarkar, N. *The Demography of Ceylon,* Ceylon Government Press, Colombo, 1957.

Snodgrass, D. R. *Ceylon, an Export Economy in Transition*, Holmewood 111., R. D. Irwin, 1966.

Spate, O. H. K. and Learmonth, A. T. A. *India and Pakistan* (with a chapter on Ceylon by B. H. Farmer), Methuen, London, 1967.

Weerasooria, N. E. *Ceylon and Her People*, Lake House, Colombo, 1970.

Weerasooria, W. *Credit and Security in Ceylon*, University of Queensland, St. Lucia, 1973.

Wikkramatileke, R. *Southeast Ceylon: Trends and Problems in Agricultural Settlement*, University of Chicago Press, Chicago, 1963.

Wilson, Pitiyage *Economic Implications of Population Growth: Sri Lanka Labour Force 1946–81*, Australian National University, Canberra, 1975.

Wriggins, W. H. *Ceylon, Dilemmas of a New Nation.* Princeton, University Press, Princeton, 1960.

Index

Note: n after a figure denotes that the reference is to be found in the footnote.